THE BEAST IN THE BOUDOIR

THE BEAST
IN THE
BOUDOIR

PETKEEPING IN
NINETEENTH-CENTURY
PARIS

KATHLEEN KETE

UNIVERSITY OF CALIFORNIA PRESS
Berkeley · Los Angeles · London

University of California Press
Berkeley and Los Angeles, California

University of California Press, Ltd.
London, England

© 1994 by
The Regents of the University of California

First Paperback Printing 1995

Library of Congress Cataloging-in-Publication Data

Kete, Kathleen.
   The beast in the boudoir : petkeeping in
nineteenth-century Paris / Kathleen Kete.
       p.   cm
   Includes bibliographical references (p.   ) and index.
   ISBN 0-520-20339-9 (alk. paper)
   1. Pet owners—France—Paris—History—19th
century.   2. Pets—Social aspects—France—Paris—
History—19th century.   3. Paris (France)—Social life
and customs.   I. Title.   II. Title: Petkeeping in
nineteenth-century Paris.
SF 411.43.F8K47   1994
305.5'5—dc20   93-32265
                                               CIP

Printed in the United States of America

9 8 7 6 5 4 3 2 1

Contents

Illustrations

Acknowledgments

I owe many people a great deal of thanks for help in the completion of this book. Friends and acquaintances who helped with source material and other encouragements include Robert W. Baldwin, Lisa Bitel, Leslie Choquette, Sarah Fishman, Caroline Ford, Leonard Groopman, David Harvey, Margaret Higonnet, Steve Jaffe, Peter Mancall, Susan Pederson, Mary Pickering, Marie-Claire Rohinsky, and Margaret Talbot. Françoise Mathieu provided friendship, knowledge, and a place to stay during research trips to Paris. I also want to thank Mary Lou and Nancy Kete.

The Department of History at Harvard and the French government provided support for a year's research in Paris during the academic year 1984–85. As an exchange student at the Institut d'études politiques de Paris, I benefited from participation in a seminar on methodology that explored the problems of post-*annaliste* history. Pierre Milza, especially, was supportive of my research project.

Maurice Agulhon guided me toward essential source material. Alain Corbin read most of an early draft of the manuscript and suggested ways of recasting the argument in stronger forms. Harriet Ritvo, whose subject is close to my own work, helped me clarify my ideas. She has also been a friend.

Generous suggestions came from Thomas Laqueur and an anonymous reader of the manuscript for the University of California Press, and from the comments of the editorial board of *Representations*, which published chapter six, "*La Rage* and the Bourgeoisie: The Cultural Context of Rabies in the French Nineteenth Century" (*Representations*, no. 22 [Spring 1988]: 89–107), guided the argument of the book as a whole to its final form, and gave me permission to reprint the article.

I would also like to thank the Minda de Gunzburg Center for European Studies at Harvard University for giving me a congenial atmosphere in 1988–89 to complete the manuscript in dissertation form and in 1989–90 to work on turning the dissertation into a book. Trinity College, Hartford, Connecticut, has been very supportive of the final stages of the project.

I am grateful to Simon Schama, who first encouraged me in the study of history and remains a valued adviser. His own work in cultural history taught me to look at the ordinary in extraordinary ways. Patrice Higonnet sustained and strongly influenced my work for many years. His contribution is incalculable.

My husband, Daniel McGrath, most of all, has shared the project's burdens and its joys. His friendship makes writing worthwhile.

This book is dedicated to Dan and to our daughter, Julia.

Introduction

Mediocre lives, it seems, leave little mark upon their world. Many histories of the nineteenth century, especially political and intellectual ones, present the ordinary bourgeois Parisian as the dull and uncomplicated object of forces greater than his or her understanding. Ideas current within high culture, like alienation, seem to be too fragile to find expression in the heavy bric-a-brac of the bourgeois interior. And yet one key to the complexity of nineteenth-century culture, like the hiding place of Poe's purloined letter, has been in full view before us.

A passing reference to petkeeping by Walter Benjamin in his essay, "On Some Motifs in Baudelaire," suggested the focus of this book. "Around 1840," Benjamin says, "it was briefly fashionable to take turtles for a walk in the arcades. The *flâneurs* liked to have the turtles set the pace for them. If they had had their way, progress would have been obliged to accommodate itself to this pace." Benjamin goes on to explain that "this attitude did not prevail."[1] Benjamin's comment about turtles and Parisian *flâneurs*, about marginal people and their referentially marginal pets, is a statement about modern life. What I realized when I came upon Benjamin's mention of turtlewalking was that the meaning of Paris to Parisians might equally be teased out of mainstream petkeeping culture.

It was in the nineteenth century, after all, that the family dog became a cliché of modern life. Many of the other familiar aspects of petkeeping had their beginnings in bourgeois culture also, either as inventions of the age or as refigurations of earlier motifs. More important than the novelty of nineteenth-century petkeeping, however, is its transparency. What immediately emerges from the sources on petkeeping in nineteenth-century Paris—the dog-care books, the *bulletins* of the Société protectrice des animaux (animal protection society), the records on the dog tax, the histories of the dog cemetery, the data on disease and medical and veterinarian records that span the century—is their strikingly self-referential nature. When bourgeois people spoke of their pets, as they loquaciously did, they pointedly spoke also of their times, and above all else of themselves.

Petkeeping involves us in the culture of ordinary people. In explaining it we suggest how the nineteenth century took shape, in everyday events, in ordinary life, and argue that the experience of modernity by ordinary people was as complicated, and just as complicit in its shaping of reality, as was the experience of intellectuals whose elitist critiques of bourgeois life have shaped our general understanding of the age.

Behind the striking development of petkeeping forms are the tensions within bourgeois culture that shaped them. Petkeeping describes the fault lines of individualism. The ever-faithful pet was a fiction that had its origin in antiquity. When nineteenth-century Parisians elaborated on it, they put into context what seemed most lacking in relationships between their contemporaries. Petkeeping imagined a better, more manageable version of the world. It described the promise and some-times displaced the terrors of class.

The role of this fantasy in building bourgeois life is significant. Petkeeping relieved the pressures of contemporary life. It also under-mined the rewards of modernity. Bourgeois domesticity was claustro-phobic, its restrictions were unhealthy—as the wilder, somatic conse-quences of petkeeping revealed. On another level, positivism itself was less promising when its values were weighed against the vulnerability of pets.

Petkeeping in Paris was bourgeois because its participants so labeled it, contrasting the "bourgeois dog" with "working-class" and "Oriental" dogs, who supposedly led unstructured, more natural, and less cultured lives. The focus of this book, however, is not class struggle but an elaborate construction in the petkeeping world of affect and fantasy—set against a recognizably imperfect world—that includes the important problem of class.

Class conflict and politics were fundamental, of course, to the build-ing of bourgeois culture and within it the fabrication of smaller more manageable worlds. In a major shift in consciousness, however, as ancien régime Paris irrevocably gave way during the Second Empire to modern commercial and domestic forms, the bourgeoisie became more concerned with the problem of modernity as a whole. This concern continued with declining creative force in everyday life from the 1850s until the First World War.

Petkeeping was not a startling innovation dreamed up by the Parisian bourgeoisie to help make sense of the world. Keith Thomas traces the development of sentimental attitudes toward small animals to seventeenth-century England and Harriet Ritvo's work on modern British history explains that culture's fascination with pets.[2] Petkeeping was an important aspect of ancien régime French life too. In a study of attitudes toward animals during the Enlightenment, Hester Hastings briefly reviews developments in petkeeping that contemporary eighteenth-century sources more graphically describe. Little dogs owned by wealthy women were already a trope of a decadent life; favored, faithful hunting dogs of nobles in the provinces resembled other canines in English country houses. In Paris rich and poor individuals alike owned dogs, creating a pattern like that distinctive of Dutch genre paintings of the seventeenth century.[3]

Other cultures also give meaning to animals, as anthropologists insist. But the notion of a *longue durée* is of limited use when considering ideas of nature in history, as Alain Corbin argues. He explains that what is needed, rather, is "to examine in what manner and by what mechanisms people of each epoch and if possible in each social category have interpreted earlier structures (*les schèmes anciens*) and have reintegrated them in a coherent ensemble of representations and practices."[4]

In nineteenth-century Paris the relation between animals and culture was especially well marked. Bourgeois Parisians insistently associated petkeeping with modernity and with themselves, an association that allows us to grasp their understanding of their culture. Petkeeping improvised solutions on a household level to the intractable mesh of postrevolutionary France.

As this book will show, Parisian petkeeping restates in another mode the century's central intellectual ideas—ideas about modernity expressed in literary and artistic representations and in ordinary nineteenth-century lives as well. Moreover, this book connects the creation of class cultures to these troubled, aesthetic responses to modernization. This book also suggests that it was the imagination—the realm of the aesthetic, as Kant explains—that largely shaped class, and that the unexpectedly esoteric realm of the ordinary is the place where we should begin our search for the bourgeoisie.

Animal Protection
in Nineteenth-Century Paris
The Case of Pets

During the French Revolution the problem of animal protection entered the public sphere. "At what point does the mistreatment of animals become a matter of ethics, of public concern, and should there be laws in this regard?" was the question set in a public essay contest in 1800. But not until the July Monarchy, in 1839, was an attempt made to establish an animal protection society, along British lines. The attempt failed. Nonetheless in the early 1840s more initiatives were taken to protect animals in France. In 1845, in the home of Parisot de Cassel, the seven founding members of the Société protectrice des animaux met. Male and representative of much of the upper-class political spectrum, they included Dumont de Monteux, prison doctor and self-described disciple of Rousseau; Parisot, doctor and self-described Christian; Count Renneville, a philanthropic agronomist; and Henri Blatin, Freemason, philanthropist, and republican. In 1846 the society was authorized by the government. In February 1848 it held its first annual convention, its *séance solennelle*, at, of all places, the Hôtel de Ville.[1]

Maurice Agulhon brilliantly analyzes the impact of the Revolution of 1848 on the nascent animal protection movement. Its first major success was the Grammont Law of 1850, which prohibited the public abuse of animals. The measure was negotiated through the Assemblée nationale, as Agulhon explains, by a man of the party of order, former cavalry officer and horse lover, General Grammont, with unexpected left-wing support.[2] The left responded to his most telling argument—"that the spectacle of suffering encourages cruelty, that the child accustomed to bloody pastimes or witnessing cruelty will become a dangerous man, that the vicious carter (*le mauvais charretier*) is latent in the child." The right had been appalled by the bloody play in February of "a subproletariat of *misérables* and vagabonds." As Agulhon further explains, it was necessary to leash the mob, this "underclass" (*sous-peuple*, in the poet Alphonse de Lamartine's words), so easily excited by the sight of blood.[3]

Even before 1848, the spectacle of popular Paris had worried middle-class minds. In its request for authorization of 1846, the Société protectrice des animaux explained to the government that popular attitudes toward animals not only were an offense to public decency, they also "nurture that depth of insolence and wickedness that moves one to do wrong for the pleasure of being bad, for instance, it prompts the carter to ram other carriages just to arrest their progress, or to respond to remonstrance or entreaty with insults and threats, in short, they provoke arguments, fights, and bloody scuffles."[4]

The abuse of animals by provincials likewise posed a threat to Parisian public health, as the animal protection society more narrowly defined it: "The calf that the Norman carter brings to Paris is forced to travel in atrocious conditions, bound, hoof to hoof, packed in with a dozen others, thrown in the back of the cart," argued the society's bulletins in lurid detail, "may become sick (*fiévreux*) and produce unwholesome meat." As Grammont more succinctly explained to the Assemblée nationale: "The poor conditions of transport of bovines . . . pose a threat to the health of consumers."[5]

Worse still were the rotting corpses of horses "in those hideous places," the knacker's yards, where the imaginative Parent-Duchâtelet saw, in horrible organic splendor, almost sublime preparations for the miasmic destruction of Paris. "There," he explained, "grow horrible masses of larvae, foul-smelling and twitching, from which emerge flies, clouds of flies that one can see spread out in the air above Paris."[6] Gratuitously, the working classes (*les classes laborieuses*) weakened the economy of France. "The horse that one so abuses in Paris is a form of capital, its destruction is truly a waste," the society argued. "The massacre of horses by Parisian carters is a loss for the national economy," added Grammont.[7]

Informed by similar utilitarian ideals, doctors and other bourgeois reformers during the early years of the animal protection movement sought to impose a benign and self-consciously bourgeois model of behavior on a ferocious working class and ignorant peasantry. A matter of social coercion, or persuasion, it is a story about a hegemonic class. But attentive readings of the later records of the Société protectrice des animaux suggest another narrative, equally drenched in the vocabulary of modernity. The haunting image of "the vicious carter" now nudges us toward metaphor.

Modernity, in this understanding, is the nebulous but given set of conditions that contemporaries experienced as material reality. Modernism is the set of aesthetic reactions to these conditions that in turn provided a cultural cast to the experience of material life. Ordinary people within bourgeois culture reshaped key images of modernity in the late Second Empire and early Third Republic. This recasting of the social imagination of the nineteenth century is apparent in changing attitudes of animal protectionism toward urban life. Initially, principles of animal protection expressed optimism about the city and were grounded in upper-class attitudes. Threats, to progress and to an orderly configuration of its signs, were located in the worker—drunken, violent, wasteful, and uncomfortably close to an unruly natural world. Urban life in itself was good—modern and bourgeois. Its problems lay in the behavior of a primitive class that education and laws might tame. But bourgeois morality soon came to embrace antipositivist themes also and in ways that illuminate our central point: by the late 1860s and 1870s the affective behavior of canines offered dramatic contrast to an increasingly cruel bourgeois and urban world, male, alienating, and relentlessly unsentimental. The pet became the countericon of the scientific, and dehumanized, age.

The dominant notes of the animal protection movement sounded forth in the context of the modern city, of Haussmann's Paris, and seemed to afford triumphant expressions of class superiority. In 1855 the Grand Exposition was the particular setting for the society's work, broadly conceived as injecting a healthful dose of morality into an otherwise beneficent materialism. Paris during the exposition was a stunning panorama of industry and genius, society members proudly remarked: "the rendezvous of nations, it presents to [our] dazzled eyes . . . innumerable products of work and genius from every latitude." The rebuilding of Paris was dazzling in itself. "In the new splendor of its streets and its activities, Paris appears as the most magnificent of spectacles," the society reported in its bulletin. The organizers of the Société protectrice des animaux were worthy of modernity's challenge. "In the midst of so many wonders," marveled the organization's president in an address to members, "is it not also noble and moving to see dedicated people like yourselves," he added, "meeting to assure protection to the weak and to strengthen that moral sense without which all the material works of civilization," he asserted with passion, "are only useless baubles."[8]

Two years later lower-class brutality toward animals still marred Paris, the reports of the society confirmed, in ways that strengthened the early organization's dominant themes: working-class attitudes and behavior—waste and violence—threatened the impressive bearing of progress. Describing Paris and the goals of the animal protection society, the reports took an exultant and self-congratulatory tone despite accounts of continued violence. "If we have not completely reached our goals," suggested the secretary general of the society, "at least we may congratulate ourselves on improvements effected in this beautiful capital of France," where, he insisted too hopefully, "the most revolting cruelties no longer occur." The society firmly situated its civilizing goals in positivistic terms, "having its headquarters," its members tellingly explained, "in the capital of civilization itself."[9]

Women had a part in the movement: they were to bolster these positivistic goals. In 1855 the society's president outlined the relation of women to animal protection. Speaking to the organization's annual convention, he explained that the support of women, of women of social position, that is, would be a "precious support." "A cause entrusted to women is a cause won," he gallantly explained. Other leaders of the society stressed the logical connection between women's interests and animal protection. "The cause of animal protection, that is, the protection of the weak against the strong, of moral and intellectual force substituted for brute physical power, in short, of civilization . . . cannot fail to interest the ladies," the secretary general explained.[10]

Sentiment was women's forte in the society's predictable reading of gender. Feeling needed constraint, however, if it was not to slip into sentimentality and interfere with the work of protection. "We have no sympathy for those irrational passions that inspire people weakened by age or otherwise subject to blind caprice. . . . We are looking for generous hearts that are guided by lofty intelligence," he told the assembly, feeling sure, he said pointedly, that his meaning was clear.[11]

Women's role in animal protection throughout the 1850s and 1860s was decorative, symbolic, and marginal. It was represented at annual conventions that figuratively expressed the concerns of the society. Next to richly dressed ladies sat notables from the worlds of science, arts and letters, and government; scattered among the assembly were prize-winning peasants, distinctive in their blouses. By the early 1860s *dames patronesses*—women whose social position and contributions to the society were especially noteworthy—were grouped on stage, in the places of honor. Occasionally they read poetry. In 1861 the assembly enthusiastically applauded Madame Ségalas, whose verses, "The Devil in Paris," sadly, as the minutes to the meeting explain, contained nothing particularly relevant to the work of animal protection.[12]

Complacent assumptions of male superiority were shaken in a series of debates on vivisection in the 1860s and 1870s that opposed affect to effect. The former, tautological, relation of the modern to the good was dislodged: in an unstable doubling back on itself the notion of danger traveled figuratively from the irrational classes—women and workers—to rest uneasily on the modernizers and on their city itself as well.

Prompted by a study at the Académie de médecine on the merits of regulating vivisection, the Société protectrice des animaux formed a committee in 1860 to examine the problem of vivisection.[13] The committee's arguments set the tone for a discussion of rationality that encouraged the participation of a wider public. In principle, vivisection was good. It was scientific; it was beneficial. Insofar as it was useful, vivisection could not be cruel. A safely positivistic definition of abuse was proposed. "To merit approval, vivisections must be strictly kept within the limits of their noble goal," the committee warned, "they must only be the means of verifying a hypothesis that has been well defined in advance." The suffering of the subject must be limited to that which "is absolutely indispensable" to the experiment. "Beyond that begins cruelty, since there also begins the gratuitous, the absence of utility."[14]

Many Sociétaires (members), however, questioned whether vivisection could ever be useful. As early as the 1850s critics drew attention to notorious examples of excessive experimentation to show its ineffectiveness.[15] "To attach an animal to an operating table, to plunge a lancet into its palpitating flesh, to dissect it alive, to make its blood pour out, to elicit its cries or howls of pain, of rage, or of fright, to incite its anger or stupefy it with terror," such acts could hardly serve any useful purpose, argued Doctor Roche, for instance, member of the Académie de médecine and vice-president of the Société protectrice des animaux.[16]

Victor Meunier, animal protection society member and editor of *Ami des sciences*, one of the first illustrated reviews of science aimed at a general audience, pointed out that vivisectors themselves sometimes admitted the futility of their work. In a description of a typically horrible experiment on dogs, "here in his own words," Meunier reported, "is how [the vivisector] explained his work to the Société médicale des hôpitaux: 'Hollow probes would not work so iron rods were inserted . . . the dogs had to be gassed, muzzled, and hog-tied, then left without food or water for three days, conditions that are not those of rational experimentation'—the scientist concluded—'they remove all meaning from the experiments.'" How, Meunier exclaimed to his audience, can you believe your ears; "it is the author of the experiments himself who declares that they have no meaning . . . that they are not performed under reasonable conditions!" Why then were these experiments performed, Meunier asks? Surely a physiologist knows what he is doing: "he knew it . . . and he did it!"[17]

As other members fumbled for answers to Meunier's rhetorical demand, the emphasis of the problem shifted from the occasional if notorious excesses of vivisection to the corrupting influence of modernity itself. One member argued that "in the old days" the great men of physiology, "the Harveys, the Asellis, the Pecquets, and the Hallers, had never had the idea of making use of vivisections the way we do today." Vivisection then, didactic historians of animal protection proclaimed, was practiced only in order "to come to some great and useful discovery." Vivisectors worked "far from the public, helped by only one or two assistants." They were deeply moved by their experiments and perhaps even "had a painful memory" of them. Haller, especially: "One knows, indeed, that . . . the famous physiologist of the eighteenth century often voiced the remorse he felt with respect to the many animals he had dissected alive, toward the goal of illuminating his scientific research."

But in modern times, as the secretary of the Académie de médecine explained, "we have a completely different spectacle."[18]

Vivisection was new and its practices were horrifying. "A word that carries with it a frightful meaning, vivisection, is a modern creation," some critics wrongly believed.[19] Modern experiments on animals were publicly, repeatedly, and crassly performed, others more reasonably observed. At the auditorium of the country's most important institution of higher learning, the Collège de France, one observer noted that experiments were completely unlike the almost reverential ones of the previous century: "There, milling around excitedly were demonstrators, assistants, the simply curious, and even students."[20] The thirst for knowledge there was often little more than idle curiosity.[21] "It is to an auditorium filled . . . with loafers coming to warm themselves in winter and to sleep during the summer, that the professor ministering to a banal curiosity performs these horrible interludes of blood more disgusting than the banquets of Atreus [who served up to Thyestes the flesh of his own children]," in the emphatic words of the Sociétaire who wrote *A Sa Majesté l'Empereur des Français: Humble supplique du caniche Médor*, a pamphlet presented from the pet's point of view.[22]

Perverted scientific reasoning led to false values. "One would think that scientists were looking for an excuse to torture animals," noted the head of the Ecole nationale vétérinaire (school of veterinary medicine) at Maisons-Alfort, "if one did not realize that their conduct is a consequence of their way of reasoning." In an attempt to circumvent the imagination and its supposed pitfalls, "one applies oneself to inventing mechanical methods [of performing research]. The physiologist transforms himself into a machine that computes, that weighs and measures; he tries to work out with his hands those problems that can be resolved only by the mind." Many otherwise respectable people, he also noted, "make no distinction between chopping a piece of wood and flaying a live animal; for the most futile motives, they martyr that animal, starve it to death, in exactly the same way as we would redo an arithmetic problem, to see the error made in adding several figures."[23]

Some antivivisectionists attacked positivist science head-on: "Many scientists are convinced that there is nothing useful in science except what they call facts." In the mind of such a critic, "In the factual sciences . . . to say that a phenomenon exists without proving so is equivalent to saying nothing." Otherwise learned doctors were swept away by a fetishism of facts. A Doctor Guardia explained in the prestigious newspaper *Le Temps* that the claims of the tormentors of animals were the "deplorable consequences of this rigid experimental method, applied too rigorously to the organic sciences by minds lacking initiative and weight," prompted by the unfortunate desire, he suggested, "to make physiology and medicine conform to its model."[24]

The experimental method when applied to physiology exposed the evil in human beings. It made them cruel: "The habit of experimenting [on animals] makes some individuals so indifferent to the pain they cause," explained Dr. Carteaux, "that as a result one finds them thrusting their lancet deeply into the tissues [of an animal] and leaving it there, unthinkingly, in order to enter into a discussion that, certainly, could have been held easily at another time." Contempt for feeling was institutionalized in the training of scientists where sense was privileged at the expense of sensibility, in an *enseignement scientifique* that never included training in the field of feeling.[25]

Ambition was also to blame for the horrors of vivisection, ambition fueling the competition among its practitioners, as members of the society imagined. No sooner did news of an apparent discovery leak out from a leading laboratory then other scientists, "envious of or allied with one another," the president of the Société protectrice des animaux explained, "race to torture other animals, here, out of jealous rivalry, in order to contest the supposed discovery, there, out of the spirit of camaraderie, to uphold the discovery and exploit it in turn."[26]

The same point about scientific ambition and its role in the abuse of animals was more dramatically made by a Doctor Joulin: "If remorse is not an empty word . . . what *danse macabre* of mutilated animals must prance in rage on the breasts of scientists!" But no, he concluded: "Remorse is not made for winners, and each of them sleeps . . . with the sweet conviction that his discoveries will make him the equal of Harvey and will permit the human race to close the great book of science."[27]

The tensions between hope for positive bourgeois knowledge and revulsion for scientific method were brilliantly embodied in the vivisector's most frequent victim, the dog. In it, in a recursive movement,

the themes of bourgeois modernity and working-class behavior disturbingly united. Other animals were of course subject to experimentation:
frogs, guinea pigs, rabbits, the occasional cat, and in the veterinary
schools for training purposes, horses. Dogs, however, were cheap, docile,
easy to obtain, and present in the minds of the bourgeoisie.[28]

The crux of the issue was a sacrifice of virtue. Arranged around the
dog were attributes that had little to do with scientific values. The
selfless affection of the dog set off the extreme egoism of the scientific
search for discovery; its helpless canine devotion framed the disturbing,
even sexual, thrust of science. In the complaint of Amadée Latour,
editor in chief of the Union médicale: "Why this preference on the part
of experimenters for inoffensive animals like the dog? I will never forgive the sacrifice of that animal. It is abominable that an animal so loyal
and so loving is subjected to the knife and the tongs. . . . What you do,
and the way you do it, is abominable and immoral," he insisted. A
refreshing understatement of the problem appeared in the 1860 bulletin
of the Société protectrice des animaux. It developed the same contrast
of higher canine worth, of sentiment, in a cruel scientific world: "These
unending tortures, cruelly inflicted upon sweet and submissive animals,
upon poor beings as defenseless as they are speechless, these are not, for
many of us, the most legitimate of actions."[29] Or, as Dr. Carteaux,
Sociétaire, helped his audience of fellow members to imagine, when,
after multiple experiments, the subject was brought back for more operations, "it is not unusual, if it is a dog, to see him, anxiously, fearfully
submissive, drag himself half-mutilated back up onto the torture table
all the while trying to touch the hearts of his tormenters with caresses
and pleading looks."[30]

The most telling icon of positivist cruelty for antivivisectionists was
the image of the dog victim appealing for mercy. British audiences in the
1880s would be outraged by a typically French scene of a dog begging
for mercy. Dogs brought up from the cellar to Claude Bernard's laboratory, a speaker would explain, "seemed seized with horror as soon as
they smelt the air of the place, divining, apparently, their approaching
fate. They would make friendly advances to each of the three or four
persons present, and as far as eyes, ears and tails could make a mute
appeal for mercy eloquent, they tried in vain."[31]

The path to a devaluation of positivism was paved by the recognition that the "madness of French physiology," as some critics called it, marked by gratuitous violence, sexuality, and waste of life, was uncomfortably close to the impulses of working-class culture. The vivisector too was driven by base needs. He had a passion to destroy and a love of gain, marked by an uncivilized disregard for pain. As Victor Meunier, in his article in *Ami des sciences*, wondered: "The strikes of the knife by the vivisector, are they less blameworthy than the blows of the carter?" Either the mutilation of animals is a wrong, or it is not a wrong, another critic insisted. "One cannot deplore too bitterly the suffering inflicted on horses by drivers or owners motivated by greed," he explained, but with respect to vivisection, "the one practice leads to prison and a fine while the other leads to the Institute [of France, which includes the Académie des sciences] and to riches."[32] In another powerful image, the vivisector was also a thief, "stealing neighborhood dogs and cats in order to amuse himself at what he calls experiments or operations on those poor dogs."[33]

Like *le mauvais charretier* but paradoxically more dangerous because they were modern, vivisectors now stood as a threat to bourgeois values. Self-assurance was undercut when representative figures of bourgeois rationality were exposed, didactically, as occasionally bloodthirsty, cruel and potentially beastly echoes of the working class. Vivisection undermined bourgeois and haut-bourgeois values, just as surely as did working-class politics. It underlined the weakness of their overall position, the absence of absolutes that might bolster their own sense of class.

Mentally, this shift from optimism implied a corresponding distancing from the scientific nature of the debate on vivisection. It was not just medical men who worried about the collapse of morality and class. Indeed the marquess of Montcalm, the society's vice-president in 1860, stressed the power of ordinary people's views. "In speaking before you on the subject of vivisection, I do not feel restrained in the least by my complete lack of medical knowledge," he admitted. Distanced from any professional concerns, he could speak on behalf of other, ordinary, fellow members. "I can say then that I am going to deal with this subject not only *in spite of not being a doctor*, but even and especially *because of not being a doctor*," he explained.[34] In a lighter but similar vein, Cham of the satirical newspaper *Le Charivari* asked in a public letter why one could not, "in the interest of science, perform these same operations on those gentlemen—the vivisectionists—whose internal organization must, fortunately for humanity, differ completely from that of other men."[35]

By the end of the 1860s the silence of the Académie de médecine on the proper procedures for vivisection dampened professional men's enthusiasm for discussion of the subject. Interest in vivisection was kept alive in the 1870s by female members of the Société protectrice des animaux, who articulated the widespread discontent with its principles and practice. The comtesse de Noailles (an older relative of the poet), for instance, donated 1,500 francs for an essay contest on the pros and cons of vivisection. The widow of Henri Blatin also succeeded in stimulating discussion of the issue. After twenty years of silently following the debates of the animal protection society, in 1878 nine years after the death of her husband she was moved to a *cri du coeur* against vivisection. The society had proposed a moderate stance on vivisection to be taken at an impending international conference on animal protection. "The protectors of animals," the widow said in response, "must not accept any situation detrimental to their protégés. Leave the plea of extenuating circumstances to others than their protectors," she added, in obvious criticism of the official position on vivisection. Mme Blatin and another member, a M. Decroix, pointedly described as a single man, exchanged words on the subject. Decroix claimed (correctly) that Henri Blatin had approved of vivisection in principle if it were regulated. Mme Blatin insisted that her husband had been always and completely against vivisection. The minutes suggest a contentious meeting.[36]

In the 1880s antivivisectionist societies, with prominent and distinguished female members, were briefly fashionable.[37] La Société française contre la vivisection, for instance, was founded in 1882 with support from the comtesse de Noailles. It prided itself on its honorary president, Victor Hugo, who commented that "Vivisection is a crime." Although Hugo's level of engagement in the antivivisection society was less than complete, throughout the fin de siècle the organization continued to attract supporters among the literati, including Aurélien Scholl, Villiers de l'Isle-Adam, and Léon Daudet. Unlike its offshoots in the Belle Epoque that drifted into radical vegetarianism and seemingly ludicrous revelations—such as that vivisection leads to cannibalism—the Société française contre la vivisection remained, tenuously, within the paradigm of official science.[38]

More confrontational was the Ligue populaire contre les abus de la vivisection directed by Marie Huot (less well known as an active member of the Parisian animal protection society) and Maria Deraismes; this group explicitly joined antivivisection with women's concerns. In a speech sponsored in 1883 by the Ligue populaire, Deraismes reiterated objections to vivisection voiced within the Société protectrice des animaux in the 1860s. In her speech against vivisection, Deraismes argued that vivisection was useless and that scientists were prompted by "an unhealthy curiosity." She added, "They are intoxicated by the blood they spill, drunk on the suffering they produce."[39]

In a departure from conventional animal protectionist tropes, Deraismes probed the consequences of the devaluation of sentiment that was distinctive of science, of modern male scientists, she emphasized: "One of the most striking characteristics of the man who calls himself a scientist is his great disdain for feeling." In the principle that held that the end justifies the means, Deraismes foresaw the perversions of eugenics. She warned: "In the human race, as in all others, alongside an elite there exist pariahs, outcasts, in a word, misfits, crazies, and criminals. Why would not science dispose of them? Nothing, really, differentiates them from animals. They are only poorly organized matter and consequently harmful despite the fact that they are human. An intelligent animal is infinitely more precious than they."[40]

Marie Huot, a member of the Société protectrice des animaux's standing committee on the dog pound in the late 1870s, became secretary of the Ligue populaire contre les abus de la vivisection; from this position she dramatically joined battle with male science. She attacked Charles Edouard Brown-Séquard (after Claude Bernard and Paul Bert, one of the most well known vivisectionists), beating him with an umbrella while he was operating at the Collège de France on a live monkey. Later she spit at a statue of Claude Bernard during its inauguration ceremony not, she claimed, out of particular malice toward Bernard, "but because they had felt the need to place an eviscerated dog at his side."[41]

More quietly around 1880, in response to antivivisectionist appeals, women began to set up and run private refuges for persecuted animals.

The fashionable journal *La Vie contemporaine* recalled the campaign against vivisection during this less fervent decade: "The ladies occupied themselves with rescuing dogs and cats, spending all their small resources on the creation of animal shelters."[42] Individual rescue efforts that the animal protection society had financed in the mid-1870s included those of Mme Lamargo, rue de l'Evêque, who, the society learned, rescued and cared for abandoned dogs, and Mme Graye, rue Feutrier, a seller of offal who, a society member told its prize committee, "has become the salvation of the stray dogs of her neighborhood."[43] Alain Corbin's research on smells suggests the success of these measures. Between 1810 and 1820 Parisians complained about cowsheds in the city. In the 1850s it was pigs that offended. From 1859 onward the smell of animals in general grew troublesome, and in the 1880s, Corbin writes, "one hears complaints of the odor emanating from dog hospitals."[44]

A significant network of feminine patronage existed throughout the 1870s and 1880s for the rescue of lost dogs, extending from rich bourgeoises like Mlle Fanny Bernard or Mme d'Este Davenport, "who spends the major part of her fortune on animals," to the so-called dog and cat ladies of Paris who used their meager, occasionally supplemented, income to buy bread for the homeless animals in their neighborhood.[45]

Nineteenth-century animal rescue was for many women an escape from a dangerous and masculine scientific world. The case of Claude Bernard's daughter illustrates the collision of feminine sensibility with these troublesome norms that parallels the history of antipositivism in Paris. We are told in a surely apocryphal story of Fanny Bernard's abrupt disenchantment with her scientist father. As the story goes, one day Fanny's best friend comes to her in despair. My dog has disappeared, she cries. Fanny tells her not to worry. Papa will know what to do. The two girls run to the Collège de France. A foolish attendant lets them into the vivisection chamber where Claude Bernard is working. We guess the rest of the story: Bernard is caught in the process of cutting up alive the friend's dog.[46]

Fanny Bernard's experience was traumatizing, of course. She lay sick in bed for weeks afterwards. Later in her life, one contemporary asserted, "It appears that the idea of expiation moved her and that in redemption for the suffering formerly imposed by the great physiologist on the animals he studied, she determined to bring happiness to those specimens of the same species that fall into her hands."[47]

Bernard's charity supported a number of private refuges and pensions for dogs in Paris. She paid an allowance to Mlle Mazerolles, for example, who lived on the rue de Buci and took care of old and sick cats. Mlle Bernard herself succored some eighty dogs at her retreat at Bezons-la-Garenne.[48] In her work of expiation for her father's sins—the funding and establishment of canine refuges in and around Paris—the focus shifted, significantly, from animals in the hands of scientists to dogs lost in the city. The prism of her life and work with refuges came to overshadow the issue of vivisection itself. In protectionist praxis in general the image of a dangerous city came to predominate. Virginie Déjazet, the actress, was well known for her habit of rescuing stray dogs. Her obituary in *Le Figaro* in 1875 described her habitually stooping to pick up dirty and wet dogs in the street.[49]

At the end of the century Valentin Magnan, psychiatrist and physiologist, described how one déclassée antivivisectionist spent her time: "She collects all the stray dogs she finds in the streets, taking them home with her or placing them in another shelter. She has made a will in favor of five or six of them she cares for at home. She has left each 25 francs a month but, fearing that sum is insufficient, she has decided to increase it." Clinically Magnan accumulated details: "Scarcely in the street and her work of protection begins. She picks up pieces of glass and other sharp objects, for fear that a horse might, in falling, cut itself on them, increasing its pain. One day she spent, she," Magnan repeated, "in her fine lady's dress, more than a half-hour in this ragpicker's work."[50]

In France as in Britain, the antivivisection movement seems to have been fueled by women's keen identification with helpless animals who lived at the mercy of controlling scientists.[51] Theodore Zeldin notes, "It was said that women led the movement against cruelty to animals as a consolation for the brutality they endured from men."[52] Claude Bernard himself, in Coral Lansbury's reading of his *Introduction à l'étude de la médecine expérimentale*, "described nature as a woman who must be forced to unveil herself when she is attacked by the experimenter, who must be put to the question and subdued."[53] In feminist discourse in general, "la science masculine" came to be posed against "les malheureuses femmes" as in the later work of Cleyre Yvelin who argued in

1910 that vivisection would end when women were allowed into the Académie de médecine.[54]

In the shift from triumphant modernity to modernism women had an increasingly important part. They were involved in the day-to-day work of the Société protectrice des animaux, work whose central goal was the definition of class. Second, and more interesting, the ideas associated with women pushed against the limits of bourgeois ideology. Sentiment, once imprisoned within the private sphere, came during the work of protection to settle in the public sites of bourgeois life.

For men and women alike, the qualities of pets—vulnerability and sensitivity, qualities long identified with femininity—broadly contrasted with the nature of urban life and undercut the city's positivistic intent. Throughout the 1870s members of the Parisian animal protection society such as Mlle Lilla Pichard, M. Charbonnier, and Mme de Charmel demanded the establishment of a home for lost dogs, "reiterate[d] the view, so often aired among us, that a refuge for lost or abandoned dogs be founded."[55] In 1885, the society did found a refuge at Arcueil (figure 1), but it soon closed for lack of funds.[56]

Individual Sociétaires occasionally rescued dogs. M. Hadamer, for instance, announced proudly at the June 1876 monthly meeting that he was rescuing dogs from the streets, dogs that if sent to the dog pound, the Fourrière, "would be hung without delay." Less anecdotal was the contribution of Dr. Bourrel, whose dog hospital on the rue Fontaine-au-Roi was also an unofficial animal shelter. The society was continually sending homeless dogs to him. A typical request resolved in this way was that of one member, M. Montanger, who asked the society in 1874 "if some member of the society would agree to adopt [a blind dog] whose masters have just died. The concierge of the house where the animal lived took him in temporarily but the owner has forbidden her to keep him any longer."[57]

Private refuges were an alternative to the Parisian pound, "the morgue for things" in the evocative phrase of a *Revue Britannique* author. Established in 1811 as "a depository for things and animals taken from the public thoroughfares," by the middle of the nineteenth century the Fourrière was functioning inadequately as a dog pound. Dogs were abused, neither fed nor watered before, finally, being hung.[58] They might be sold to vivisectionists. "It is better for the dogs to be hung

Figure 1.   The refuge of the Société protectrice des animaux at Arcueil. Collection Roget-Viollet.

rather than be released to medical students who would use them for vivisection experiments and subject them, therefore, to prolonged agony," as one corresponding member of the animal protection society argued in 1873, voicing common neighborhood fears that behind closed doors medical students were experimenting viciously on animals.[59]

The sounds of the Fourrière, of dogs slowly dying from blows or asphyxiation or hanging, mingled in Parisian minds with the equally chilling howls of the victims of vivisection. As a Doctor Condier complained in a letter to the Société protectrice des animaux about the Parisian dog pound, "not only are these unfortunate [dogs] hung there, but they are beat on the head with a stick, which makes them cry horribly to the great disgust of the neighbors."[60]

The aural imagery presented in a much publicized court case on vivisection in 1879 between the city of Paris and a Mme Gélyot, owner of a lodging house on the rue de la Sorbonne, gives a more vivid description of how animal pain, real or imagined, affected and unnerved neighborhood life. Mme Gélyot sued the government for damages caused to her business by Paul Bert's vivisection laboratory, which was located across the street at the Sorbonne. Tenants moved out because the sounds of dogs crying in the night disturbed their sleep. An officer carefully collected evidence that supported Mme Gélyot's case. "He had even taken the trouble to distinguish between the various types of howls that he heard when he went to the rue de la Sorbonne," it was explained. One dog, he reported, "barked in a deep mode," another "in a sharp, high-pitched mode," and a third, most pathetically, "wailed in tones that resembled a human voice." Gélyot's bourgeois, petit-bourgeois, and artisan neighbors supported her suit and testified to the disturbing character of the problem. M. Chaffotte, an attorney, claimed that "several times in the night he had rushed out of bed believing that someone was being murdered in the street."[61]

Anxiety invested in a hostile city now overlapped the enduring tensions of class in animal protection discourse for pet owner and antivivisectionist alike. Bourgeois rescuers continued to save animals from hard-hearted workers.[62] But what emerges clearly is the contribution by the animal protection movement in its varying gendered modes to a redefinition of public life. In the early years of the Société protectrice des animaux, in the late 1840s and 1850s, the organizing image of danger for bourgeois and haut-bourgeois reformers was "the vicious carter." The behavior and beliefs of working-class people were to blame, Parisians believed, for the nastiness of modern life, for its violent nature. The goal of animal protection initially was the reshaping of popular Paris to fit the norms of Haussmannization—utility, predictability, and controllability. By 1880, however, its goals and claims were far less secure. Parsed, the working classes and the upper classes were disturbingly alike, marked by masculine violence. And Paris, long the site of class distinctions, was the home of new and discomforting uncertainties. Dichotomies on which the understanding of modernity had rested—good-bad, bourgeois-working class, civilization-nature, male-female—became harder to maintain without a readjustment of the modernist imagination. The image of the evil scientist appeared alongside the construct of the pet. As the next chapters will show us, the ostensible emptiness of bourgeois life was filled by suprahuman, loving, and faithful pets, on an equally fictional plane.

2

The Notion of Fidelity
in a Bourgeois World

The nineteenth century's fascinated belief in canine fidelity seems extravagant and at first glance trivial. The "incredible journey," or the long trek homeward of a faithful pet, unguided and against all odds, has been relegated to the theme of children's literature. But the fact is that such striking acts of fidelity were commonplace events during the French nineteenth century and the object then of much serious concern. Victor Hugo, for example, was said to have cherished an old poodle named Baron whom he had once, in a moment of perverted generosity, given away to a Russian count. Baron, miserably unable to live without his master, trotted the thousands of miles, alone, but determined, from the count's country house outside Moscow to Paris and a joyful reunion with the remorseful Hugo.[1]

Parisians were convinced, moreover, that bereaved canines often traveled unaccompanied to the grave of their master or mistress. They also believed in dog suicide. Newspapers and journals drew attention to such events and, in the 1870s, these issues figured prominently in animal protection discourse. Cemetery keepers remarked on the daily visits of dogs to Parisian cemeteries and noted an increase in their numbers on All Soul's Day. The fixed habits of mourning dogs were carefully noted by members of the governing council of the Parisian animal protection society like the aptly named M. Cheval, who was moved several times during his own painful visits by the "sobs of a dog prostrate in grief at the tomb of his master." So widespread was members' belief in this behavior that a city ordinance of 1874 prohibiting dogs from cemeteries set off a crisis for the Société protectrice des animaux. After weeks of discussion, the society decided that although its policy was not to set itself against the authority of the prefect, in this case it had no choice. The overriding duty of the society was to support the interests of piously faithful dogs. Canine suicide, it is true, never became the focus of official attention, but spectacular cases were widely reviewed. So we learn of Chéri who leaped out of a window after her owner's sudden death, and of Trim, who threw himself into the river after being callously rejected by his owner.[2]

From our twentieth-century perspective, we might suggest that dogs do not commit suicide. They do mourn, and some have died of starvation following the death of an owner. And dogs have saved people from drowning and others have pulled people out of the snow. Animal behaviorists explain that dogs act toward humans as if humans were dogs, all of us members of the same pack. (Konrad Lorenz's notion of two dog personality types, one faithful to its master, the "pack leader," the other capable of more generalized devotion, has been nuanced in recent years.)[3] Dogs are faithful, but they do not kill themselves when bereaved or rejected. We may also doubt that dogs spend their Sundays sobbing on their owners' graves or trot thousands of miles halfway across Europe, even for Victor Hugo.

Bourgeois petkeeping has cultural specificity. The contrast between what dogs ordinarily do, and what the nineteenth century thought they did, allows us to speak of petkeeping as a construct. A sense of loss informed the construct of petkeeping in nineteenth-century Paris and, by implication, the ordinary experience of bourgeois life. Various aspects of petkeeping culture suggest this, but it is with canine fidelity that the concept of loss was most widely articulated. That fidelity, as imagined by contemporaries, has a thematic integrity. It is a statement about modernity that lacks the economy of "The Swan" by Charles Baudelaire, perhaps, or the depth of Gustave Flaubert's *Sentimental Education*. But its representations, though set in a different register, cannot be brought into doubt.

Ideologically, the production of canine fidelity was closely related to romanticism, as the indulgences of Lamartine suggest. A friend recalled the memory of a meeting at the poet's château at Mâcon:

> All of a sudden, under the tall trees Lamartine appeared on horseback, wearing a tall gray hat, dressed in a brown frock coat, with olive-green vest and buff-colored trousers, surrounded by his six greyhounds who gam-

boled about him. At the same time, above the gothic gate two peacocks spread their speckled tails. Sudden image of a prince in a feudal and fairy-tale domain.[4]

In the plunder of the past from which came so much of bourgeois culture lay, ready at hand, the emblematic representation of a virtue whose loss seems to have heightened its appeal. But if the dog was the ideal emblem of fidelity in the medieval world, the notion of fidelity in the bourgeois world is significant for its lack of resonance in French society. People owned dogs, they said, because dogs were faithful and people were not. As one theorist commented, "this fidelity, so rare in any epoch, and still more so in our own," was increasingly difficult to actualize in modern times. Dogs were appealing because "one is delighted to meet in the beast that laudable conduct that is so rarely engendered within the human species itself." "Our devotion has limits, but that of the dog, none," in the words of the author of one of the century's most popular dog-care books. Canine devotion was disinterested and selfless. The dog, another noted, "loves his master more than he loves himself." For a human being's sake, "they forsake their own kind."[5]

Canine fidelity was a dream image of the past brought into being with its nostalgic virtue in full view. The striking image of the (soon-to-be) republican Lamartine pretending with his greyhounds to an ancien régime life is even more effective when we recognize that its substance was deliberately empty. Lamartine gave up hunting and was rewarded with a medal of honor in 1855 from the Parisian animal protection society for his essay, "My Last Gunshot," whose content is still familiar to us today:

> When the smoke of my gun dispersed, pale and trembling, I confronted my crime. The poor charming animal was not dead. He looked at me, his head resting on the grass, his eyes swimming with tears. I will never forget that look to which surprise and pain, the unexpectedness of death, appeared to give the profundity of human sentiment, as intelligible as words; for the soul speaks through the eyes, especially as it dies.[6]

Lamartine loved greyhounds for their "heraldic graces." So too did Walter Scott and Byron.[7] Paul Adam, a writer less familiar today, explained in response to the death of his pet that "Jack's airs of heraldry allowed me to summon up an old and gracious dream in place of my unhappiness. They saved me." Like other artifacts of the chivalrous age, of course, the canine association was generalized. Dogs of all sorts, the French insisted, appeared as virtuous in the novels of Scott.[8]

There was, however, a particular material link with the more recent ancien régime that we should note. After the Restoration of 1815 certain other aristocratic hunting breeds resurfaced, notably the various *chiens du Poitou*. When they had emigrated, aristocrats had left their dogs behind to wait out the Revolution in disguise (perhaps we might even refer to *ci-devants chiens courants*). With tails and ears cut short, dogs were concealed on farms throughout Poitou, some individuals surviving in relatively unadulterated form to provide the basis of a breed.[9]

But, as with greyhounds, the various breeds of hunting dogs took on another meaning in a bourgeois setting. If nineteenth-century hunting rights were not restricted to persons of noble birth, they were limited by law and increasingly, as is clear from Lamartine's account, by sentiment.[10] For most bourgeois citizens the hunting dog had figurative meaning only, as material for a fantasy, a creatively remembered dream of a bygone age—like a novel by Sir Walter Scott. The association must have been metonymic, the legal adjunct of the nobility calling to mind a chivalrous breed of humanity, an aura of a better world, when individuals were still faithful one to another.

In short, during the nineteenth century, faithful dogs took the place of faithless people. This arresting fantasy was presented in all sorts of different contexts, but its appeal is underscored by the differing fate within French culture of two medieval dog stories. The legend of Saint Guinefort, the holy dog, survived in rural France as the basis of a peasant cult. The other, the dog of Montargis, the dog avenger, engaged the bourgeois imagination.

Guinefort, a greyhound, belonged to a knight. One day, as the story goes, the knight, his lady, and their child's nurse each had occasion to be absent from the castle. The dog was left in charge of the baby. The knight returned first and found Guinefort, his jaws bloodied, standing above the overturned cradle of the child. Thinking that the dog had killed the baby, the knight then killed the dog. But the baby was soon discovered to be safe and sound and lying underneath the cradle. The body of a large and dangerous snake, torn into bits, was found scattered about the room. Obviously, faithful Guinefort had saved the child's life; the greyhound had been unjustly killed.

Guinefort is known to us today mainly through the work of Jean-Claude Schmitt, who traces the twists and turns of the story in narratives and rites from the eleventh through the nineteenth century. It is a story of how a dog became a saint, how a legend became a rite, or how a story set within learned culture took on its own potency when adapted by the folk. For within peasant culture it was Guinefort, the saver of children, who became a saint, and to whom, in the nineteenth century, mothers of sick children still applied for help. Pilgrimages were made to Saint Guinefort's wood, the site where the legendary knight's castle had stood, some few miles from present-day Châtillon-sur-Chalaronne, in the department of Ain. Appalled abbés and fascinated folklorists described, as Schmitt explains, "the rite in which the mothers bore their children to the place, deposited swaddling-clothes on the bushes, and knotted together branches so as to unknot the sickly limbs."[11]

The theme of fidelity betrayed disappeared as within peasant culture the healing saint supplanted the emblem of loyalty. It is not so clearly obvious why within bourgeois culture, impressed in other respects by aristocratic norms, Guinefort the faithful hound had minimal and merely tangential appeal.[12] The story of the knight and the dog was known to such canophiles as Aurélien Scholl, who claimed familiarity with its Western prototype in the *Gesta romanorum* as well as the legend's Egyptian and Islamic variations. As a child the count Bony de la Vergne learned a Creole version and noted its details in his 1858 work *Les Chiens*.[13]

Yet within the canophile topos the story of Guinefort rested sterile, anecdotal, and incidental, for the canine constellation was arranged with respect to fidelity replaced rather than betrayed. It was the dog of Montargis who became the prototype of nineteenth-century beasts, "that valiant dog" who denounced his master's murderer and forced him to confess. This dog belonged to Aubry, a courtier of Charles V who was murdered in 1371 within a wood close to Montargis and near Orléans. Only the dog witnessed the crime and succeeded in bringing the murderer, a man named Macaire, to justice. The dog followed the man everywhere, drawing attention to himself and his pursuit. Finally the king, who already suspected the villain, ruled that a duel should take place between Macaire and the dog. The dog won the duel, which took place on the Ile de la Cité. The murderer confessed to his crime and was executed.[14]

In all versions of this story Aubry's dog, an ordinary greyhound, is the only observer of the crime. When people fail to denounce the murderer, the dog becomes the instrument of the judicial duel that determines the fate of Macaire. An eccentric "monument to the French monarchy," the dog of Montargis appealed to the bourgeoisie as did other replacement figures whose purpose we can now consider in some detail.[15]

Again and again the theme of pet ownership showed up alongside the apparent emptiness of life. One owns a dog so one doesn't have to die alone, explained one contributor to the monthly bulletin of the Parisian Société protectrice des animaux. One values a dog because it is faithful beyond the grave, wrote another, so the point is that one will be mourned.[16] The discourse on canine fidelity was characterized by a relaxed confusion of the fictional and the real, but its content was organized mainly around the issue of death and dying. British contemporaries may have pointed to the ideal widow—the Indian woman who, rather than survive her spouse, would throw herself onto the burning funeral pyre of her husband. But the French, more poetically than the British, imagined the mourning dog, determinedly reluctant to live without his master, his mistress.[17]

"They follow us to the grave" is the theme of numerous little journal articles and anecdotes that purported to be true. The number of eyewitness accounts from all over Paris suggests a widespread willingness to believe in their veracity, to construe events so as to evoke the same meaning. The detail of these stories, the realist strategy at work in the organization of trivia—like Balzac's novels they are true and yet not true, a type of magical realism, we might say—underlines the purposeful impulse to fantasize within ordinary lives.

A dog found dead on the street in Paris, for instance, may have stimulated the production of the following story, which appeared in the bulletin of the animal protection society in 1875. It concerned Finot, the dog of a poor artist "on whom fortune had yet to smile," who lived on the rue Notre-Dame-des-Champs. "Several days ago," we are told, "misfortune overwhelmed the poor artist." Finot's master was stricken with pleurisy. He was taken to the hospital, where he died. Finot was bereft: "He had followed the stretcher but—one will have guessed the result—Finot was stopped at the doorstep of the hospital." He returned home and there, "refusing the hospitality offered him by the concierge," he spent the night on the street. For five days Finot maintained the same sad routine. Each day he "stayed 'put' in front of the hospital, no longer eating, drinking from the gutter only when thirst pressed him hard"; in the evening he returned to wait on his dead master's doorstep. Finally he died, "of hunger and cold, still awaiting the return of the master he loved so well."[18]

Prevented from expiring on their masters' or mistresses' graves, some dogs would die instead at the door of a hospital, or at the gates of a cemetery, wherever the final parting had occurred. Dog mourners maintained vigils, and some tried to dig the beloved human being out of the grave. What is curious about these stories, besides their number, is the level of belief, or suspended disbelief, in patently impossible happenstances.[19]

The most persistent dog mourner may be the *chien du Louvre*, the dog of a worker killed in battle during the Revolution of 1830, whose story was immortalized by the poet and member of the Académie française Casimir Delavigne. It was repeated in 1869 by another important figure, Pierre Larousse, in his monumental work, *Le Grand Dictionnaire universel*. As Larousse explained, during the attack on the Louvre on 29 July 1830, a worker was shot and his dog, Médor, his only friend, remained with the body. Several days later the corpses were piled onto an enormous hearse and driven to their final resting place. A dog was seen following the hearse. After the other mourners had left the cemetery, the dog remained behind. At daybreak he would disappear, only to return each evening to cry on his master's grave. One morning the cemetery keeper found him dead, as Larousse emphasized, "dead from grief!"— the last victim, perhaps, of the old regime.[20]

Canine deaths by mourning were given respectful publicity, but most were determinedly quiet affairs. More spectacular cases of canine suicide—"le suicide d'un chien," as headlines described it—were reported, such as that of Chéri, mentioned earlier in the chapter. Faithful and devoted pet of a Mme B., *rentière*, rue Sainte-Anne, her story first appeared in the *Petit Moniteur*. Chéri threw herself out a window a few days after the sudden death of her owner. Despite the care and attention lavished on her by the heir of Mme B., "the poor animal remained inconsolable, unable to accept the death of her mistress," as is clear from the journal's account: "The day before yesterday the young heiress, sitting by the window where her aunt had so often spent her days, placed Chéri, who was crying, on her lap and began to pet the sad dog and to offer comforting words to reassure her. All of a sudden, in a fit of despair, the dog threw herself out the window, onto the street, where she instantly died."[21]

We should consider to what degree the distinctions nineteenth-century individuals established between human and canine behavior were to be admonitory. Did mourners intend to emulate dogs and follow their spouse to the grave? Or were people to be moved—in a Dickensian sense—into becoming for a time a little more caring in their dealings with their fellow human beings? There seems rather an element of sighing resignation in these exaggerations that supports another view. Canine devotion, as some contemporaries noted, was suprahuman. "This precious model" was perhaps too noble for human behavior, one that the inhabitants of the nineteenth century could not be expected to follow.[22] We can follow this line of mournful reasoning through stories that commented on community life.

Large-circulation journals in the 1870s and 1880s appealed to their audience by offering anecdotes of city life, "slices of life" in which the denouement doubled as a moral. In these *entrefilets* of modernity, a dog often appeared as a hero, one whose romantic heroics contrasted with the morally static quality of public life. Typical of these is an article from *Le Gaulois* of 19 October 1875, whose narrative was structured around plain fact.

It was six o'clock on a Saturday evening when the reporter from *Le Gaulois* came on a crowd of people lining the quai d'Orsay and the bridge that connected the river's left bank to the Jardin des Tuileries. Joining these "spectators not less moved than curious by so fascinating a scene," the reporter saw a little black and tan dog, *un roquet*, running back and forth along the edge of the Seine near the place where the *bateaux-*

mouches were docked. The little dog was frantic, "furiously, desperately barking in a strikingly pitiable way," turning in rage toward the river, "as if accusing it of a crime."

What the dog saw, and the crowd and the reporter witnessed, was the futile attempt of the dog's master to save himself from drowning. The man's efforts were violent but unavailing. Finally, "his head disappeared, only his arms remained in view, flailing desperately, and then . . . it was over, the body sank." At the disappearance of his master, the little dog stopped short, "trembled horribly," then "violently threw himself into the river." He struggled, "swimming, panting, pushing himself through the water," toward the spot where his master had been. But, the reporter explained, "the power of the river easily vanquished the puny animal whose little paws were so inadequate to his task and who, in a last noble effort, threw his head above the water, barked a bark of desperation, then disappeared."

What the miniature dog attempted—the rescue of a drowning human being—a city crowd made no move to effect: "None of the spectators, we regret to say," the journal explained, "made the slightest pretense of going to the aid of the dying man!" Simply *flâneurs*, the onlookers were there for the show.[23]

The behavior of a crowd similarly contrasted with canine heroism in the autumn of 1875, this time in an account by the *Petit National*. In this case, the disinterested nature of the dog's heroism accentuated the weakness of human bonds. According to the *Petit National*, the drama began when a man threw his cat into the Seine from the pont de Solférino. Unexpectedly the cat survived the fall and managed to cling to one of the piles that supported the bridge. Passersby coalesced into a crowd and the scene became a spectacle. At this point, a dog who happened to be in the area came to the rescue of the cat. Grabbing it by the back of the neck, we are told, he "set himself the task of returning the cat to firm ground." Despite the uncomprehending struggles of the terrified cat, the dog succeeded in the rescue; then, "without dreaming of laying claim to the reward [routinely awarded to rescuers]," he coolly went on with his bathing. "Many people," the reporter observed, "would not do as much, even for one of their own kind."[24]

The Société protectrice des animaux cited these examples not to condescend but to underscore the pathos of ordinary lives. Together, these and other stories sketch a larger, and even poignant, narrative of Parisian life. Mindful of their significance, the society gathered these stories, originally printed in newspapers and journals, for its monthly bulletin that was distributed throughout the country. Sociétaires themselves submitted such articles as appeared in their own newspapers and at least within the circle of the society the message was amplified. But pets were ensured a multimedia deployment of their most salient characteristic.

The Salon exhibition of art in 1861 presented the portrait of a hero dog, Mustapha, whose story had appeared in the newspapers and was to be repeated very frequently in canophile literature. Mustapha was heroically faithful to a treacherous master who fell into the Seine as he tried to drown his pet, only to be rescued by the dog he had been exerting himself to kill. Sometimes in these accounts Mustapha is a Newfoundland, sometimes a poodle. Sometimes his master is an impoverished worker, sometimes not. Two endings of the story were current. In the one, master and dog return home together, the dog as happily loyal as ever, the master sadder, maybe wiser. In the other, Mustapha is purchased by a witness who subsequently commissions the portrait that is exhibited in the salon. But always we learn that the dog is a better person than his master.[25]

Stories about canine fidelity were produced and disseminated on all levels of bourgeois culture, at times anecdotal, at times more poetic. Canophile literature, for instance, can be said to begin in 1836 with Lamartine's poem *Jocelyn* and Fido, "cet ami du pauvre Solitaire," whose three-month wait for his master's return weakened his body but not his devotion:

> There, when my dusty feet struck against my poor home
> An affectionate howl was my only welcome;
> Alas, it was my dog, beneath my window crouch'd
> Worn thin, by three months' absence of his master touch'd.[26]

The "incredible wait" was itself an echo of a minor Homeric theme that in the nineteenth century was given predominant importance. It was the wait of Argus, not the return of Ulysses that, significantly, was translated into the bourgeois idiom. For example, Marshal Jean-Baptiste Philibert Vaillant, in 1854 minister of war and later household minister to Napoleon III, saw fit to mention Argus in the following terms in a defense of dogs that he published in 1866. The dog of Ulysses should be remembered, he urged, "that old blind dog who recognized his master after an absence of more than twenty years and who died making one last effort to lick his master's hand."[27]

We might compare the process that privileged Argus to the one that assured the dog from Montargis a hero's welcome in the bourgeois world (and a place also in the minister's caniography). Freely borrowing from Homer for a section of *Les Quatre Vents de l'esprit*, Victor Hugo shifted the center of the story from the homecoming of an aged sailor to the wait of a faithful dog. The dog has grown old in his master's absence and lies still, lifeless, on the day the sailor's ship at last arrives in port. As evening falls and the master approaches his house,

> Old, himself, and hastening his step that age had broken
> He murmured the name of his dog in a low voice.
> Then, raising his eyes full of shadow, exhausted,
> The dog looked at his master, and wagged
> For one last time his poor old tail,
> Then died. It was the hour when under the blue canopy
> Like a torch shining forth from the depths, Venus shone
> And I said: From whence the stars? Where goes the dog?
> Oh night![28]

Canine fidelity, like the timelessness of a literary form, stands in contrast here to the dominant, punctuated, nineteenth-century experience of time. Equally important is the presence of "the incredible wait" in anecdotes of everyday life. Sir Hector Pinpin, one of Emile Zola's dogs during the 1890s, was a failed Argus but was no less admirable for the effort. According to Zola's sister, he died of grief during Zola's exile in England: "He was simply incapable of living away from his master," she explained.[29] As with "the incredible wait," so too with themes that operated on parallel levels, such as "the incredible journey," which we mentioned in the introduction with respect to Victor Hugo and Baron, and "the incredible rescue," a theme whose content is now sufficiently obvious.

In a weave of fiction and fact, the notion of canine fidelity developed in response to perceived shortcomings in contemporary life. The potency of this device had much to do with its association with medieval times and to a lesser extent with ancient history, both real and imagined. But the theme of canine fidelity expressed itself as a continuing statement of protest against bourgeois individualism. It outlived the romantic mode, and the longing for an organic and integrated life wrapped itself around other articulations of discontent.

It found expression in concrete sentimentality at the end of the century in that most pathetic of inventions, the public pet cemetery. The Parisian dog cemetery was founded in 1899 by Marguerite Durand, the editor of the feminist journal *La Fronde*, and by Georges Harmois, a lawyer and animal advocate. A place in the outskirts of Paris was chosen, Asnières, already a petit-bourgeois fantasy—a picnic ground—and the inspiration for Georges Seurat's painting of self-absorbed swimmers, *Une Baignade à Asnières* (1883–1884). For five francs, in 1902, one could bury one's pet in a common grave. But for fifty francs one could assure the favored beast a private plot for ten years—and for one hundred francs, an undisturbed rest of thirty years. Restrictions were placed on the type of monuments allowed, and graveside services were forbidden. "Ceremonies and decorations that mimicked human burial," the regulations explained, were expressly prohibited.[30] The line between human and canine was carefully drawn in ways that suggest a de facto pastiche, an insistent confusion of canine and human.

The epitaphs engraved on canine gravestones are moving. Visitors to the cemetery in the early twentieth century remarked on the frequency of the still familiar, "The more I know people, the more I love my dog" (a favorite expression also of Sociétaires who variously attributed it correctly to Pascal and wrongly to Montaigne). Bereaved owners could choose between a number of such expressions. A list of epitaphs to British dogs published in 1898 by a Parisian veterinarian and canine publicist included, "One would have thought he was human, but . . . he was faithful!"[31] And the touching, "Deceived by the world, never by my dog," engraved recently on a monument to a dog named Jane echoed the sentiments of the owner of Emma who, in 1900 on an immense monument that interests visitors today (figure 2), engraved as if to a

Figure 2. The pet cemetery at Asnières: monument to Emma. Collection Roget-Viollet.

lover, "To the memory of my dear Emma . . . faithful and sole companion of my otherwise rootless and desolate life."

All dogs were faithful, unexpectedly, in a world that rationed human virtue by class. Petkeeping was a class-conscious activity, as well: "As there are social classes, so there are canine ones," commentators often noted.[32] It is striking to consider, therefore, that the manufacture of fidelity in everyday imaginary life was, in a sense, class-blind. The nineteenth-century canine, "that friend of the last hour," was faithful no matter what sort of master it had, good or bad, worker or bourgeois.[33] The chien du Louvre, Mustapha the hero, Chéri the suicide, as well as Baron, that intrepid friend of Victor Hugo, all obeyed the same ambivalent impulse. These histories of faithful dogs contained an acknowledgment of class and an empathic transcendence of it. The duality emerged quite clearly and powerfully, for example, in an article from the *Petit Journal* in the 1860s that was reprinted and broadcast by the animal protection society. An apology for pets, it reads also as an indictment of modern life.

As the story goes, the reporter had been wandering along the rue de la Sourdière, "one of the most melancholy streets in Paris." The street itself, the unlikely neighbor of the busy marché Saint-Honoré, was, as its name suggests, an obstinately silent protest "against the brouhaha and the activity that surround it."

Some little way ahead of the author walked an elderly woman "of the people." Her dog, the reporter noted, "was simply repulsive." A mongrel of indeterminate color, fat, short, and small, on a loose leash, Azor moved sluggishly in response to the gentle commands of his owner. All of a sudden, two street urchins ran up to the elderly couple and jumped on the leash. The impact threw the dog into the gutter where he began to tumble head over paws, the leash wrapping itself around his neck, until he was strangled. The woman fainted and the reporter was solicitous. He brought her to a pharmacy where she recovered herself a little and then, gathering up the body of the dead dog, she wandered off, "without knowing where."

"She'll die of it," the pharmacist said, and the author learned a lesson that he imparted to his readers: "Ever since that day, I dare not laugh at the last affections of old people!" Pets, the author reflected, "take the place, perhaps, of dead or departed children, of daughters who have been seduced, of spouses who have been ungrateful." At the time of life when "a great emptiness begins to surround those who have reached sixty or seventy years of age," pets are there, "inadequate objects (*objets insuffisants*) for feelings ready to expire." Like the rue de la Sourdière, perhaps, oblivious to the activity that surrounds it, a pet is comforting to those who are out of step with their times. The moral of the reporter's story was more simple: "Don't, therefore, laugh at animals. Who among us can be sure that our last regret will not be for an Azor?"[34]

Bourgeois empathy extended the boon of canine fidelity to marginal people—to the blind, of course, and to the elderly. The dog ladies of Paris who fed strays caught Baudelaire's imagination, "certain sexagenarian maidens, whose deserted hearts are devoted to beasts because stupid men no longer want them."[35] But less articulate contemporaries also sensed the depeopling of a burgeoning Paris, the "capital of the nineteenth century."[36] Underlying their obsession with canine affect and beastly devotion was bourgeois' apprehension at the fragility of life, as one last anecdote of modern times suggests. The following article appeared in the *Gazette de France*:

> One evening last month around eleven o'clock a *barbet* made the rounds of the cabarets still open in the outer boulevards. First, he would attract attention by yapping, expressing himself almost as if in a human language. Then he would begin to howl and seize people by their clothing, pulling them toward the door of the cabaret. In several places these maneuvers only brought him kicks, but at a cabaret frequented by retired soldiers, he met with a more sympathetic reception. The soldiers followed the dog, who led them to a place where a man in workers' attire lay senseless. . . . Several minutes later and he would have died.[37]

The contrast between our perception and contemporary reception of these stories is significant. Their absurdity has illustrative value and may make us rethink the meaning of kitsch. Fidelity appears in this context as pointing toward the troubling and problematic core of modern life. A reification of essential humanity and its concentration onto nonhuman beings was at once a solution to and a recognition of the breakdown of human potential. The producers of canine fidelity expressed conservative resignation to a world that held little insurance against loneliness and isolation. They acknowledged alienation as the human condition; at the same time they used a deliberately ironic ploy to arrest its progress: canine fidelity looked backward toward the Middle Ages, but the normative ideal it presented was prima facie ridiculous.

We easily recognize that the appeal of canine fidelity was not a mere ideological figment. The love bestowed on stray dogs by the elderly women with whom Baudelaire identified was real. So too, certainly, were the feelings of the owner of Azor, killed by street urchins in the rue de la Sourdière. And a relationship whose termination triggered suicide was surely intense, such an experience as occurred when "a former schoolteacher living in Paris killed himself . . . out of grief for his old dog, run over by a carriage."[38]

Petkeeping has a universality that neutralizes many peculiarities of time and place, as studies often attest. Medical research suggests that the quality of contact between human beings and pets is of a higher level than that between individuals and most other human beings. Blood pressure, for instance, generally remains the same or rises when people are talking to other individuals but falls when they are speaking to a pet. People's "voice tones and facial expressions," in the terms of the researchers, "resemble those used by lovers or by mothers with small children." Physiologically, pets function as intimate companions. Researchers found that people treated their pets like children and thus the impact of the loss of a pet is great, especially to the elderly. "Having to give up one's pet," psychiatrists say, "can be a severe source of stress leading to depression, physical illness, or suicide."[39]

The signs and symbols of petkeeping loosely enclose both the nineteenth and twentieth centuries. Engraved on tombstones or acted out in suicides, the affect registered as powerfully in nineteenth-century Paris as it does in recent psychological case studies. And treatment prescribed in dog-care books supports the notion that pets were like people; it appears provocatively in an 1899 study, *L'Enfance du chien*.[40] Pets function metaphorically, we might say. But the exaggerations of Victorian canine fidelity argue against a wholly ahistorical explanation and suggest that dogs may have functioned as ersatz humans for many individuals in the nineteenth century. Of greater consequence to our subject is to reflect on the exaggerated place of canine affect as an idea within bourgeois culture.

Canine fidelity was a construct, and as such is comparable, *mutatis mutandis*, with constructs that inform the nineteenth-century novel. I suggested above a comparison with the Balzacian strategy of piling detail onto detail to create an imaginary world. On another level of interpretation, if the secret of a novel's appeal is the coherence of the fictional world it creates—positing a totality against the fragmented lives of readers—canine fidelity appealed by offering itself as a completion to an imperfect world. Within bourgeois and petit-bourgeois culture, in elite and ordinary life, stories paid attention to canine fidelity, energetically depicting faithful dogs and patching up a damaged social fabric—behind the facade of genre, unexpectedly, modern life was bleak.

The image of the city presented in these stories suggests that ordinary nineteenth-century citizens found their experience strangely disconcerting. The same disaffection that prompted Emile Zola in the 1870s to describe the Haussmannization of Paris as the hacking to death of a sentient being emerges here, albeit on an anecdotal level.[41] The source material on petkeeping is coincident with that on the modernization of Paris—the series of changes in the physical plant that, beginning in the 1830s and reaching its climax in the late 1850s, 1860s, and 1870s, doubled the population and area of the capital and replaced, seemingly, neighborhood life by boulevards. The relation of material change to *mentalité* can be debated. But the evidence suggests that the terms of modernism were equally accessible to culture builders on elite and mass levels alike. For it seems a useful and telling paradox that, amid an equally powerful discourse on family life, the bourgeois themselves were exclaiming (as the Goncourt brothers commented about the modernity of Poe) that people seemed to be gone—to be replaced by empty things.[42] For many, this was the void that canine loyalty might fill.

3

The *Embourgeoisement* of the Beast

Daumier captured the new configuration of bourgeois and beast in 1839 in a series of twelve drawings he made for *Le Charivari*. "A Day in the Life of a Bachelor" is a day that revolves around pets. The appropriately named M. Coquelet awakens early each morning to the touching spectacle of his cat, Minette, and his dog, Azor, fighting over who will receive the first paternal kiss. By eight o'clock Coquelet has tidied his apartment and pauses by his window to refresh himself with nature, to listen to the song not of the [wild] nightingale (the caption includes but strikes out the adjective) but of the caged canary. This young rooster Coquelet stays single, the caption tells us, out of selfishness and is content to share his frugal breakfast with Azor and Minette. Self-centered and antisocial, Coquelet and Azor spend the day out in Paris in a parade of rejections—of women, children, and the poor—that affirms the perverse importance of his pet. Coquelet refuses a beggar's plea for money as he buys a treat for Azor: "What would you have me do, my dear man? This animal has only me; but you, you have all the world." Later, with Azor's help he cheats a friend at dominoes. Coquelet's day ends as it begins, in his comfortable bachelor's bed with his dog and cat, "a portrait of the single life."[1]

In defining the pet, bourgeois petkeepers during the nineteenth century drew on themes similar to those Daumier mocked. But they used a different medium and evoked more profound effects. Daumier's caricatures in pen and ink displayed petkeeping's egocentric character while bourgeois petkeepers employed the characteristics of pets to point to the discomforts of modern life, the problems of modernity that made petkeeping such a striking response to the age.

A vocabulary of modernity accumulated within bourgeois petkeeping culture that differed from categories of the ancien régime. As we will see, the bourgeois imagination clashed with the bureaucratic language of the previous century over issues associated with a tax on dogs. French lawmakers sought in the tax of 1855 and in subsequent legislation to define pets using categories of function, outmoded concepts from the eighteenth century. To the bureaucratic mind a pet was a luxury, a useless taxable item. Parisian petkeepers, however, insisted on their own definition of a pet as an essential champion of domestic sentiment and warmth.

Bourgeois ideas about the place of animals in contemporary life shaped a newly popular genre of literature also. Histories of animals and petkeeping explained that the dog was an artifact that changed as people did. Many authors suggested that the history of the dog paralleled the history of the world, culminating in modern times in Paris by withdrawal into a private phantasmagoric realm.

Petkeeping came to express bourgeois modernity in many significant ways. We can read the process in the evolution of the dog tax in France into a battle of wills between bureaucrats and ordinary people. Bourgeois' insistence on their own understanding of nineteenth-century needs resulted in reluctant legal acceptance of the modern notion of the pet, the concession of new categories of meaning. Nineteenth-century petkeeping becomes then not just an example of bourgeois life as in Daumier's critique but the invention of a medium, a means of communication: it was the way bourgeois talked about themselves.[2]

The bureaucratic imagination cast backward for models and precedents to the eighteenth century when reforming ministers of the crown first proposed a tax on dogs. The measure was suggested in 1770 as a means of increasing the food supply. A census confirmed officials' suspicions about the inordinate number of dogs in France. Four million of these hungry animals were counted. If two dogs ate the bread that might go to one person then, in the harrowing arithmetic of the age, dogs were consuming one-sixth of the French population. To reduce the number of these beasts and ensure that only the rich could afford the luxury of a dog, an enormous tax of 6 livres per dog was proposed. As with so many eighteenth-century reforms however, the dog tax remained as a proposal; in 1788 thirteen *cahiers de doléances* (lists of grievances), from all three estates, demanded its institution.[3]

Food alone was not at stake. The dogs of the poor, authorities claimed, were a health hazard. They spread rabies—for Nicolas-Toussaint Le Moyne, called Des Essarts, lawyer and author of many books on law, here was the most pressing problem. Rabies was believed to develop typically among dirty and hungry animals, so day laborers "and other people who can scarcely feed themselves" should not be allowed to own dogs, Des Essarts urged. Sébastien Mercier, too, objected to the number of dogs kept by the poor of Paris. "All of these animals, in too great a number, contribute neither to the health nor the repose of the city," he suggested in *Le Tableau de Paris*. Dogs ate bread that should have nourished children; they dirtied the stairwells, disturbed the neighbors, and caused disease.[4]

Among the rich, pet dogs were equally useless, though their owners were better able to tolerate their perniciousness. The eighteenth century was "a kind of Golden Age for dogs, or at least for ladies' lap-dogs," one historian observes. Women cared more for their pets than for their husbands and lovers, according to misogynist satires: "Step on the paw of a little dog," Mercier complained, "and you have lost the esteem of the woman; she may pretend otherwise, but she will never forgive you." In the expansive sexuality of the age, little dogs were playthings in a salubrious sense. Donald Posner's monograph on Watteau's painting *La Toilette* makes clear the nature of the pleasure to be had from a pet. Eighteenth-century pornography dwelt on the same theme.[5] But while the *scène galante* remained an important motif in nineteenth-century imagery, the French Victorian century can be said to have begun in 1790 with the burning of these little dogs (called *lexicons*) at the place de Grève, "for a crime that morality prevents us from naming."[6]

The bureaucratic authors of the 1855 tax on dogs thought in terms of these same ancien régime categories. Two classes of dogs were recognized: useful ones and useless ones, working dogs and luxury dogs. Utility was defined in economic terms. The purpose of the tax was to limit dog ownership to those for whom it was a means of making a living, shepherds and blind people and the like, and to those with the means to care properly for a pet. Echoing eighteenth-century terms, officials blamed stray dogs for the incidence of human rabies. A telling point in the 1840s when the law was first debated in the Chambre des députés was Malthusian: a rising dog population reduced the amount of food available for human consumption.[7] So dogs integral to the economy of the working classes were to be taxed minimally, but dogs of no economic value were to be made expensive, so that only the rich could maintain them. The midcentury pet was by definition a luxury, reserved as the privilege of a small class, a matter of consumption. The tax was meant as a sumptuary law, hailed as such by the recently formed (1845) Parisian Société protectrice des animaux.[8] In contrast, as part of the system of production, the public function of the working dog was sanctioned.

Guidelines were set by the law to enforce the bureaucratic understanding of dog ownership. Communes were directed to establish a tariff of ten francs or fewer for luxury dogs and one franc or more for working dogs.[9] The luxury tax was directed against poor people's dogs in a system that recognized "rich" and "poor," "useful" and "useless," but ignored the distinctive categories of modern bourgeois life.

The tax on dogs shows the tenacity of eighteenth-century structures of thought. Of even greater interest is the way in which ordinary bourgeois individuals undermined these structures. The tax on dogs became a text in which a narrative of bourgeois and petit-bourgeois life was inscribed. Its openness lent itself to competing representations; its shifting authority encoded ordinary attitudes to the bourgeois experience. For if the central bureaucracy formally issued the tax, the town hall was where it was constructed and interpreted. Official representation of dog owners described a simple world of luxury and industry. But declarations by dog owners made at Parisian town halls charted a more complicated story of modern life.

We can observe the bourgeoisification of the law in the construction of the tax rolls (*état-matrice*), in the confrontations between tax assessors and pet owners, and occasionally in the assessors' encounters with the taxable items themselves. The tax was annual, and between 1 October and the following 15 January, all dog owners were obliged to declare formally at their city halls the number and type of dog they owned. Then, from 15 through 31 January, tax officials drew up a master list of taxable people (*état-matrice des personnes imposables*). The following table is a translation of the *état-matrice*. Note that one section transcribed the dog owners' declarations while two other sections verified and commented

Table 1. Master List of Taxable Dog Owners

Names and Addresses of Taxpayers	Taxpayers' Declarations				Facts Established by the Mayor and Tax Assessors			Observations of the Mayor and Tax Assessors
	Date of Declarations	Number of Dogs Declared			Number of Dogs as of January 1			The Commissioner of Direct Taxation, having stipulated various increases in the tax owed for dogs who are not declared or for otherwise incomplete or inexact declarations, directs these observations toward a clarification of the data in columns 6 and 7.
		1st category	2d category		1st category	2d category		
(col. 2)	(3)	(4)	(5)		(6)	(7)		(8)
Abraham (Isidore), Signy	1 January 1857	—	2		1	1		Inexact declaration [with respect to function of dogs]
Autoine (Pierre), Signy	—	—	—		—	2		No declaration made
Isaac (Nicolas), peddler, Signy	2 January 1857	—	1		—	1		—
L'Homme (Louis), Saint-Fargeau	—	—	—		1	—		No declaration made—omitted to make one
Norbert (Jean), wood merchant, Signy	10 January 1857	—	1		—	2		Has previously made an incomplete declaration
TOTALS		—	4		2	6		

Source: Ministère des Finances, Bulletin des contributions directes et du cadastre (Paris, 1855), 220. This table was presented as an example in a collection of government documents on direct taxation.

on the owners' statements to bureaucrats: the whole is a document of official anxieties overlaid by bourgeois concerns.[10]

The categories seemed clear enough to the early authors of the tax. Category one included all dogs for "pleasure" (*chiens d'agrément*) and hunting while category two identified the useful dogs: "Dogs used to guide the blind, to guard herds and flocks, dwellings, stores, workshops, etc.," and, much more ambiguously, "in general, all those that do not fall into the preceding category."[11]

The authors of the tax had envisaged a simple process of categorization. On the basis of an interview between dog owner and tax assessor every dog in France would find its place, in category one as a luxury dog, or in category two as a working beast. Hopes in Paris ran even higher. In 1855 the prefect of the Seine advised his mayors that, in Paris, all dogs were luxury dogs ipso facto and only the highest tax rate was applicable.[12] But correspondence between the prefecture and the town halls and the latter and the taxpayers recorded the reluctant adjustments the bureaucracy made to the realities of petkeeping in Paris. It was only a matter of months before it was recognized that working dogs existed in Paris. Guard dogs and guide dogs were subject to the low rate, after all, in 1856, the first year of tax collection.[13] But real confusion set in and a mass of paperwork resulted when officials came to defining what indeed was the distinction between a working dog and a pet.

The office of the prefect of Paris repeatedly warned mayors to have dog owners questioned precisely as to the type of dogs owned and "principally about the uses to which they are put."[14] From the correspondence emerges the increasing difficulty bureaucrats had in determining in which category a dog should belong. In 1859 the profession of the owner was included in the evaluation of the dog.[15] And during the following decades more factors were brought under consideration. The Conseil d'Etat issued literally dozens of decrees on the subject of pets. By 1887 there were fifteen subcategories that defined dogs whose owners were liable for the luxury tax; perhaps the most baroque subcategory was the thirteenth, whereby, "A dog living with a deaf person who alerts that person when a stranger comes to the door must be taxed at the high rate since that kind of dog cannot properly be considered a guard dog."[16]

A dog was a pet rather than a worker if it accompanied its master on walks, if it was allowed to wander freely within a home, or if it was allowed to play with children. A dog "habitually confined in a house that was situated in a built-up area of a city, when that house is enclosed on all sides and when it contains neither large store or shop" was a pet, as was the dog "of small size that by its nature cannot be understood as being intended exclusively to guard a house." As the law imagined, a dog must be deemed a pet if its state of health or age rendered it useless, and if it was constantly in the living quarters of a house, or "though serving as a guard dog is also admitted inside apartments or offices."[17]

Elsewhere in France such unexpectedly difficult distinctions were disregarded for a time, quite in opposition to the intent of the law, as some experts continued to argue. Until 1867 when the minister of the interior "expressed anew the view that it was not according to breed but solely according to use" that a dog should be classified, in many communes dogs were sorted out on the basis of size. Little dogs were placed in the first category and large ones in the second. Jurisprudence followed pragmatism. Only small dogs could be considered as having "un caractère d'agrément," according to judgments published in the late 1850s and early 1860s.[18]

Categorization of French dogs became so tricky that in 1886 ultimate responsibility for this task was placed in the capable hands of the commissioner of direct taxation. In Paris that transition of power into the hands of the authorities in charge of direct taxes was effected in 1855 by Georges Haussmann. As the prefect explained to his mayors, the tax collectors in charge of indirect taxes lacked sufficient knowledge of the inhabitants to establish the *états-matrices*. Under the supervision of the commissioner of direct taxation, the Parisian tax assessors were charged with door-to-door investigations, meant to be more accurate but the difficulties of which were initially underestimated. In 1856 Haussmann characteristically claimed to have obviated all confusion. "In order that any uncertainty that may yet exist in the classification of dogs be entirely dissipated," he wrote in a memo to tax officials, "I have given instructions to the tax assessors that by aiding them in their investigations . . . will allow the *états-matrices* (the establishment of which they are specially in charge of) to be drawn up without any hesitation whatsoever."[19]

A series of caricatures by Cham published in *Le Charivari* belied this vision of bureaucratic ease. Bewildered tax assessors found themselves presented with bald-faced lies, a dog disguised ineffectively as a cat, for instance, a feline-type tail stitched over its own. As the ingenious dog owner explained: "This a dog! But, no, monsieur: it's a cat. Notice, rather, the tail. Well, perhaps there may have been dogs in his family—it's what may give him some resemblance [to a dog] but, to be sure, it's a cat."[20]

Of course, it was in an individual's best interest to lie about pets. And at least one-third, possibly one-half, of all dog owners at any one time outmaneuvered the tax assessor. But even optimists like Haussmann realized that the difficulties in tax collection went beyond the self-interest of citizens. "Be certain," he urged tax officials, "that very specific questions are asked when those making declarations about dogs first present themselves." All in good faith, dog owners were apt to make a false or incomplete statement.[21]

At issue was the meaning of utility. To bureaucrats, only working dogs were useful. For bourgeois pet owners, affect and defense against the onslaughts of modern life were essential functions of the dog. Decrees from the Conseil d'Etat were thought to settle matters to the benefit of the law, but the official dual definition of a dog—useful or useless—was a feeble attempt to contain modernity within bureaucratic bounds. Dog owners' statements in the form of claims and counterclaims elicited accommodating legislation that slipped ordinary bourgeois views of utility into the legal understanding of the pet. A closer look at those views brings us closer to the changing categories of experience neatly webbed within nineteenth-century petkeeping.

As canophiles responded to the tax, their views developed into an apology for the bourgeois dog and, coincidentally, for the bourgeois home. The sentimentalized canine we know today was given its full development in works that linked him inextricably with family life. We read of the Gordon setter who goes shopping with his mistress and the dog who meets the mailman, who "takes the *Petit Journal* [the news-paper], and letters if there are any, and triumphantly carries them to his master." Fans of 1950s family situation comedies will recognize the supporting characters of the genre and readers of canophile literature today—one thinks notably of J. R. Ackerley—will note some familiar themes.[22]

As the multifunctional family beast took shape in the bourgeois imagination, it vehemently contradicted the bureaucratic notion of the useless dog. Decrees ruling that a canine could be either pet or guard dog but not both went against the grain of the bourgeois experience and angered canophile authors. Writing when the official definition of a pet comprised five subcategories, Jean Robert dismissed the rulings. When was a guard dog not a guard dog? In the legal mind, when it went for a walk with its master or wandered around the apartment or played with the children. "To let children ride on its back, instead of biting or threatening them, is to act in a manner unbecoming to any serious dog," this spokesperson for the family pet wrote, mockingly. A guard dog wasn't allowed to grow old: "'Your old servant isn't good for anything anymore; you'll have to kill it, poor devil, or you'll be taxed more.' Good intentions are a luxury, and we place a surtax on pity," he more caustically continued.[23]

To their owners, the guard duties of bourgeois dogs were inseparable from duties of an affective nature and bound up with private life. The functions overlapped. Alexis Godin, editor of an animal protection journal, explained in the year the tax was enacted that a dog "does not stop being an object of *pleasure* even though he makes himself more or less *useful.*" As canophiles would argue, he noted, "the apartment dog, the same one who shares a bed with his master or mistress, is for them a *useful* guardian as much as if not more than if he were set loose or chained in the courtyard." The largest as well as the smallest dog might be cast in these roles. A dog of any breed could be an object of affection. "One might say," Robert explained, "that in general [the dog] is so amiable that it is always a pleasure to own." Hunting dogs, for instance, made delightful pets, he insisted. "A Pont-Audemer spaniel is perfectly at home on a rug; there are pointers who strike a very good figure in a salon." And all dogs were guard dogs, Robert optimistically detailed, "the tiny terrier as well as the mastiff; they may, for example, fulfill the office of guardian, if not by flying at an intruder's throat then at least by sounding the alarm."[24]

As bureaucrats splintered an outdated legalism to fit contemporary reality, insisting on a legal and expensive distinction between useful working dogs and (inessential) pets, other distinctions increasingly formed the basis of ordinary bourgeois categorization. Deliberate class articulations took the foreground. As Laure Desvernays explained to the petit-bourgeois readers of the series of Little Handbooks for the Home, an essential function of the bourgeois pet was guard duty. In these times when "ruffians have proven themselves capable of any audacity," she asked in her contribution on the well-run household, "what more important service may we demand of our dogs than to defend our homes and ourselves?" The dog dependably recognized class enemies: "He guards discriminately, almost never failing to nip at the heels of poorly dressed strangers whom he suspects of criminal intent."[25]

The bourgeois dog stood guard not only against class enemies. The family pet presented an interface between the home and the outside world and maintained the isolation of the family unit as effectively as architectural "strategies of isolation."[26] As locks, peepholes, later doorbells did, in the bourgeois imagination, the family dog functioned as a statement of privacy and control. "The dog immediately recognizes those friends of the household he must always make welcome," and those he was bound to rebuff, we are told. The dog knew friend from foe—as a family retainer might, in the pretensions of another age; "He has an unshakable authority. . . . We may enter with confidence if he indicates, by his affability, that we have his support. Presented by him, we will be welcome."[27]

The pet dog guarded the morals of *petits rentiers*—individuals of small but independent means—who "without the pleasure they find at home or on a walk with these docile and faithful companions" would ruin their health, waste their time and resources, and sink into iniquity at cabarets.[28] The dog trained the children in an ethical life. The dog had "the gift of exciting sentiments of good, of humanity, of love among children," suggested one canophile.[29] The pet signaled the alienation of the family from public life yet performed what was perhaps its most important duty as guardian of the soul. In a heartless world, these sources repeatedly suggest, utility no longer differed from affect. Consider the following statement that began Alfred Barbou's authoritative account of the French dog:

> We turn now to the role the dog plays within the home. Good to all those who approach him, always ready to defend the weak, and the children, friend of the house and recognizing *only* the friends of the house, he plays a large part in family life. Often he proves himself not only a supporter, but a consoler. More than any human being, the dog is able to give his master, after the most dreadful misfortune, brief moments of joy.[30]

Barbou touched on the isolation of the individual within the family home. We can make the same distinction here between intimacy and privacy that a reviewer notes in discussing architecture and the domestic interior in nineteenth-century London, Paris, and Vienna. "An architecture of flats that was designed to protect the privacy of the family from the outside world did not at the same time foster family intimacy." The family apartment kept parents separate from children, and the family from servants.[31] We can read petkeeping culture as a comment on this architecture of distance and as an even more telling parallel statement of modernist withdrawal.

"The caressing regard of a dog, the sweet touch of a cat, the rhythmic modulations of a bird in a cage, the triumphant trills of a canary, have they not, on occasion, chased away our melancholic thoughts?" asked Laure Desvernays, adding, "we have good reason . . . to surround ourselves with animals." The presence of pets made an apartment come alive: "If it were not animated by the presence of animals, dogs, cats, birds, every house would be somewhat like Sleeping Beauty's castle. The presence of 'our animal friends' in our apartments, our gardens, adds an invigorating note."[32] Though later chapters explore petkeeping culture's domestic interior per se, note here the mixture of dead interior and affective animal, of disappointing humans and rewarding canines: "The grief and sadness of a dog in the absence of his master and its exuberant joy at the master's return, are truly startling"—in a world otherwise still.[33]

Petkeeping culture existed quietly within the history of private life on an everyday level. Not every home had a dog, of course. But for the same cluster of reasons, perhaps, that within high culture the prostitute became an icon of nineteenth-century Paris, so the canine, on a more banal plane, projected a set of representations of the bourgeois experience. Prostitution has existed in other times and places, but the selling of women's bodies took on harsher meaning in a culture uneasy with the effects of commercial capitalism and aware on a metahistorical level of its own alienation. Pets, too, belonged to the age. The tax on dogs disturbed the growing importance of the home as a place of essential emotional retreat and in the 1860s, 1870s, and 1880s displayed the experience of ordinary dog owners themselves.

Other sources plotted the same narrative of bourgeois life, using canine history as their guide. In the burgeoning field of canine literature, the history of human society was linked, "intimately," as some canophiles liked to emphasize, with the history of the dog.[34] From the dawn of history through the Middle Ages, the dog was a practical companion, necessary for human beings' survival on an elemental level. Only in modern times, in urban society, did the dog begin to lose that function to become, in the nineteenth century, essential primarily for people's emotional life.

Borrowing heavily from Alphonse Toussenel's *Esprit des bêtes*, Dr. Portanier (a veterinarian from Nice who wrote also about rabies) in a lecture published in 1889 suggested that the history of the dog was indistinguishable from that of early human society. In the beginning of our common history, dog and man hunted together. The canine was an essential auxiliary to man in his primitive fight for survival in a hostile world. "Alone and isolated, in the midst of nature . . . how else would mankind have survived, and more than that gained mastery over his world?"[35]

The same theme was expressed as panoramically by Oscar Honoré in 1863 in *Le Coeur des bêtes*. Imagine, he suggested, with what joy the first human beings realized that with the dog, the hunting of large game was successful. Dominion was assured: "The dog is probably the first conquest of man, and it is thanks to him that man has conquered some tens of other species of animals without which there would be today neither city, nor road, nor nation, nor maybe mankind itself on the earth."[36]

The dog made civilization possible for, after a while, the dog became a shepherd. Humankind moved into a pastoral mode of existence, and continued progress was assured: "Without the dog, no herds; without herds, no sustenance, no clothing, no time to waste, consequently, no astronomical observations, no science, no industry. It is the dog who has given leisure to man." Aurélien Scholl, quoting the naturalist Georges Cuvier, described the domestication of the dog as "the most useful and most remarkable of conquests, 'perhaps essential to the establishment of society.'"[37]

In prehistoric times man and dogs were allies, "unable to live without each other," but once the survival of the human species was assured, "the role of the dog was wiped out." With the advent of the arts and sciences, Henri Lautard explained in 1909, "the influence of the dog on the progress of civilization became more and more secondary." Nonetheless, canine and human remained close. In the Middle Ages, Lautard noted, we find, "the dog . . . very involved in feudal society, either in the great hunts where he takes his place beside the falcon, or in the life of the château where he enlivens, a bit, its heavy monotony."[38] According to Pierre Mégnin in an exhaustive history of the dog that appeared in 1877, in the Middle Ages the dog was still a practical animal. In his summary Mégnin explained, "From the time of its domestication until the point where we are in this history, the dog has been an unceasingly useful animal, an indefatigable auxiliary to man in hunting, or a faithful guardian of his flocks." The greyhound was the only dog "admitted into intimacy" and could not be considered exclusively a luxury dog, since it was used for hunting as well. But in the seventeenth and eighteenth centuries in courtly and urban culture a taste developed for new species of dogs, little apartment dogs, while "small landowners and rural bourgeois who had begun to free themselves from noble tutelage" introduced new breeds of recreational hunting dogs.[39] With the advent of the bourgeoisie, these historians noted, came the bourgeois dog.

The dog appears in these accounts as a form of culture, whose essence changed as society did. But though the writers agreed on the dog's role in the past, they differed as to what it had become in the nineteenth-century world. Some critics suggested that in the modern world no one needed a dog; it should be destroyed. Nicolas Fétu, for instance, in his *Requête à mes concitoyens pour l'extinction de la race canine à Dijon*, reviewed the familiar approving history of the dog but concluded that now it was obsolete: "What needs to be decided is whether, in the fullness of civilization (*en pleine civilisation*) the dog retained its raison d'être, and what were the consequences of its conservation in the midst of us."[40]

The hunting dog had lost its place: "Modern man, for seizing prey and feeding himself, has no need anymore for the help of the dog." The guard dog was useless in the modern policed city. So too was the butcher's dog that had had its place "in the beginning of things" but in the modern city was extraneous. Pets, especially, had no place in modern life.[41] Later Fétu clarified his views: it was the modern city that held no place for dogs, the city of Dijon where he lived, but his argument applied to any city like it, "a supervised city, where industry flourishes, with a modern police force, where the funeral cortege of a poor person is always accompanied by some old comrade." He added: "If the fate of civilization still depended on the presence of the dog, we would indeed despair of the intelligence and heart of man!"[42]

Such condemnations of the modern dog were troubling but in their one-sidedness rare and countered by influential canophiles such as Marshal Vaillant, Napoleon III's minister of the household, whose defense of dogs in the form of a letter to Fétu appeared in journals. The Société protectrice des animaux reprinted Vaillant's response in full in its monthly bulletin of July 1866 and in part in subsequent issues throughout the remainder of the century. After a brief history of famous dogs and their notable deeds, Vaillant introduced testimony from his own family pet:

> Your fury would direct itself even to the dog who is here, resting against the hand that writes to you, fixing his eyes on mine and letting me read in them the indignation that moves me against you! Scold this monsieur, he seems to say to me, scold him well; tell him how I love you, how we love each other! how I love your sister, your niece, all those who are dear to you; tell him how I watch over you at every instant of the day and night.[43]

For Vaillant and other canophiles, the dog was necessary for emotional survival, for the protection of the private realm of family and self. Canine historians of this sort liked to emphasize the voluntary nature of the dog's liaison with humankind throughout the centuries. "The dog himself," wrote Aurélien Scholl in 1897 in his introduction to the baron de Vaux's *Notre Ami le chien*, "I scarcely doubt, took the initiative in his own domestication." We can imagine, he added, "the first caress of the dog, placing his wet nose timidly on the hand of his master, or licking it. We may imagine him following, hesitatingly, his benefactor in the street, half fearful at first, but encouraged little by little and finally adopting the habit of accompanying him to the fields and identifying himself to a certain degree with his life."[44]

Animals could live without human beings, but not the reverse.[45] Dogs willingly followed people throughout all the periods of history, and in the modern world, dogs became bourgeois. Of course, some dogs remained workers, "so many masters! so many different [fortunes], those who give pleasure, and others who work!" Does the classification of dogs not follow that of our own world, asked A. L. A. Fée, "may we not make categories of dogs as we make social categories: patrician dogs and plebeian, bourgeois dogs and proletarian, rich dogs and poor."[46] A census of dogs provided by dog tax returns indicated to Alfred Barbou in 1883 that "working-class neighborhoods" contained working dogs, and "rich neighborhoods," pets.[47] The following chapters concern themselves more fully with the life of the bourgeois dog. The dog-care book, for instance, provided a wealth of information about the intimacies of a deliberately bourgeois fantasy—how to travel by rail with one's dog; how to groom and dress it; how, in occasional circumstances, to mate it (buy beach costumes in shops along the Palais-Royal—a wedding is nice but unnecessary). Here we are concerned with ordinary bourgeois perceptions of the trajectory of bourgeois history as it unfolded in the history of the dog and as it found expression, on an even broader level, in the new language of petkeeping.

By the end of the century legal and moral attempts to contain dog ownership within the categories of the ancien régime had clearly failed. More and more people owned dogs as the years progressed. "Undoubtedly the taste for dogs is expanding," wrote Jean Robert in 1888. "Today," he explained, "in spite of the tax, [hostile] concierges, and the exiguity of apartments, almost everyone has a dog, if not several." *Le Petit Moniteur universel* noted in 1876 that in Paris there was one dog for every twelve humans.[48]

A good many of these dogs escaped the fiscal census. In the 1840s it had been estimated that there were 100,000 dogs in Paris and 3 million in France.[49] Officially these figures were not reached until the 1880s and

1890s respectively. In 1856, the first year of tax collection in Paris, 75,286 dogs were declared. But the rate of increase in the number of dogs during the Third Republic based on official figures alone is nonetheless impressive. Between 1872 and 1885 the number of dogs in France increased by 450,000: in 1872 a tax was paid on 2,240,000 dogs, and in 1885 on 2,690,000 dogs; by 1896 that number had become a little more than 3 million. In the Department of the Seine (which includes Paris), in the four years between 1888 and 1892 when a total of 131,395 dogs were registered, 8,000 dogs were added to the rolls of taxable items. The impossibility of reducing the numbers of dogs was generally conceded by bureaucrats.[50]

As we have seen, the dog tax was the subject of much debate in the 1860s, 1870s, and 1880s, debate that reshaped the century's understanding of the place of pets in modern life. Although many health officials continued to believe that, if properly enforced, the tax would reduce the number of dogs, others came to recognize the quixotic nature of this goal. As one public health official complained, dogs could not be taxed away for "the dog has become someone with whom we must reckon."[51] Another official explained that, in general, police measures against dogs were unenforceable. The minister of the interior might direct his prefects to execute such and such a measure, and the latter might successfully prevail on his subprefects to order the mayors to enforce it, but no amount of persuasion could prevail on the local police; "They do nothing, being careful not to appear lacking in consideration for those dogs who are so influential and well thought of in their commune."[52]

Contemporary explanations for the failure to limit dog ownership focused on the status of the dog, on its new personality. In later caricatures, Daumier conceded that the tax itself conveyed a new status on the dog. "There, now you have become a citizen," one proud owner remarked to his pet in a print published in 1856 by *Le Charivari*. Another scene in the same series on the tax and family life showed an owner commissioning an artist to paint his dog's portrait: "Now he's one of the family, he needs his picture too" (figure 3).[53] The argument of a doctoral thesis published in 1907 dwelt on the conceptual contradictions involved in considering as sumptuary the tax on dogs. The opinion of the law notwithstanding, the author argued, a pet is not a luxury.[54]

Figure 3. Honoré Daumier, caricature of artist painting a dog's portrait: "Now he's one of the family, he needs his picture too." From *Le Charivari*, 1856 (by permission of the Houghton Library, Harvard University).

By 1907 the point was obvious. Luxury and pet ownership were now contingent themes. The definition of a pet had changed. Its indispensability was acknowledged and the old categories of function could not be maintained. The dog, useless when considered in light of its productivity, had become an essential household figure—a "love machine," a *machine à aimer*, in nineteenth-century terms.[55] Ensconced within the family, the dog had become an affective end in itself. Not so much a replacement person, a metaphor, but an adjunct, a dream image was constructed in the shape of the family pet, as the next chapters detail.

4

Dreamworlds of the
Bourgeois Interior (1)
Pets and Private Life

Dogs formed only a part of nineteenth-century petkeeping culture. Fish, birds, and even plants, as well as cats, the anti-pet par excellence, complement the beings within the fantasy universe of the ordinary bourgeois. The domestic interior reveals itself here as the setting of a vision at once utopian and parodic, a worldview that hovered somewhere between the dreams of Charles Fourier and the later fantasies of the science fiction novel.

What do we make, for example, of Victorian enthusiasm for the *épinoche*, or stickleback, whose family life highly recommended it for French aquariums? Florent Prévost, whose popular pet-care book was awarded a medal of honor in 1861 by the Parisian animal protection society, instructed home aquarists in the art of stickleback watching. Provide the fish with a tangle of aquatic plants from which a nest can be built, he explained: "We see the male set immediately to work, sorting and making his selection, carrying these bits of plants in his mouth to a place he has chosen, laying them one on top of another, fixing them in place with butts of his head, attending to his work with very great attention."[1]

When the nest is built, the male looks for a mate: "The male throws himself into the midst of a group of females to attract the attention of any who might be disposed to lay eggs, offering a shelter for her offspring." Stickleback lovemaking takes place privately in the nest. The book invites aquarists to imagine the lovemaking of sticklebacks by following its traces, to note by the female's tail, sole portion of the body visible, "the convulsive movements [that] indicate the efforts she makes to lay her eggs," to witness the male's encouraging behavior toward his mate, then imagine his own vital activity: "He follows the same path as she, gliding over the eggs while wriggling and depositing the reproductive liquid."[2]

Domesticity is the male's preserve: "The male is left as the sole guardian of his precious deposit." Not only do females take no part in protecting the eggs, "they become their most dangerous enemy, forming large raiding parties that attempt to invade the nest to satisfy their ferocious appetites." The male's task is difficult, having to guard the nest against "these devastators," then after hatching, "to watch over the education of his large family." Relentlessly devoted, he fulfills his new function with great care, "not permitting any of the newborns to leave the nest; if one of them escapes, he takes him in his mouth and brings him home." In the process "the male" becomes "the father": "At the end of ten to twelve days, the little ones are hatched, but the father must still protect them for a rather long time since, if he abandoned them, they would soon become the victims of their enemies."[3]

Grandville's animals lived in the shadow of middle-class propriety.[4] So too did plants, such as the *Rossolis*, whose habits, like the stickleback's, French Victorians assiduously collected. The *Rossolis* was a carnivorous swamp plant common in outlying areas of Paris, a "very curious aquarium plant," as Prévost described it. Flies attracted by its color would come to rest on its flower: "Woe betide them! The downy hairs of the flower immediately bristle and envelop the fly, entangling it at a thousand points. The leaf itself curls up and the insect, suddenly imprisoned . . . flounders about in a battle that ends only with his death agony."[5]

This violence came highly recommended to the Parisian bourgeoisie: "It does very well in apartment ponds, and the bodies of the flies that it kills serve as nourishment for little fish."[6] In fin-de-siècle Paris, an environment in miniature—manufactured ruins, sunken ships—intensified the statement of domesticated otherness.[7]

The aquarium—wildly, if briefly, popular on both sides of the Channel between 1850 and 1880—fits with deceptive ease within the conventional framework of Victoriana. Scientific discoveries by the British chemist and philosopher Joseph Priestley and others allowed the development of a sophisticated system of exchange between water flora and fauna that superseded the goldfish bowl of early modern Europe. More prosaically defined as "a glass container holding a community of animals and plants in such concentrations as to reflect as nearly as possible the conditions in the wild," the home aquarium was popular, standard accounts tell us, because it satisfied the desires of bourgeois pet owners to be instructed while entertained, to be busy while at leisure.[8] This conventional point of view intersects contemporary commentary only superficially—the surface story is the same but the underlying meaning is not.

Predictably, French and British vied for the honor of the aquarium's discovery. According to H. Bout in his 1886 work, "Notes pour servir à l'histoire de l'aquarium," which was summarized in the supremely positivist *Grande Encyclopédie*, the aquarium was invented by a Frenchman, Charles Desmoulins, a professor from Bordeaux. As early as 1830, Bout carefully explained, Desmoulins "proposed that in receptacles in which one wished to conserve living freshwater fish one would place aquatic plants, of either floating or submerged varieties, in order that the vegetation would ingest the carbon dioxide that was the end product of the respiration of animals while emitting oxygen that those [animals] needed for survival."[9]

Despite French claims to precedence, however, British enthusiasts undeniably established the aquarium as a fashionable diversion of middle-class life. Nathaniel Bagshaw Ward, a Whitechapel surgeon who, according to David Elliston Allen, was "the true inventor of the aquarium," had discovered in 1829 (or early 1830) that enclosing plants in bottles created a self-sustaining universe—an invention that triggered a craze for collecting and displaying ferns, plumed "emerald green pets glistening with health and beadings of warm dew," as one smitten contemporary explained. In 1837 Ward suggested to the British Association for the Advancement of Science that principles he had previously developed for plantkeeping be applied to animal life.[10]

But it was Robert Warington, a chemist, who first publicized the principles of the aquarium and probably, as Lynn Barber suggests, warrants credit as the inventor of the aquarium. In 1850 he presented a paper on the principles of the freshwater aquarium to the Chemical Society, and in 1852 a description of the saltwater system was publicized in the *Annals of Natural History*. At the same time in Devonshire Philip Henry Gosse was conducting essentially the same experiments. Gosse, already a best-selling author, "with a faithful public behind him," as Barber notes, "precipitated the huge popular craze for the invention" by describing his experiments first in 1853 in his still fascinating work, *A Naturalist's Rambles on the Devonshire Coast*, and a year later in *The Aquarium*, a handbook that, *La Grande Encyclopédie* also explains, had an enormous popular success.[11]

In 1861 Florent Prévost could note that "Paris and London now stock their apartments with these miniature fish ponds with transparent walls, mounted on pedestals." Aquariums, "instruments of progress (*appareils de progrès*)," as *La Grande Encyclopédie* described them, were status symbols.[12] They were commercialized and in an apparently trickle-down movement were available to enthusiasts at many levels of society. "Aquariums have become fashionable, and the industry that admirably exploits this new taste has made aquariums into elegant household furniture from which simplified versions, more or less rich, are adapted to the taste of children, of workers, of the garret and the salon." A simple glass globe, Prévost observed: *voilà l'aquaire de l'amateur* (the enthusiast's aquarium). *La Grande Encyclopédie* reproduced one of these pretty globes of glass on sale at all the crystal shops, for instance, those of M. Boutigny, Palais-Royal, 22, galerie Montpensier, who, Prévost noted, "has a wide variety of models for the salon, globes and small aquariums of all sizes that are very elegant."[13]

In England, one contemporary observed, "it has now become one trade to supply tanks and vases for aquaria, and another to collect and supply plants and animals for stocking." Lynn Barber credits "the efficiency of the railways [that] made it possible to transmit live specimens from the seaside into London within one day." And while Gosse in *The Aquarium* optimistically claimed that "in London sea-water may be easily obtained by giving a trifling fee to the master or steward of the steamers that ply beyond the mouth of the Thames, charging him to dip it in the clear open sea, beyond the reach of the rivers," Prévost recommended to his French readers the use of salt water made from a formula.[14]

The London Zoological Society opened the first public aquarium in 1853, attaching Gosse's private collection of sea life to its London zoo. The French followed suit and the Société zoologique du jardin d'acclimatation added an aquarium to its holdings in the Bois de Boulogne.

In the 1870s more spectacular aquariums were built, like the underground sea palace at the Trocadéro whose eerie deep spaciousness—3,200 square meters underground—was described in its illustration.[15] The Brighton Aquarium, "the largest and most beautiful building devoted to piscatorial science in the world," as its promoters believed, opened in 1872, and Southport's and Manchester's exhibitions each opened two years later. New York and Berlin built aquariums that same decade and Britain built another in Sydenham, site of the Crystal Palace.[16]

From 1850 until around 1880 "the infatuation of the public for aquariums was considerable, as much in England as on the continent." Yet *La Grande Encyclopédie* wrote shortly thereafter, "now that infatuation has somewhat abated." Aquariums continued to be built at Le Havre, Roscoff, Vimereux, Concarneau, Arcachon, and Banyuls-sur-Mer, but for exclusively scientific purposes.[17] The Reverend J. G. Wood, a credible observer of natural history fads (his 1858 work, *Common Objects of the Country*, sold 100,000 copies its first week of publication), marked the abatement of "aquarium fever" as he called it, as early as 1867. He recalled the recent past: "The fashionable lady had magnificent plate-glass aquaria in her drawing-room and the schoolboy managed to keep an aquarium of lesser pretensions in his study. The odd corners of newspapers were filled with notes on aquaria, and a multitude of shops were opened for the simple purpose of supplying aquaria and the contents. The feeling, however," he continued, and his metaphor is apt, unwittingly, "was like a hothouse plant, very luxuriant under artificial conditions, but failing when deprived of external assistance."[18]

Although the introduction of tropical fish into fin-de-siècle Europe and America permanently reinvigorated interest in aquarium keeping—the aquarium still has a place in Western culture—its precipitous decline by around 1880 elicited significant comment. In France, *La Grande Encyclopédie* explained in 1886, medical warnings about pernicious miasmas accounted for this decline. It was "above all after the doctors had suggested that effluvia released by evaporation could well produce intermittent fevers" that aquarium keeping fell into disfavor.[19] British explanations were less theoretical, as the Reverend Wood's musing suggests. "Perhaps," he wrote, "the beautiful plate-glass aquarium fell to pieces, discharged the several gallons of sea-water over the fashionable furniture with sea-anemones, crabs, prawns and other inhabitants of the waters." Or, perhaps, he continued, "some of the inmates died, and the owner was too careless to remove them." The water became fetid, and in either case the room where the aquarium was kept became uninhabitable.[20]

What these contemporary explanations strikingly share is the locus of interrogation, the home, a consideration absent in histories of aquarium keeping that place their subject within the context of Victorian interest in natural history. Lynn Barber suggests that when professional scientists established marine zoological stations, "not open to the public or to interested amateurs," parlor enthusiasm died: "For when the lay public could no longer hope to understand, let alone contribute to, the latest development in marine zoology, they naturally lost all interest in the subject."[21] David Elliston Allen in his social history of British naturalists explains the "national craze" for aquariums during the 1850s in social and economic terms. Along with Barber, he notes that removal in 1845 of the glass tax helped cause the craze. But there was also a social reason: "A whole new stratum, the 'middle' middle class, had surfaced and exposed itself to cropping. . . . What had been small and rather dilettante coteries became engulfed by huge crowds of zealots. What had been mildly eccentric pastimes ballooned into pursuits of fashionableness and respectability."[22] For the coincident craze in France, no studies exist; the subject seems completely neglected by historians.

A cultural reading of nineteenth-century petkeeping, however, avoids the limitations of those based on social history alone. As Allen points out, contemporary evidence is meager: "As so often with major social changes of this type, it is difficult to find allusions to it in the writings of contemporaries."[23] Yet contemporary explanations of aquarium keeping abound and if we read them along with other aspects of petkeeping culture, they yield important insights into the nature of the bourgeois world.

Consider first the apology of the British naturalist George Sowerby, whose 1857 *Popular History of the Aquarium* was recommended to French enthusiasts:

> In tide-pools of the shore we see the most picturesque miniatures of oceanlife. Surrounded by a reef of small rocks, fringed with overhanging

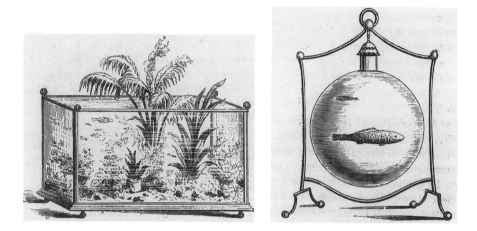

seaweeds and branching corallines, these little nooks afford grotto-like dwellings for animated beings.

Crabs . . . shrimps . . . sea-flowers . . . seaworms, . . . barnacles . . . and small fishes glitter in the brine as they seek to elude the stranger's sight. Could we but transport this little picture to our dwelling—could we place it in our gardens—could we examine the contents at leisure—could we watch the habits of these living creatures in their native element but far from their native retreats, what an endless source of amusement would it be!

Sowerby asked, "Can we do it? Can we raise the grotto, and carry it home, water, rocks, plants, animals and all?" Of course not, "but we can realize the idea, by collecting the materials and imitating the arrangement, and this will be a 'marine aquarium.'" The same impulse accounted for fresh-water tanks: "Imagine again a section of a river, pond or lake, with its weeds and rushes flourishing, water-snails creeping on the leaves, and fishes gliding among the stems: suppose this section enclosed within glass walls, and placed in your parlour or conservatory and you have a 'fresh-water vivarium.'" The fresh-water aquarium was an "imitation . . . tide pool or pond"; unabashedly Sowerby stressed its

Figure 4.   Aquariums with plants.
From Florent Prévost, *Des animaux
d'appartement et de jardin: Oiseaux,
poissons, chiens, chats* (Paris, 1861)
(by permission of the Harvard College Library).

artificiality.[24] In salt systems, another enthusiast said, the sea anemone,
"at once pet, ornament, and subject for dissection" lived on "mimic
rocks amid mimic forests of algae in mimic oceans."[25] In French homes,
the aquarium was an imitation window onto an imitation world:

> In the wall separating the aquarium from the salon or room, a piece of
> glass, simulating a window, in which the ledge would be at the same level
> as the base of the aquarium, is placed, through which across the peaceful
> water and aquatic greenery shines into the salon, as into a dark chamber,
> a halcyon day, serene and calm. And so, without leaving the salon one may
> study the most curious phenomena.[26]

The home aquarium had a deliberately private function. Unlike the
huge aquariums at the Collège de France, for instance, which offered
scientists a look at "a countless number of plants and animals belonging
to the most curious and lesser known species that live in the sea," the
domestic aquarium "is set out in the actual conditions of pleasure, of
ornamentation, between the greenhouse and its flowers, the aviary and
its birds."[27] Prévost's illustrations are a representation of this promis-
cuity as the French envisaged it (figure 4).

The nineteenth-century aquarium was a dreamworld. Like the panorama that petkeeping made private, the aquarium was a mixture of real space and fantasy.[28] Exotica, role-reversal, ruins, imitation—an interrogation of aquarium keeping tells us less about natural history than about the imaginative context of bourgeois life. Much the same is true of birds. Caged, even elaborately at times, their appeal to the haute bourgeoisie was somewhat limited. Prévost complained that in Paris where greenhouses filled with exotic flowers were fashionable, few aviaries were to be found.[29] Flaubert may have better captured the appeal of birds in his projection of parrot-loving sentimentality onto a lower-class woman in *A Simple Heart*.[30]

We can pursue this imaginative panorama more vigorously in the parallel case of dogs—obviously, more emotive and plastic than fish but calling up rhymes for the same metaphor of otherness. Nineteenth-century breeds, new or newly defined as we will see, were a narrative, a characteristic story, interchangeable among individuals. The King Charles spaniel, for instance, wept always and everywhere as Charles I was beheaded, while the Saint Bernard dog saved snowbound travelers—even as it slept on drawing-room floors. Transporting their owners into classless time and space as puppets or dolls do, dogs were the instruments of fantasy. The confusion of real and imagined animals points up an enchantment of the home, a fairy-tale-like quality underlined in contemporary manuals of dog care. This reading of petkeeping culture invokes a denatured world, a controlled, contained, imagined world, a corrigible universe of little worlds whose intersection is the bourgeois interior.

The history of dog breeding hints at the impact of petkeeping on everyday life. Though the fact is little known, canine types such as collies and retrievers—contemporary, standard, reproducible types—are inventions of the Victorian age.[31] Familiar breeds took definite shape only in the last century and first acquired consistency in the imagination of the age. In 1788 the influential naturalist Buffon described fourteen varieties of dogs. Some thirty years later Delabere Pritchett Blaine, a dog breeder and canine pathologist, counted at least twenty-four.[32] Pierre Larousse, adopting Frédéric Cuvier's grouping of three major categories of dogs ("distinguished by the shape of the skull"), described well over fifty types of dogs in his 1869 essay on dogs.[33] Thirty years later again, in a three-volume work on French dog breeds, *Les Races de chiens*, Pierre Mégnin held the line at two hundred. In amazement, Mégnin noted that his listing hardly represented the activity of the century. Like compound interest perhaps: "The number of varieties that have disappeared and of new varieties is such that, in order to conserve the memory of them, we would need to classify them every twenty years."[34]

How should we understand the proliferation of nineteenth-century breeds? One line of thought runs in the direction of natural history. An eager cataloging of plants and animals into separate species, subspecies, and types quite naturally included canines and measured human beings as well. The new discipline of anthropology was the application to humans of the methods of natural history, as Sigismond Zaborowski-Moindron explained in his *Grande Encyclopédie* essay on the subject. Anthropology, "one of the most fertile areas in the philosophic movement of our day, has envisaged man . . . as a being who must be studied according to the same methods and classed according to the same principles, that is to say, according to the determination of the same characteristics [as other species]."[35] Joseph Boyer's 1876 work, *Recherches sur les races humaines de l'Auvergne*, more wide-ranging in argument than its title might suggest, is a good example of the application of these principles. It described the French "races" of humans in terms similar to those that distinguished types of dogs, in appearance and disposition, and ranked humans on a scale of superiority. And Boyer's discussion of *dégradation* perceived the same danger in a mélange of races that structured pet owners' attitudes toward breeding, as we will see in the next chapter.[36] The relation of the Société d'anthropologie (founded in 1859 by Paul Broca) to the Société impériale d'acclimatation bears investigation.

Competing systems of classification also account for Rabelaisian divisions of canines. Buffon claimed one ancestor for all types of dogs, an archetypal *chien de berger*, and his ranking of canines was based on resemblances to this *race primitive*, as Larousse explained.[37] Frédéric Cuvier grouped dogs in three major divisions, or categories of types, while Pierre Mégnin in the 1890s remained idiosyncratic in the face of British acceptance of one single species for *Canis familiaris*. The familiar categorization (family Canidae, genus *Canis*, species *familiaris*) was rejected by Mégnin in favor of three species of domestic dog: "Thus, we have at least three types of dogs in Europe that are relatively fixed and whose origin is lost in the night of time: we are, consequently, right to consider them as *species* in the zoological sense of the word."[38]

A compulsive cataloging of the natural world accounts for the appearance on various nineteenth-century naturalists' lists of exotic dogs, the Eskimo and the dingo. But, as Harriet Ritvo's recent work on Victorian animals reveals, of still greater interest was the construction of new breeds. Even breeds with time-honored British pasts, the bulldog and the collie, were reinvented, "newly imagined," Ritvo explains, along arbitrary lines, vigilantly maintained through class-bound institutions such as the dog show and the kennel club. Indeed, Ritvo places dog breeding in the context of class anxieties. "The structures evolved in the third quarter of the nineteenth century to regulate the breeding and the showing of pedigreed dogs," Ritvo argues, "figuratively expressed the desire of predominately middle-class fanciers for a relatively prestigious and readily identifiable position within a stable, hierarchical society."[39]

The institutions of middle-class petkeeping were modeled after aristocratic pursuits, especially high stock breeding. But this formal conservatism was undermined by the business of dog breeding itself. "The prizewinning pedigreed dogs of the late nineteenth century seemed to symbolize simply the power to manipulate and the power to purchase— they were ultimately destabilizing emblems of status and rank as pure commodities." The Victorian dog fancy, Ritvo concludes, was insistently self-referential. An expression of the middle classes, "its goal was to celebrate their desire and ability to manipulate, rather than to produce animals that could be measured by such extrinsic standards as utility, beauty and vigor." Therefore, "it was an index of their paradoxical willingness aggressively to reconceive and refashion the social order in which they coveted a stable place."[40]

With dog breeding as with aquarium keeping, however, neither amateur interest in natural history nor sociological explanations of petkeeping fully describe the meaning of race and pedigree within ordinary experience in Paris. France's institutions of dog breeding, first of all, were embarrassingly secondary to Britain's. Consider the history of the dog show. The first French dog show, the Exposition universelle des races canines, was held in 1863 under the auspices of the Société impériale zoologique d'acclimatation at the society's Jardin zoologique d'acclimatation (15 hectares of land carved out of the Bois de Boulogne in 1857 for the influential society, leased from the city for the nominal sum of one thousand francs per year).[41] The organizing committee included Baron James de Rothschild, the eminent anthropologist Jean Louis Armand de Quatrefages, Albert Geoffroy Saint-Hilaire, various viscounts, and a prince. Such Parisian canophiles as Baron Couteulx de Cantelou and the painter Théodore Rousseau also participated in the show.[42]

Despite the backing of prominent scientists, French dog shows never came to represent success in animal husbandry. The business of breeding was not taken very seriously and unlike in Britain not linked to microdivisions within the social scale. French attitudes toward the physical characteristics of breeds were cavalier and, to the British mind, frivolous. Particularly revealing were the difficulties encountered by Pierre Larousse, the sponsor of a half-shepherd, possibly half-wolf dog, Moustache, at the 1863 show (the name also of Napoleon Bonaparte's dog, Moustache was a popular name for canines throughout the century). The dog was excluded and Larousse, disappointed. At the dog show Moustache appeared with the following pedigree:

Name	Breed	Age
Moustache	Sheepdog	8 months
Place	Mother	Father
Grignon Imperial Farm	Catherine	Unknown

Yet despite what Larousse assumed were suitable credentials and amid the admiration of all viewers, as his owner proudly recounted, Moustache was placed *"hors de concours*, under the pretext that he came from an establishment of the state."[43]

Larousse had a casual attitude toward the official business of dog shows.[44] So too did the judges, at least with respect to the provenance of dogs shown. Standing in significant contrast to British regulation were the relaxed pose of most French participants in dog breeding and the misfounded optimism of Quatrefages, whose speech at the exposition of 1865 claimed for French dog breeding what only the British actually and metaphorically achieved: "To form breeds, that is almost to create new species."[45]

Surprisingly, the French rarely succeeded in promoting and developing French breeds, despite the patient urging of influential canophiles. "A good many years," le baron de Vaux lamented in 1897 in this regard, "are needed to repair faults caused by our carelessness and thoughtlessness."[46] Twelve years later Paul Mégnin echoed the complaint: "So many breeds created, so many have disappeared, either because of mistakes made by fanciers or because the fashion for them has passed. One is content to say and say again that our neighbors the English are the premier sportsmen in the world and masters in matters of breeding."[47]

In an age when Desmoulins asked in the title of his famous book, *A quoi tient la supériorité des Anglo-Saxons?* British models set the tone, in part, for French dog envy. For every club intended to promote a French breed, for every *réunion des amateurs de chiens d'arrêt français* or *club du basset français*, there was a pointer club, a Gordon setter club, a spaniel club, a fox terrier club, and a *club du setter anglais.*[48]

But the French interest in breeding operated on a more flamboyant register than the British. Most French dog shows were held in the capital—beginning in 1865, on the Cours-la-Reine, Champs-Elysées—and favored society canophilia, unlike in Britain, where, though high society was also involved in dog showing, the many shows were in good part "small-town or regional affairs, offering local fanciers the chance to show off their pets and perhaps prepare for the big time."[49] The more central location of the 1865 show signaled a decisive turn toward high fashion that French dog shows were to take in the 1880s, when the newly constituted Société centrale pour l'amélioration des races de chiens en France—always called the Centrale—took over the organization of *expositions canines*, holding them first at the Cours-la-Reine, then in the Tuileries, on the terrasse de l'Orangerie.[50]

The majority of Centrale members were fashionably titled. A survey of the society's monthly bulletin for February 1888 indicates that out of one hundred seventy or so *membres fondateurs* and *membres souscripteurs*, there were thirty-eight counts, seventeen viscounts, nine marquesses, and twenty-one barons. Two others were princes and three were dukes. Twenty-one simply carried the particle *de*.[51] The Centrale membership set the tone for the expositions, and participants seem in good part only slightly less secure. We meet, for example, in the *liste des exposants* at the ninth canine exposition in 1890, Mme Levavasseur with the fashionable address of 73, rue Saint-Honoré, whose white poodle was named Léa; and a Mme Renouard, 2, place Vendôme, with a remarkable eight entries: Miss, a toy terrier; Tobie, a terrier-griffon; Charley and Darling, Yorkshire terriers; Mouche, a young greyhound; Prince, a King Charles spaniel; Daisy, a Blenheim; with last, and perhaps least, Coquette, a Maltese.[52]

A distinctively French interest in dog breeds emerged in a comparison of French and British attitudes, one that blended fashion and fantasy to express interpretations of modernity. Consider the review of the 1880 Parisian dog show that appeared in a short-lived but ambitious society journal, *La Vie élégante*. The story of progress, a Promethean triumph over nature that French scientists looked for, was overlapped by a postscript, a postromantic disenchantment of humanity or eulogy, a "reenchantment" of subdued nature. After the beautiful dogs, the pampered and coiffured dogs, came packs of hunting dogs:

> They were superb. . . . I noticed, however, between these hunting dogs and the other dogs an absolute difference. There was between them the same difference that exists between civilized man and primitive man. I found on the hunting dog the same heavy features, the same bestiality, that look devoid of subtlety, thus of incomplete intelligence, that one finds on the savage. In the great forests, in the profound echo of their victorious fanfare, they present a triumphant image of the first instinct that was born in the heart of man, combat! of his first virtue, bravery! of his first joy, triumph![53]

The construction of French breeds took place, first of all, however, not in the kennel, or the show ring, but in the provincial and, especially, the Parisian home through amateur reading about dogs. The dog-care book gave readers easy access to categories of fictive imagery. Unlike its prototype across the Channel, the French dog-care book defined a breed completely, with reference not merely to its appearance or even its disposition, but to its character and habits. A difficult task, as Florent Prévost complained in 1861: "To distinguish a good dog from a bad dog and to appreciate, even after a detailed study, the qualities or faults of an individual is not as easy as some may believe."[54] The French invention of breeds was epistemologically idealist. The "moral" qualities of a breed were often described in a sketch or story, a fictive signature that fixed the type as distinctly as did body size, color, or shape of ears and tail. These narrations, though sometimes couched in the past tense, actually functioned in the present, as literary critics often argue that the novel does. Peter Brooks explains (though he adopts a rival point of view) that "the preterite tense used classically in the novel is decoded by the reader as a kind of present, that of an action and a significance being forged before his eyes, in his hands, so to speak."[55] Dog ownership quite literally articulated this process since the actual manipulation of character traits was realized by the dog-owning reader of dog-care books. In the confusion of fact and fiction that was an inescapable part of all thinking about nineteenth-century breeds, individual merged with type.

Canophile literature followed the conventions of the dog show, categorizing breeds into three major groups for discussion and examination: working dogs, hunting dogs, and pets. Jean Robert observed that this classification was not entirely accurate, since all dogs were useful dogs, but he himself adopted this taxonomy that was in common use. In *Nos Chiens: Races, dressage, élevage, hygiène, maladies* Paul Mégnin did so too, for similar reasons.[56] But it was the idea of the breed, not its supposed use, that mattered.

Consider the first of the major categories of dogs defined by dog shows and in dog-care books, *"chiens de garde et d'utilité,"* which included guard dogs, sheep dogs, and other working dogs; these were *chiens de trait*, bred for a specific character. All these breeds, formally, were exotic in Paris, though Parisians proudly owned them. At the Exposition internationale de chiens held in Paris in 1885, all four *dogues de Bordeaux* (the French equivalent of the mastiff) that were shown belonged to Parisians: Lion and Lionne belonged to M. Eugène François who lived at 71, boulevard de Vaugirard; Turco belonged to M. Pouy who lived at 90, boulevard Mortier; and Jean-Bart's owner, M. Iffernet, lived at 35, rue de Fontarabie. Three out of four Great Danes shown were Parisian: Luxor belonged to M. Boyer, 140, boulevard de la Villette; Sultan to M. le comte Durand de Beauregard, 56, boulevard Haussmann; and Bravo lived with M. Franz-Case at 87, rue Vieille-du-Temple.

Similarly, mountain dogs (*chiens de montagne*) lived in Paris: Turc, a Saint Bernard belonging to M. E. Lamané, lived on the rue Chabrol. Tom, a Pyrenean mountain dog belonging to M. Charles Rochard, lived on the rue du Pont Neuf; Fidèle, another Pyrenean, lived on the boulevard Exelmans with M. Maury; Vermouth, belonging to M. Jean-Marie Garlon, lived on the boulevard de Belleville; another Turc belonged to M. Alexandre Bourceret, who lived on the rue de Sèze. Sultan lived on rue Chénier with M. Labbé; yet another Turc lived on the rue de Lyon with M. F. G. Cauchois; and Porthos, belonging to a Mme Ciceri, lived on the rue Montmartre. Other lists to the same end could be made for other types of rugged dogs, Newfoundlands, for example, and varieties of sheepdogs.[57]

In the imagination of owners not particularly interested in breeding, what did a mountain dog or a sheepdog represent? Florent Prévost's descriptions of breeds suggests the configuration of that thinking. The various mountain dogs, for instance, are very intelligent, we learn, and excellent guard dogs: "the Pyrenean mountain dog, notably, is thought highly of, it is used to guard houses and flocks." The Saint Bernard was a cliché already in 1861: "The whole world knows the services that these dogs render, trained by the monks of mont Saint-Bernard to go in search of travelers lost in the mountains." The sheepdog, also quite bright, "is very serious and attached to his master." What does a sheepdog do? Of course, "it is used above all to guard flocks."[58] Fifty years later the point was more poetically made. Writing about the sheepdog from Languedoc, one of the many French breeds of sheepdogs, Paul Mégnin described a pastoral world of beauty:

> It is he who guards the flocks that spend the winter in lower Provence or lower Languedoc and he who when spring begins drives them to the plains of Camargue or Crau.
> In general, a dog and a man drive four hundred to five hundred sheep; and nothing is more picturesque than to see the summer's or winter's migration of flocks from several villages reunited: ten thousand to twenty thousand sheep covering the pastures.[59]

The story of the Saint Bernard (figure 5) developed in no less elaborate fashion. "It would take a poet to suitably sing the praises of these heroes who spend their lives saving people," suggested Jean Robert in 1888:

> Carrying suspended around his neck a little keg filled with eau-de-vie designed to restore the strength of those unfortunate people who have been vanquished by cold and fatigue, the Saint Bernard takes off through

Figure 5. Typical illustration of a Saint Bernard rescuing a traveler. From Alfred Barbou, *Le Chien: Son histoire, ses exploits, ses aventures* (Paris, 1883), 105 (by permission of the Houghton Library, Harvard University).

snow, ice, and precipices in search of travelers in distress. These he revives, fanning their faces, giving them air, encouraging them with his caresses, pulling them by their clothing, he leads them toward the hospice, sometimes even carrying them.[60]

An Alpine past was invented for the *chien du Leonberg*. A cross between the Saint Bernard, the Newfoundland, and, possibly, later, the Pyrenean mountain dog, the breed was created by the so-called baron Essig (to capitalize, critics in the 1870s claimed, on the "rage for big dogs that has long existed"). Vero Shaw, one of Britain's most respected dog writers whose work appeared in translation in France, declared that "the breed, as a pure one, is apocryphal."[61] Yet by the end of the century the Leonberg formed a separate class at French (and European) dog shows and was associated with deep time. "The Leonberg," Paul Mégnin explained in 1909, "has existed, some people would have it, from time immemorial in the Alps."[62]

In faraway Kamchatka life for "the four-footed guide," as Alphonse Toussenel imagined it for the benefit of many readers and popularizers of his *Esprit des bêtes: Zoologie passionnelle*, was more profoundly difficult. Toussenel, an anti-Semitic Fourierist whose only objection to Fourier seems to have been the social theorist's baffling dislike of dogs, described a day in the life of a snow dog. After safely guiding visitors through the snowy steppes the pack headed toward home:

> Good-byes exchanged and task completed, the pack again takes up the path toward home. . . . On their return, one scratches lightly on their master's door, not to demand a place by the hearth, not to demand a share of the feast . . . ; he scratches quite simply to make their presence known . . . 'Don't disturb yourself, it's us; everything went well.' Then, unharnessed and in a circle, each beds down in a hole hollowed out in the snow, with an empty stomach but a clear conscience.[63]

Little dogs by contrast were associated with the historically exotic, with the Renaissance, for example, in the case of the Blenheim, a toy spaniel that, the French understood, "takes its name from a château located in the neighborhood of Woodstock, in Oxfordshire, where Queen Elizabeth was imprisoned for a time during the reign of Mary," and more directly with the English Civil War.[64] The King Charles spaniel or, rather, its prototype became popular on the continent during the exile of Charles II and his dogs. French Victorians, curiously, added a more poignant feature: King Charles I's spaniels had cried, they said, as the king was beheaded.[65]

The image of the greyhound also had a particular resonance, an association with the medieval past that we glimpsed in chapter two, even if, as Jean Robert explained, given the law of 3 May 1844 that prohibited hunting with greyhounds, this popular breed was now a mere *chien de fantaisie*.[66] French hunting dogs—*les chiens de Gascogne, les chiens de Saintonge, les griffons de Vendée*, and even more spurious types, *les chiens du haut Poitou* and *les chiens d'Artois*—were similar products of an impulse to recapture the past. A lineage was claimed for them that led back to the four types of royal and aristocratic hounds (*chiens courants*) mentioned in medieval texts, the white, the gray, the fawn, and the black.[67]

Despite the propagandizing efforts of Count Couteulx and other breeders of ersatz medieval beasts, the more likely inhabitants of bourgeois salons were English breeds of hunting dogs, Gordon setters notably, reference points to other worlds as well as to days gone by. On a more minute level, the residents of apartment-house life included even the Pomeranian (Spitz dog), "formerly called the *loulou de Poméranie*—the good old *loulou* of the stagecoach" as well as the Dalmatian, "the horse's friend [who in England] . . . often guards stables and accompanies coaches on the major routes."[68]

Quite obviously, the particular story of any breed is of little significance in itself. What matters is that the identification of owner with pet was a function of image that the pet acquired, however arbitrarily that meaning came about. We note, therefore, that Félix Faure, the French president at the end of the century, owned a Gordon setter, while composer Camille Saint-Saëns was fond of a griffon, whom he named Lisette. And that Emile Zola owned a little black Pomeranian named Pinpin. As Zola explained in a letter to the veterinarian and canine publicist Lucien Richard, the dog was a *loulou* Pomeranian, formally called le chevalier Hector Pinpin de Coq-Hardi but in private life known as Monsieur Pin.[69]

Various breeds were in vogue at different times during the century. Beginning in the First Empire, the trajectory of demand for little dogs went from pugs (*carlins*) to miniature spaniels, greyhounds, and terriers until the Belle Epoque, when pugs came into fashion again. Saint Bernards began to be popular at midcentury while collies in fin-de-siècle France were almost as popular as they were in Victoria's England. The Third Republic's favorite breed was the poodle (*caniche*), a sophisticated version of the *barbet*.[70] But what seems most consistent about each vogue is its ephemerality, its detachment from fixed points of reference.[71]

The construction of breeds in nineteenth-century Paris represents an "escape from narrative," or to borrow from Walter Benjamin, dialectics at a standstill.[72] Like the aquarium, it describes a metaphoric space outside of conventional time, which we should associate with other collections of exotica. The vocabulary of the bourgeois interior uses not the idiom of nature but of fantasy. Petkeeping relates to the syntax of the home, to the omnipresent arrangement of the imaginary in ordinary life. Animals as objects reveal a denial of nature and a vigilant system of self-referential control. It is to the recovery of this system that we now turn.

5

Dreamworlds of the Bourgeois Interior (2)
Domesticity and the Dog-Care Book

Odile Marcel reflects on the complex ideals of bourgeois life in her autobiography, *Une Education française*, the story of growing up well-to-do and Catholic in the conservative 1950s. "The bourgeois universe," she explains, "with its pot-bellied bankers, its splendid tables, its epicurean rites, its restaurants, and its Sunday roasts," was at the same time "haunted by the ideals of the hermit in the desert," self-denial, discipline, and control. Early childhood was an initiation into the distinctions between humanity and bestiality. "Don't eat like a pig," Odile and her siblings were told: "One must eat properly and act like a human being." Satiety was a base pleasure, "one must curb one's animal desires by limiting the signs of their gratification." Such injunctions were quickly internalized. "We have no wish to be beasts," Marcel writes in the words of a child. And whether in one's own being or in others, "an avid body . . . is abominable."[1]

Hunger and thirst were involuntary natural responses that had to be subjected to reason. "One must master them, check grossness, enfeeble and frustrate its drives." Emotions were equally subjected to restraint. "Good form presumes that one's anger and dislikes will lie hidden, as it places a limit on appetite and a brake on gluttony." A world was at stake in Odile Marcel's training: "*La bonne éducation* defines the world as it should be, a civilized, human world, where everyone is kind, obliging, and refined." No small task, it is "an enterprise, a vigil, which lasts for twenty years, the task of mothers, aunts, and grandmothers who pass on the secret of those principles by which one belongs to one's family, one's class, and one's nation."[2]

Marcel accurately locates the origin of her family universe in the anxieties of the previous century. Like the corsets packed away in her attic, the principles of Marcel's youth were constructions from another time. The best of recent scholarship supports the image of domesticity poetically presented by Marcel. A universe filled with precautions predicated by the notion of difference—between culture and nature and public and private—emerged alongside commodity capitalism.[3] Animals in the home would seem to contradict the rules of domesticity as articulated by Marcel and her grandparents, but prefigured in nineteenth-century petkeeping culture was, nonetheless, the outline of regulated domestic life.

The paradox of a culture bent on banishing nature from the home resolved itself into the construction of a shadow world of denatured animals. Critics and canophiles alike remarked on the fetishistic qualities of pets, speaking of "living dolls" and of eternal children, whose care absorbed the family.[4] Parisian merchants and veterinarians catered to dog owners' daily concerns, and dog-care books made a midcentury appearance in middle-class culture to outline suggestions on toilette and toilet—sexuality and obedience training—that marked the transformation of beastly behavior into quasi-human conduct.

The pages of the Didot-Bottin, the very useful annual almanac of commerce, are a help here. In 1863 they listed no dog stores (though dogs were sold on Sundays at the horse market along the boulevard Arago and privately through breeders).[5] Only one vendor advertised in 1873 (Ravery, Etoiles-Ternes, 4), and in 1883 a handful of other dog merchants had joined him under the heading "chien." By 1910, however, we find dozens of advertisements for purebred puppies and for dog accessories, collars, clothes, and *biscuits pour le chien*. Consider also the reification of the home-away-from-home fantasy of bourgeois life, the evolution of the "bourgeois pension for healthy dogs" that a kennel such as the Chenil des Pyrénées (offices: rue des Petits-champs, 64; kennel: rue de La Fontaine, 46) presented in the 1910 Didot-Bottin.[6]

In these texts, members of the middle class found themselves "consolingly reflected in a world of their own creation."[7] Petkeeping reveals a culture of domesticity in its first stage, at the separation of nature from culture, from which the norms of middle-class life elaborately emerged. Gender and class distinctions among pets express the exoticism of the nineteenth century as, following Odile Marcel in a final point, we reclaim for bourgeois culture its place "dans le musée de la bizarrerie humaine."[8]

Nineteenth-century petkeeping was at once an extension and denial of medieval and early modern tropes. Perhaps the earliest dog-care manual is a hunting book, the *Livre de chasse* of Gaston III de Foix, called Phébus, count of Foix (1331–1391). The oldest English book of hunting is for the most part a translation of Gaston's work: *The Master of Game* by Edward of Norwich, second duke of York (1373?–1415); it was composed between 1406 and 1413.[9] More comprehensive than these is *La Vénerie* by Jacques du Fouilloux (1521–1580), whose 1561 work included not just advice on hunting and breeding but also instructions on how to care for sick dogs. Cardinal de Rohan's copy from around 1566 shows *La Vénerie* to have been a working manual for kennel masters. The cardinal's copy includes a manuscript, lists of the Rohan hunting dogs, and additional remedies for treating dogs and horses.

Jacques du Fouilloux's dog-care book encompasses music and verse. The inclusion of an account of his adolescence testifies to the opacity of *La Vénerie*, as does the following remedy for canine sterility: "Take two heads of garlic and half a testicle from an animal called the beaver (*Castor*) with essence of cress and a dozen Spanish flies." Boil the concoction up together with some mutton, he says, feed it to a bitch, and she will never fail to come into heat.[10] *La Vénerie*'s illustration of a kennel also expresses nicely the imperatives of another age. Its dictates of hygiene (fresh air and water, drainage and warm bedding) are, by contrast, familiar and seem very rational to the Belle Epoque's reigning dog expert, Pierre Mégnin.[11] But the kennel as adjunct to hunting lodge represents an essentially masculine and aristocratic pursuit.

Surveying pets in early modern culture, Solange Bélin remarks that in contrast to the well-articulated principles of kennel keeping, pet-keeping during the ancien régime was a more or less makeshift affair. Dogs ate what people ate. According to Bélin, the *Encyclopédie* mentions that dogs were fed table scraps, which for luxury dogs in the eighteenth century might be quite delectable, consisting of "fat chickens, consommé, little cakes, and morsels of sugar." In the absence of veterinar-

ians, for another instance, pet owners themselves cared for their sick or
hurt pets.[12] The Ecole nationale vétérinaire of Maisons-Alfort was
founded in 1767, but graduates cared primarily for horses and cattle.[13]
It was only in the middle of the nineteenth century that urban veterinarians began to specialize in the care of dogs and cats.

In the course of the nineteenth century the definition of a pet lost its
association with luxury, its affective properties becoming allied with a
new notion of utility (as we saw in chapter three). At the same time, the
kind of dog considered appropriate for petkeeping expanded to embrace
all types—rugged as well as delicate, large as well as small—Dalmatians,
poodles, Saint Bernards and Newfoundlands, pugs and miniature greyhounds.

The early modern motifs in dogkeeping were modified—modern-
ized—in the nineteenth-century care of these beasts. What had been an
exclusively aristocratic pastime developed in English society into an
upper-class country house style of kennels, stables, and dog-care books
that harked back nostalgically to Jacques du Fouilloux and his English
counterparts. The British doggy world influenced in turn more "sci-
entifically" inclined French kennel keepers and breeders, self-important
practitioners of so-called cynographia, writings about canines.[14] To a
greater degree the typical French dog-care book is thematically indebted
to the urban eighteenth-century world of luxury dogs. The concerns of
French dog owners centered around the reconciliation of the dog and
the city, of apartment living and animal life, and the authors of dog-care
manuals had a primarily Parisian audience in mind.

Nineteenth-century dog-care books systematized this audience's
concerns. Typically, introductory chapters defined the dog in terms of
natural history, world history, and the history of the home. A description
of breeds ordinarily followed. More to our point are the central chapters
of these books, essays on training (*éducation*—this is the mot juste for Jean
Robert: "I do not say *dressage*, I say *éducation*") and hygiene—morals,
cleanliness, and sexuality. The purpose of dog training, Robert explains,
being "to make the dog into as agreeable a companion as possible," it
was a matter of deanimalization, feminization, and control.[15]

The pet-care book was invented in France in 1856, claimed Alfred
Bonnardot when *Des petits chiens de dames, spécialement de l'épagneul nain*

was published in Paris in a limited edition of one hundred copies. His book would fill a gap—pet dogs were increasingly popular among the comfortable classes of society, but Parisians had no place to go for information on taking care of them. Perhaps, he suggested, one could find such books in England, but he knew of only one, *Pathologie canine* by Delabère-Blaine; even in this French version, it was hard to get hold of.[16]

Bonnardot, however, exaggerated the dearth of contemporary British dog books. Harriet Ritvo's research on Victorian pets shows that although these books were rare before the nineteenth century, "an expanded market inspired a sudden stream of dog books beginning with Sydenham Edward's handsomely illuminated *Cynographia Britannica*, which was issued in parts between 1800 and 1805."[17] Yet a search through French bibliographies does support some of Bonnardot's claims to novelty, as does a comparison with those English works available to French readers; as Bonnardot noted, they were concerned with the care of robust breeds and thus had little relevance to Parisian pet owners: "It is scarcely a question of *chiens de dames*."[18]

On one level the purpose of dog-care books was quite simply to impart information to well-meaning pet owners. As Laure Desvernays explained in the introduction to *Les Animaux d'agrément* (one of the household manuals published by Colin, a series that also included *L'Art et le goût au foyer,* by Mme M. Hennequin, and *La Cuisine, simple et à bon marché,* by Mme Augusta Moll-Weiss): "To explain how to care for these various kinds of animals, how to breed them, as much for our enjoyment as for the profits we might gain, to insist on the observance of the rules of hygiene that are essential to success [in these endeavors], such is the goal of this little work."[19]

Echoing Bonnardot's lament on the dearth of pet-care books, Jean Robert also claimed to be filling a gap: "There are a number of very learned, witty, and literary works in France on the dog in general, but almost all the specialized studies are on hunting dogs, the breeds called *d'utilité* and *d'appartement,* although the most common have been very unjustly neglected."[20]

Pierre Mégnin, in the pompous introduction to his authoritative work, *Le Chien: histoire, hygiène, médecine* of 1877, drawn from a series of his articles published in the journal *Acclimatation*, made a similar claim: "Indeed, the works that exist now and that treat the same subject are simply undigested compilations made by completely incompetent authors or, worse, reproductions of books written in the first part of the century, a time when the most irrational and deadly theories reigned in medicine."[21] Pierre Mégnin's son, Paul, presented his father's theories in accessible form to a wider audience in *Nos Chiens: Races, dressage, élevage, hygiène, maladies*. With charming self-deprecation Mégnin fils explained that he had no pretensions "to produce an original work." He had, he said, "simply tried to raise, alongside the monuments that have been consecrated to these good and brave dogs, a tiny little chapel."[22]

Our interest in the crucial elements of bourgeois petkeeping, however, leads us to consider dog-care books on another, deeper level. Far from being a prosaic tool for household husbandry, dog-care books functioned as maps for the imagination, manuals of world making.[23] In petkeeping culture we note the ultimately saddening but perhaps salutary attempt to create—with more faithful, affective, and malleable companions—a newer and better world.

The first French dog-care book suggested this impulse quite strongly. Its object was to help dog owners make for their pets "a sort of terrestrial paradise." In a participatory world where dog and dog owner acted in symbiotic unison, the owner worked with and on the inherent qualities of canines—affection and devotion, for example—as thinkers dealt with concepts of essence and existence. The petkeeping world came into being as a book comes into being, through the realization of a text. As Bonnardot explained the obvious, "It's not enough to own a good instrument, one must learn to produce beautiful music."[24]

The curiosities of petkeeping culture—the dressing of dogs in human clothing, and hair dying and styling, like the games and tricks that make up the repertoire of the well-bred dog (one source has a dog playing "soldier" at the turn of the century), even the prosaic and flexible game of fetch—are relevant items in a discussion of bourgeois culture.[25] Like the tactics of deodorization that form a significant section of dog-care books, they help reorganize the themes of bourgeois life on a fictive plane. Recursive to bourgeois life but not reductive to it, petkeeping is a system of control that parallels domesticity. As we work our way through the themes of nineteenth-century dog-care books, we can trace the dyadic relation of fiction and reality in everyday life—apparent also in the creation of the faithful and affective family pet.

Infantilization is the first of these themes. Dogs were eternal children, captive outside of narrative, without a past, a future, or a culture. Dogs were uniquely malleable and controllable, nineteenth-century authors insisted, "they live in an eternal childhood, a minority without end."[26] Pets doubled as children in didactic tales for youth such as *Chat et chien, ou les enfants volontaires*, published by the Bibliothèque morale de la jeunesse and approved by the archbishop for Christian families.[27] Postcards at the end of the century frequently featured canine and human children playing together, a motif pointedly elaborated by E. Leroy in *L'Enfance du chien*.[28] Diagnosing canine illnesses posed problems similar to those children's doctors faced: "Dogs, like very young children, are unable to indicate the location of their sufferings; it must be guessed."[29]

Like children, pets needed to be trained, gently but firmly. "It is the same with dogs as with children, if one wants them to be loved they must be well brought up," Mme Charles Boeswillwald explained to the Belle Epoque readers of her manual for rich pet owners, *Le Chien de luxe: Comment élever, dresser, et soigner nos chiens*.[30] Ideally, consistency, logic, and rationality governed pet pedagogy. With respect to the rules of propriety—not soiling the carpet, only sleeping on one's own bit of cushion or rug, and not jumping on forbidden furniture, perhaps, above all, refraining from jumping up on dinner guests—Jean Robert was optimistic: "It's simply a matter of patience and firmness." Predictably, he was less sure of feminine than of masculine pet owners' success in this realm (Robert divided women into three categories—those who refuse to own pets, those who treat them like a doll or a bibelot, and those who love dogs sincerely: "and these are the only true women").[31] Laure Desvernays nicely summarized the rules governing these as well as more difficult lessons in obedience. "Punish only disobedient, not clumsy or maladroit, behavior. Punishment should be appropriate to the fault," was the enlightened advice.[32]

In model lessons for well-bred pets, their childlike aspect, in obvious references to women and children alike, reveals a deeper and more powerfully manipulable realm for the nineteenth-century imagination.

The doll-like ideal of nineteenth-century pets, set in lessons that mimic human behavior, evokes the urge to reproduce a controllable image of self.

The lesson "Portez arme! (to arms)," in which the dog poses as a soldier, is to the point here. Also interesting is "Attention!" as Boeswill-wald calls the exercise consisting of "placing a morsel of sugar or cake on the nose of one's dog and making him stay still until one gives the order to snap up the treat." The game is also described in detail by Leroy, whose cocker spaniel puppy, Maggie, is his model pupil. "Fais le beau!" asks the dog to stand on hind legs as a person does, "En marche!" to walk like a child.[33]

We can see how Boeswillwald's system of pet training works as we look more carefully at the exercise "En marche." "You make him stand on his hind legs without giving him his treat but instead holding it out about two paces in front of him" (Boeswillwald recommends rewards for tricks well done). Inevitably, he immediately returns to four paws and runs toward you. Conceal the cookie from him, tap him lightly on the nose, and repeat the command, "Fais le beau!" When he is again standing up on two legs, hold the treat in front of him while saying the words. If he still does not grasp the command, "have someone hold him who will make him walk as one makes a little child walk. Then, give him a cookie."[34]

Boeswillwald wrote about ladies' dogs and suggested that the salon after dinner was the proper setting for performances. But it was pets of all kinds, not just ladies' dogs, who mimed for bourgeois families. Leroy chose a cocker spaniel for the leading role in his puppy-care book. Very large dogs were less his concern, he believed (he was more certain of the principles than the facts of bourgeois petkeeping), for they had "the grave inconvenience of being too cumbersome in these times when everything is becoming smaller in consonance with our current needs and ideas about the comfortable: apartments, furniture, parks, gardens."[35]

Jean Robert in his dog-care book of the 1880s used different breeds for examples of training exercises. He clearly presented the goals of pet training as the manufacture, from any breed, of a *chien de fantaisie*. The discussion of "Fetch" is instructive. After noting the value of this trick—

"one of the most amusing, sometimes the most useful [of these exer-
cises]"—Robert set before his readers the essential qualities of a pet. A
choke collar, often employed in training a dog to fetch, was antithetical
to petkeeping, "inadmissible when it is a question of an animal having
to fetch all sorts of things for fun for the sole purpose of amusing its
master and when it is important above all to inculcate in him a taste for
retrieving." "To amuse you," Robert explained, "it is essential that a
chien de fantaisie retrieve gaily and with pleasure"—with willing subser-
vience, we might add.[36]

The impulse to impose quasi-human, quasi-toylike qualities on pets
appears also in the matter of clothing and coiffure. Paul Mégnin was
indulgent: "Some think it criminal and grotesque to impose quasi-
human practices in this way on these little dogs (*mignons toutous*)." As for
himself, he was resigned to the fashion. A decade earlier, Jean Robert also
defended the practice of clothing dogs, especially in winter. Surprisingly,
he was a gallant supporter of the miniature greyhound, the *levrette*, a
breed somewhat out of fashion in the 1880s. Clothing these delicate dogs
was, he thought, a matter of common sense.[37]

Some motives were more extreme. The wardrobe, the *trousseau complet*, of an elegant *toutou* in fin-de-siècle Paris might include shirts,
handkerchiefs, dressing gowns, traveling cloaks, tea gowns, and rubber
boots. Dog collars might be made of gold or silver; they were works of
art, according to Alfred Barbou in the 1880s. The Didot-Bottin of 1910
included under its heading "collars, muzzles, and *articles pour chiens*," a
dozen or so listings of places where dog accessories might be purchased
including Lochet aîné et Dedertrand, established 1864 (and gold med-
alist at various international expositions); Bouyer and Gotschif, founded
in 1835 and also "Aux Etats-Unis," which advertised "collars of the latest
style, overcoats, and kennels" and was located prominently on the rue
Saint-Honoré. Fashionable dogs, as Barbou in careful detail explained,
wore "costumes of a certain richness, pretty embroidered coats, silk
jackets, warm outfits for the winter, light ones for the summer." The
maison Ledouble, 29 galerie d'Orléans at the Palais-Royal, advertised in
Jean Robert's dog-care book, offering shirts, housecoats, and raincoats
for little apartment dogs along with "collars of superior quality, brace-

lets, clips, brushes, combs, and clippers for poodles, and special collars for Great Danes."[38]

The Parisian dog in its idealized elaboration was feminized. Duplicating the costumes for middle-class women was a proliferation of canine outfits for many occasions that could be coordinated with their mistresses' clothing, "in color always," Mégnin insisted, "in design, as closely as possible." The place to shop for canine clothing was the Palais-Royal, "absolutely [that is, exclusively, as in women's clothes] like Worth's or Paquin's." The fashionable dog had a costume for afternoon visits, for the evening, for travel, and for the beach. Some authors recommended canine underwear. For the beach, Mégnin explained, "our chic dogs have a special bathing outfit—in blue cambric with a sailor's collar hemmed in white with embroidered anchors in each of the corners; and on one of the sides, embroidered in gold, the name of the beach—Cabourg or Trouville." For travel, "a checked cloak of English cloth with a turned down collar, belted, with a small pocket for the train ticket." Boeswillwald recommended underclothes—"these little shirts . . . decorated all over with narrow bands of Valenciennes lace that will extend a half a centimeter around the coat giving a special cachet to the outfit"—and described in the following illustration (figure 6) the complete canine costume.[39]

Like people, not all dogs were equally well dressed. What mattered—to borrow from Lévi-Strauss—was that "in the economy of objects and identities that make up [the bourgeois] environment," dogs functioned as signatures for human nature.[40] Clothes marked off bourgeois from beast; but more than that, the clothed pet was a double, a doppelgänger, a personalized expression of control.[41] Canine clothing was clearly as restricting of movement, as denaturing, as that of contemporary women's fashions, brilliantly analyzed in these terms by Philippe Perrot.[42] Owner's initials embroidered onto pet's clothing would further intensify this somewhat pathetic process of personalization, or superposition, a powerful doubling back of metaphors—of culture and nature, of bourgeoise and beast. "One will add, as one likes," Boeswillwald's directions to pet tailors read, "a pocket, with embroidered initials."[43]

Figure 6. Costume of the well-dressed dog. From Mme Charles Boeswillwald, *Le Chien de luxe: Comment élever, dresser, et soigner nos chiens* (Paris, 1907), 233 (by permission of the University of California, Berkeley, Library).

Canine coiffure also ingeniously removed beastly characteristics from animals in the home. Canine fur was shaped to resemble clothing, most obviously so in hairstyles for poodles: the "lion cut," the "English cut," and the coil shape (*tonte en macarons*), to name three of the most common fin-de-siècle cuts.[44] The effects of breeding could also be hobbling. Note the description of the Yorkshire terrier given by Desvernays: "Small luxury dog. Body of a terrier with very long and abundant silky hair parted down the middle of its back. . . . Very sweet, walks with difficulty. Needs a lot of care, is very delicate."[45] There was a summer cut, also called the "seaside cut," which was suitably bare. The fur was shaved close except around the muzzle and paws. The "winter cut," or *tonte à la zoave*, was more complicated, predictably. The most stunning styles perhaps were effected on the *caniche royal*, or *caniche cordé*, a type of poodle very popular among dog fanciers. Illustrations show that the lion or demi-lion cut was most suited to these animals. *La vie élégante*, for instance, in 1882 depicted a fashionably dressed lady with her fashionably coiffured poodle in a warming room at the racetrack.[46]

Other breeds, too, had hairdressers, either one who clipped ordinary bourgeois dogs (*les toutous bourgeois*) on the banks of the Seine or a *coiffeur pour chiens* who made house calls for the more pretentious. Very large dogs as well as little dogs received this service. Mégnin reported that not only poodles had haircuts, but so too did Newfoundlands, Saint Bernards, and Pyreneans. Among little dogs, Havanas were sometimes coiffured in the lion or demi-lion cut. The Yorkshire terrier had a special hairstyle, "very fin-de-siècle," popular at the resorts of Normandy, which consisted of tying its hair back from its face with ribbons of the same color as its owner's dress.[47]

The poodle's hirsute malleability certainly had much to do with its unrivaled popularity among Parisians by the end of the century.[48] The historical trajectory of the poodle takes it from disrespect for the lowly but intelligent *barbet*, a hunting dog and blind person's companion, to high status for this same "elegant, fine, and fashionable dog." Many writers described the transformation. Boeswillwald contrasted the dirty, disheveled, badly groomed, and, as she believed, white *barbet* with the brown or black poodle, svelte and silky, whose coat "expert scissors had shaped and trimmed" (figure 7). No longer the blind person's bread earner, the *caniche* was to be found at the Bois de Boulogne or on the boulevard des Italiens, "well combed, freshly clipped, its legs ornamented with bracelets of fur, a pompon on the tip of its tail, wearing a handsome collar set off by silver bells."[49]

Alfred Barbou in his 1883 essay on Parisian dogs described two Parisian industries whose business was dog care, hair clipping and bathing, which took place along the banks of the Seine particularly near the

Figure 7. Illustration of a *barbet*, or *caniche vulgaire*. From
Mme Charles Boeswillwald, *Le Chien de luxe: Comment élever,
dresser, et soigner nos chiens* (Paris, 1907), 121 (by permission
of the University of California, Berkeley, Library).

Pont des Arts. On Sundays, most usually, Parisians brought their dogs
to be washed. The dogs were soaped and brushed, dunked in sulfur water
to deflea them; then to rinse them off they were sent to retrieve a stick
tossed into the Seine.[50] The clipper and the dog washer have histories
that reach backward to the ancien régime. Solange Bélin tells us about
les demoiselles Demoncy et Varechon who lived on the quai Pelletier. In
1774 they charged clients 1 livre 4 sous, a day's wage for a laborer, Bélin

notes, for various services, including bleeding, trimming coats, and clipping ears. Sébastien Mercier sent his dog, Diogène, to a certain Thomas for grooming. Thomas kept shop under the Pont Neuf while Thomas's wife tended more fussy clients, "making house calls to comb, perfume, and powder spaniels . . . or other pets (*chéris*) of a *dame de condition*."[51]

A qualitative as well as quantitative difference, however, separates eighteenth-century concerns from nineteenth-century ones, and Mercier's observations from Barbou's. To anticipate our next point, we note that the mode of nineteenth-century petkeeping evolved very strongly within class terms. A fantastic statement of deanimalization, petkeeping among the bourgeoisie set out a dialectics of exclusion and inclusion, of "outside and inside" in Bachelardian terms, with surprisingly profound implications.[52]

Canine death was a weak intrusion of reality into the insistent fiction of petkeeping. In the 1850s Bonnardot counseled pet owners to kill their aged and infirm pets. "Sometimes in old age they contract repulsive and incurable illnesses"; he recommended the use of chloroform, "that vapor that kills by numbing the senses."[53] In the 1870s Robert deplored the practice of canine euthanasia, castigating pet owners who would replace a pet when it was no longer pleasing, "by caprice, out of distaste." This act stemmed from false values: "When young and attractive, [the dog] is pampered and spoiled, for as long as the vanity of his owner is nourished by possession of a pet. Come old age and its infirmities, and the unfortunate dog is relegated to some obscure corner." Neglected and in pain, he suffered until, Robert imagined, "moved by egoistic pity Monsieur or Madame says, in a forced and artificial manner: 'Poor dog! For humanity's sake, someone put him out of his misery!'"[54]

Evasions swept away the fact of death and doubled animal and object in the midcentury practice of stuffing one's pet, a macabre fashion offensive even to Bonnardot. "This mode of remembrance repulses me," he admitted, explaining in choice detail: "It's a sad thing to see one's little companion whose look was once so lively and bright forever immobile and staring. Moreover, if one kept all his successors in this way, one would end by having a somewhat cluttered and encumbering museum." Yet some pet owners kept only the head of their pet. "It is true that one could limit oneself to having the head prepared in this way; that's even the fashion these days," Bonnardot noted. As for himself, it was enough to have an image of his pet, "at the time of his brilliant youth," captured by a photograph or painting, a practice he recommended to other pet owners. He went on to confide, however, that if he neglected this "act of foresight" he would arrange to have his dead dog's coat kept "as long as it had not lost its silkiness"—an act of tenacity not less bizarre, in our eyes, than the taxidermy.[55]

How to dispose of a dead pet remained a problem throughout the century. Pet owners had few options until the Parisian pet cemetery at Asnières was founded in 1899. Although some pet-care books continued to recommend having one's pet stuffed and mounted for posterity—as Boeswillwald did in 1907: "Or you could have him stuffed in which case you will have with you, always, something that will recall your favorite to you"—most pet owners must have had recourse to less expensive solutions.[56] The only legal expediency was to send a dead pet to a knacker. Most people simply threw a dead dog out with the garbage, and dog bodies ended up in the Seine or in ditches on the outskirts of the city. As early as 1830, concerns about the pollution of the Seine from dead dogs led to the occasional proposal for a city dog cemetery, for instance, by M. Changeur, a veterinarian, who wrote to the prefect along these lines.[57]

In the 1890s, when Marguerite Durand and Georges Harmois lobbied for the establishment of a pet cemetery, hygiene and sentiment were linked goals. In the appeal for funds, the prospective Société anonyme du cimetière pour chiens et autres animaux domestiques (later the Société anonyme du cimetière des chiens) announced its first goals: "To improve the sanitation of Paris where, in spite of the rules and regulations, dead animals are often buried in conditions that are detrimental to public health. To put a stop to the waters of the Seine being poisoned by dead animals thrown into it and spreading anthrax by being drawn by the current of water below Paris." Not less important was the sentimental goal of the cemetery, the due recognition of canines' real and imagined contributions to modern life: "To secure a patch of land to the animal who was a faithful companion, a consoler of pain, who often has to his credit the rescue of human life and who in recompense of his devotion is tossed on the garbage heap like the vilest refuse."[58]

A brief glance at the Parisian pet cemetery, however, suggests that the distinction between animal and object was lost in canine mortuary art. Tombstone motifs were a pastiche of everyday life, clichés that evoke otherworldly fantasies within the ideal of petkeeping culture. We note the doghouses, dogs' heads and bodies in beautiful relief, as well as testimonies of canine goodness (that we glimpsed in chapter two and saw in figure 2), all set within lush funereal vegetation.[59]

"Wanting to perfect nature," Dr. Henri Blatin (presiding officer of the Parisian animal protection society) commented about fashion-conscious pet owners, "they allow the beast to die without posterity."[60] What Blatin says figuratively about fashion (in a fad of the 1860s Parisians sported red-, green-, and purple-dyed pets) holds true literally, we suggested, about death. We can extend Blatin's insight to other aspects of petkeeping—to canine diet, sexuality, and bodily excretions—that also denied the animal nature of pets.

We turn first to a consideration of diet. As early as the 1830s, British experts were insisting that a meat diet was harmful to dogs. Francis Clater, for example, argued that meat-eating dogs were susceptible to mange and cankers as well as various inflammations. Some thirty years later, Delabere Blaine, the influential canine pathologist, recommended a mixed diet for dogs. Active outdoors dogs could be fed, he said, a diet containing a high proportion of meat. The constitution of apartment dogs, however, who were "always confined," demanded a primarily vegetable diet, "containing fewer nutrients," as Pierre Mégnin expressed the warning in his distinct treatise for French readers.[61]

The British makers of the first and widely successful commercial dog food, Spratts Patent (boasting in 1907 foreign factories in Berlin, New York, and Sydney), translated Delabere Blaine's strictures into profits. Spratts Patent manufactured a dog biscuit consisting, its French advertisement read, of "25 percent beef, vegetables, all incorporated in a mixture of cereals." For little apartment dogs, for those spaniels and terriers and little *loulous*, "who could tolerate meat only in small quantities," Spratts produced a special biscuit.[62]

Normative statements about bourgeois life appear with surprising clarity in discussions about the type of food dogs should be fed. British and French experts agreed in a mistaken assumption that once—in the ancien régime, as the French explained—dogs lived an outdoor life, subsisting on the raw leftovers from hunting.[63] In what is now a familiar theme, they recognized that in the modern world, the lives of the most important of companions had changed with those of their owners. As one canine advocate approvingly noted in the 1870s, a dog's "power of assimilation to the customs, to the nourishment of human society, and the ease of his training is recognized by all."[64] People were omnivores, so too were pets. The French promoters of Spratts explained: "Today, since he shares not only our roof, but often our table, [the dog] has become completely 'omnivorous.'" M. Baron, of the Ecole nationale vétérinaire of Maisons-Alfort, went further in his reasoning. He "not only acknowledges that the dog is omnivorous but believes that he may become a vegetarian like his master."[65]

La Grande Encyclopédie presented the conventional diet for French dogs in the 1880s. "A large dog will eat a kilogram or more of this food a day: bread, soup, meat, beets, carrots, and potatoes will form the base of his nourishment."[66] Similar recipes are to be found in standard French dog-care books of the century. But this manifestly practical approach to canine diet uncovered other concerns. Pet diets described domesticity and set the basis for a criticism of bourgeois life, paradoxically itself a construction. Pierre Mégnin identified a common problem of bourgeois pets and owners in the 1899 edition of his second work on dogs (*Le Chien: Elevage, hygiène, médecine*). Mégnin described strangles (*la gourme*), a disease often confounded with distemper, he said, but caused not by germs but by modern civilization. "The dog, from the time he accepted the domination of man, has been subjected to the same influences, the same food, the same lodging, that is to say, has been more or less completely deprived of his normal food, meat, and of an open-air life."[67]

Mégnin tapped a theme widely diffused in French culture but focused dramatically in ordinary peoples' fear of rabies, as we will see in the following chapter. Here we note not general fears of modernity per se but French experts' concerns about diet that also reflected dog owners' needs for mimetic pets. Meat-eating was associated with the natural life of canines. Robert warned pet owners not to deprive their dogs of meat—"something that goes contrary to their carnivorous nature"—and contrasted a healthful, meat-eating regime with the one he believed harmful to little apartment dogs.[68]

Laure Desvernays also scolded pet owners for withholding meat from pets, noting that in Belle Epoque France: "The prejudice against including meat in a dog's diet has begun to decline a little." Still, three times a week was enough, it was advised, or else the dog would gain weight. Meat was too exciting for most of these dogs. Canine nymphomania and satyriasis might be controlled by eliminating meat from the diet of suffering dogs.[69]

Boeswillwald, too, urged pet owners to remember that pets had exigent needs and echoed Robert's insistence that pets were not dolls: "In order to maintain our dogs in good health, we must love them like friends in need of our protection and not like dolls." But we might ask if the ordinary pet owner followed her or his own inclination in this matter, treating a pet to mocha and *le petit déjeuner* (as Leroy did) or, more extravagantly (as Bonnardot suggested), to buttered bread, sugared milk, and pastry.[70]

Infantilization and control come together in nineteenth-century pet-keeping culture and most obviously in the treatment of canine sexuality—a problem that underlies all consideration of animals in the home and sets the terms for a discussion of class and gender. The problem was embarrassingly present to owners of female dogs, who come into heat twice a year. Many experts recommended cold baths to calm otherwise docile bitches. Desvignes warned readers in 1869 that if they wished to try this method the baths should be given before the onset of heat (*la folie*, it was called), to prevent chills, "always [so] dangerous when [bitches] are in that state." Bonnardot believed that unlimited exercise, runs in the woods, could make pets forget these "mad" ideas but admitted that there were times when recourse to this method was impossible. Various recipes and regimes were proposed throughout the century whose object was the prevention or masking, rather, of animals' sexual maturity. Desvignes directed concerned owners to her preferred method, a light diet consisting of crustless bread, three to four grams of ground hempseed, and a little milk. Some years later Boeswillwald suggested, "One may delay the appearance of these episodes by giving the dog a light diet, laxatives, and anti-spasmodics."[71]

Failure to exert proper control over female sexuality could lead to adverse results. Nymphomania and false pregnancies, experts explained, were its dysfunctional extremes. So too were dizzy spells and rabies, as we see in the next chapter. Pierre Mégnin, for example, related the history of a terrier kept in seclusion during heat: "From that moment onward the animal was sad, uneasy, still eating well but walking about the room, unceasingly, raising her front paws in front of her like a horse . . . , that is to say like an ataxic."[72]

Canine "marriage" could forestall histrionics. The phrase first appears in Bonnardot. But mating itself had to be controlled. Paul Mégnin attended a canine "wedding" and reported, credulously, that it was customary for the "husband to present a marvelous set of wedding presents, for everyone to lunch, then for guests to leave the newlyweds 'finally, alone.'"[73]

The so-called canine wedding was the fin-de-siècle formal consequence of an idea whose function had more obvious prosaic expressions. Bonnardot warned that when one's female dog came into heat, it was essential that she not be allowed to play with "undesirables."[74] He meant that spaniel should mate with spaniel, but undesirability had also a class nuance, explicit in discussions of what British sources called *telegony*, the influence of the previous sire, the contamination of future generations by the first male to mount the bitch.[75] It would be disastrous, Boeswillwald warned, "if a moment's distraction would leave [one's bitch] vulnerable to a dog of a common breed, or even to a dog that was good-looking but of another breed than she." Future generations would be contaminated. "All of her litters will be marked by the breed of the first male who approaches her. That imprint will be indelible." She illustrated the danger: "If your fine miniature greyhound, or your pretty little spaniel accepts the approaches of a 'bumpkin' when she is still a virgin, her tenth litter still will bear the stigma of her violator."[76] Joanny Pertus in his dog-care book of 1893 explained the process in more scientific terms. "The procreator, by coupling, and through the resulting impregnation, leaves in some way a trait of his own in the [female's] system (*économie*) and one that can be discovered much later in his descendants, even indirectly."[77]

A *mésalliance* demanded remedial action, a prudent douching with vinegar and water according to Boeswillwald, or, if this failed, abortion. See the recommendation along these lines of Mme H. Ducret-Baumann in *L'Education et l'hygiène du chien* published in 1913.[78]

Other dangers also demanded vigilance; the fear of lower-class contagion inspired prescriptions of isolation. A chance encounter with a mongrel could soil one's pet and the benefits of an "éducation" might be shaken in a thirty-second encounter with a beast. "It takes only a half-minute in the street, when your maid is walking the dog, for a dirty dog to contaminate your pet (*votre favori*)" with mange.[79] In a universe fraught with invasions, lower-class people could spread fleas to upper-class pets, in a significant collapse of categories. "The princess Vaudemont goes without personal maids," Robert explained to his curious readers, "for fear they would give fleas to her dogs."[80]

Inside exercise could take the place of risky walks, while the exigencies of evacuation posed serious concerns. In what seems another unavoidable association with nineteenth-century women, subject to the "green disease" (a condition caused by the fear of "breaking wind" in public), canines could be victims of their own pudency. In certainly another of petkeeping's myths, nineteenth-century dogs were known to die rather than soil the carpet with their excrement.[81]

The physical presence of animals in the home was shaped to bourgeois expectations of self, though a large gap undoubtedly exists between prescription and practice in petkeeping culture. Indeed, it is the interplay between fiction and reality in everyday life that is at issue here, or, rather, the dual landscapes of the imagination that insist on our appraisal. Petkeeping mirrored and mimicked bourgeois culture. The infantilization (read, feminization) of canines was part of a larger process of objectification that sets before us the bourgeois understanding of its own experience. Staging and framing bourgeois culture were such extravagances as portraits, later, photographs of pets (such as those by Th. Migneaux, a photographer located at 110, rue du Temple, Paris, who advertised "modest prices" at the 1890 canine exposition).[82]

The projection of bourgeois personality onto canine behavior allowed for self-referential criticism, for the evaluation of modernity on an imaginary plane. "Man, after having created a work worthy of himself out of something primordial not altogether his," wrote an unabashed canophile in the late 1870s, "beholds himself in his work, and admires himself there, body and soul."[83] But other participants in bourgeois petkeeping had more somber reflections, as the following chapter explains.

6

La Rage and the Bourgeoisie

Rabies kills by attacking the central nervous system. It is understood today to be an acute viral disease. Infection occurs when the virus is introduced into the system from an open wound, ordinarily through a bite. The virus travels along nerve tissue to the brain. The incubation period is highly variable but lasts on average from four to eight weeks. A prodromal period, preceding clinical disease, is marked by fever, headache, malaise, vomiting, nausea, and other indeterminate symptoms. Excitation and agitation characterize the onset of the encephalitic phase, followed by confusion, hallucinations, combativeness, bizarre aberrations of thought, and various seizures and muscles spasms. Hyperesthesia is common and hydrophobia appears in about half the cases. Priapism and spontaneous ejaculation are possible. Death follows these symptoms by a few days.[1] Rabies is a fatal disease but, as the most superficial investigation will reveal, its rate of incidence is woefully inadequate to account for pre-Pasteurian fears.

Fewer than twenty-five people died of rabies each year in France during the period 1850–1872, according to statistics compiled by the Comité consultatif et des conseils d'hygiène publique,[2] but contemporary attitudes, intensely phobic as they were, would seem to bear little relation to these figures.[3] Informed commentators did indeed dwell on this surprising aspect of the disease: "A horrifying disease, fortunately very rare, despite the commotion it makes," wrote the author of a popular dog-care book.[4] "Although relatively uncommon," rabies, one prominent veterinarian noted, is "one of those diseases that frighten us the most."[5] But despite such learned warnings, fear of rabies became positively obsessive for those unfortunates who were bitten by dogs suspected of being diseased. For them, life became a sleepless hell of anxiety, a dread anticipation of the appearance of symptoms that would confirm the inexorable movement toward death.[6] Even a lick could elicit a doubt and the tiniest scratch could cause alarm.[7] The client of another prominent Parisian veterinarian believed he had caught the disease from a handkerchief contaminated by his rabid dog's saliva.[8]

Fear of rabies could result in hysterical symptoms notoriously difficult to distinguish from those of the actual disease. Louis Pasteur himself was occasionally fooled.[9] Hysterical rabies was in some ways as challenging to pathologists as its prototype, "the most difficult case" being that of an individual "bitten by a healthy dog but so disturbed by the event that he imagines himself rabid and becomes hydrophobic."[10] Whole communities such as the "rabid village" of Lorraine succumbed, while newspaper and journal reports triggered seasonal panics.[11] Public health officials joined editors in warm weather campaigns that sometimes ended in "great dog massacres" called variously, but deliberately, canicides, hecatombs, or canine Saint Bartholomew's days.[12] The already immensely famous Pasteur was repeatedly urged to discover a cure for rabies. An anticipatory rhetoric of resistance called forth a hero: "Humanity will recognize you as its deliverer," promised Ernest Renan as he welcomed Pasteur into the Académie française.[13] Three years later in 1885 his prophecy was fulfilled as thousands of supplicants flocked to Pasteur's laboratory during the first months following the announcement of a successful treatment for rabies. But we may wonder, as did the anti-Pasteur lobby in the Académie de médecine, if a good many of these victims were less in the grips of a disease than of an anxiety characteristic of its age.[14]

In the phobic imagination of the nineteenth century, the signs and symbols of rabies centered on violence and sexuality, and its etiology on repression. To a list of "meaning-laden" Western illnesses—medieval leprosy, modern tuberculosis, contemporary AIDS—we clearly must add rabies as nineteenth-century France experienced it.[15] The fear of rabies lies at the intersection of the organizing themes of bourgeois life and can be read as an expression of uneasiness about modern civilization and its tolls, about the uncertain conquest of culture over nature. Indeed, the ubiquitous fear of rabies allows us to test for the existence in mass culture of concepts that are ordinarily applied exclusively to elite culture. The same distancing from contemporary life that informed the works of nineteenth-century painters and writers had quotidian echoes, ones expressed, unexpectedly, in modernist terms.

Ambiguity and indeterminacy marked the mediation of man and beast in the French Victorian century. In an obvious analogue to Poe's 1841 tale, "Murders in the Rue Morgue," an elision of differences between species allowed conflicts apparent in the making of modern life to find expression on a household level. Fear of rabies is revealing of the implosive nature of the bourgeois interior. The retreat from an increasingly alien world, signaled poetically by Walter Benjamin, was a self-perpetuating construction that implied a negation of human nature and was, as we will see, only uncertainly maintained. The *mentalité* that created the realm of privacy was concerned above all with control. The fear of rabies allows us to recover the anxieties that fostered the desire for control. Beliefs about rabies formed around fears of the breakdown of this defense mechanism and of its demolition not from without, but from within. We turn now to that concern.

Rabies transformed human being into beast, wild, uncontrollable, and dangerous, as the disease unfolded in the imagination of contemporaries. Lecturing to a provincial academy in 1886 on *La Rage: Deux jours chez M. Pasteur*, a Dr. Fredet, assistant professor and local public health officer, describes a rabies patient in these macabre terms: "The wretched victim attacks his surroundings. Lunging at things, he crushes them, breaks them into a thousand pieces. He beats his head against the wall, as if to split it open. He bites himself. Seizing the flesh of his arms and his hands with his teeth, he devours himself." After this introduction Fredet warms to his theme: "His convulsions become more forceful and generalized. Fits begin in earnest. His voice turns hoarse and convulsive, sounding like the barking of a dog, the howling of a wolf." He concludes, in a confusion of extrarhetorical bounds: "Is this an animal? Is this a man?"[16]

Descriptions of rabic fits almost always included the patient's attempts to bite others or himself, or the bedclothes. Throughout the period, the *Dictionnaire de médecine* called to the attention of prudent practitioners the exceptionality of such cases: "As to this belief, today [1865–1884] still quite widespread, it is obviously erroneous."[17] But the symptom continued to be considered within the profession as diagnostically important. For instance, in an 1887 report on juvenile rabies presented to the Conseil d'hygiène publique et de salubrité du département de la Seine, the climax of Dr. Ollivier's case study of a typical child victim was her cry, "all of a sudden, to her keeper: 'Watch out, I'm about to bite you!'"[18] Indicative of the internalization of beastly associations is the prevalence of the symptom in cases of hysterical rabies. A resident of the rue de Rivoli, for instance, a Monsieur X., as he appeared in the writings of Dr. Bourrel (veterinarian to the Parisian rich, officer of the animal protection society and author of several works on rabies), was bitten by a dog that Bourrel certified as healthy. Nonetheless, M. X. lived in terror of a rabies attack. For two years, anticipating symptoms, he would from time to time call out to his servant, "Get out of here, I have the urge to bite you!"[19]

Beastly impulses, emptied systematically out of domestic life, slipped back in to fill the interstices between phantasmagoria with devastating effect. Within the haven that was home, insults, blasphemies, shrieks—"horrifying howls"—issued forth from the sickroom. Biting and hitting, the sick family member overturned everything within reach, shattering the bric-a-brac of predictability. Exhibiting prodigious strength, the patient could easily break the most secure restraint. Defying gravity, he bounced about the room, "leaping, skipping, bounding distances with stunning dexterity," and could drop just as suddenly, "like a rock," into death.[20] The rabid fit was the denouement of the narrative pathology of the disease, "the moving spectacle of a fit," those scenes of "the last hour" that, as played by contemporaries, "leave such a profound impression that it is impossible for witnesses to free themselves from its recall."[21] The bourgeois imagination routinely became entangled in this aspect of rabies, and the impression that so disturbed the nineteenth century was the image of a bourgeois self out of control.

Consider the case of Mme E., a rabid woman from Avignon. Her personality, once docile and unassuming, became suddenly and bewilderingly aggressive and abusive. Her doctor noted during an initial examination that "her face showed its usual mild expression." But as the illness developed, "she became irritated with her husband who was trying to get her to drink and she threatened to throw the bowl at his head." And as the intensity of the fits increased, the wife "violently grabbed her husband by the arm, lunged at his eyes with her nails, and tried to bite him." It became necessary to restrain her. She began a verbal attack on other associates, "delirious, vociferant, she raved, insulting people who were not there." The transformation of Mme E. must have been as shocking to herself as to her husband and her doctor. For as the first fits took hold she implored her doctor in "these moving words: 'If I must become rabid, make me die.'"[22]

As Dr. Jekyll knew himself as Mr. Hyde, so the victim remained conscious of her or his monstrosity. Accounts of rabies insisted on the special dreadfulness of the self-conscious patient. "The terrible fear," we learn, "comes from the dreadful sufferings [rabies brings] while leaving to its victims their intelligence, the ability to appreciate the gravity of their condition."[23] Death by rabies was certain, slow, and horrible, "leaving to the patient all the faculties of his intelligence intact, he sees himself die."[24] Vain attempts were made to maintain self-control, to restrain the *monstrum horrendum* of self. A valiant effort in Rouen, for instance, was observed in 1882: "She said she felt the need to bite, while resisting the desire to do so."[25] Many tried to control the situation by protecting bystanders. Sensing the onset of a fit, "they demand to be restrained so as not to cause any harm or beg those around them to keep their distance."[26]

The violent explosion of the rabid fit revealed the pathetic nature of the illness. A sudden, shocking confirmation of disease, reminiscent of demonic possession, it appeared to contemporaries as "a kind of madness."[27] Here bourgeois individualism became demonic and self-destructive, as if turned back on itself. Fear of rabies was focused on the pathology of the disease in humans and what matters to us as it did to nineteenth-century bourgeois, obviously, is that the most frightening aspects of that pathology were constructions. Fear was of their own making. It was the beastly appetites of humanity that were expressed in the symptomatology of rabies and it seems striking that in an age typified by repression of appetites, *la bête humaine* attracted fascinated, if horrified, attention.

We can follow this line of reasoning also with respect to sexuality. Studies published in the late 1850s described rabies in terms that brought it close to nymphomania and satyriasis.[28] Drawing on earlier research, these studies established the place of "la rage amoureuse" and "la fureur utérine" in the cortege of commonplaces with which rabies was associated. Nymphomaniacs or satyriasis victims foamed at the mouth, suffered from fits and hydrophobia, and felt an overwhelming desire to bite—the very symptoms, as it happens, that were distinctive of rabies. Rabid humans were almost always obsessed by an "erotic fever raised to its highest degree, exactly like those poor victims of satyriasis." And, of course, if rabies was fatal, so too was nymphomania. While chronic slow-acting cases accounted for prostitution, lesbianism, and bestiality, sudden intense cases of nymphomania led quickly to death: "As the symptoms intensify, a FROTHY FOAM dribbles from the lips, the victim's breath becomes fetid and her THIRST, BURNING. Often these symptoms are accompanied by an intense FEAR OF WATER . . . , GNASHING TEETH, the DESIRE TO BITE, and death is not slow in putting an end to these horrible afflictions."[29]

Premodern authors had made of painful priapism an aspect of rabies, but nineteenth-century rabies became instead the occasion for lewd pleasure, for licentious behavior ordinarily associated with sexual disorders. "The release of semen is almost always accompanied," we are assured, "by intense pleasure, evidenced by the patient's own lubricity."[30] Rabies victims experienced this pleasurable sensation to an excessive degree. Like sufferers from satyriasis, a rabid man would "abandon himself thirty times in twenty-four hours to the act of coitus" according to an authority quoted in the staid *Dictionnaire de médecine*, while a parallel process in women, "la fureur utérine," was observed and "confirmed" in an occasionally complete autopsy.[31]

The first indications of illness, in nymphomania and satyriasis as in rabies, were discreetly signaled. Uneasiness and sadness, an unaccountable malaise, marked the onset of each and, in an analogy impossible today, the condition was equated with a *post coïtum animal triste*—or, rather, as the phrase was reworked, an *antè coïtum animal triste*, the indulgence of sexual feelings giving way in the one condition to satisfaction and physiological balance, and in the others to obscene compulsions, to convulsions, and to death.[32] Though syphilis did not share the spectacular pathological features of rabies, the two could also be compared, insidiously: Rabies "is the type of virus that conceals its power over an organism until after a corresponding process of hardening occurs at its point of entry. This is also the case with respect to the signs of syphilis."[33]

In the beast the bourgeois found his double. As might be expected, the same theorists who speculated that nymphomania and satyriasis in humans could result from prolonged sexual abstinence saw canine continence as the cause of spontaneous rabies. Disease was more frequent in canines whose sexual well-being was hampered by an awkward anatomical arrangement: "The structure of the genitals is such that, anatomically speaking, the ejaculation of sperm occurs only with great difficulty, and in order that it may occur at all, copulation is essential."[34] Masturbation in dogs is impossible, and a comparison with humans was provocative food for thought: "For those individuals who do not indulge in that deplorable habit that one calls ONANISM, and who have the courage to condemn themselves to an absolute continence," inadvertent nightly emissions sufficed to purge the body. The same was unfortunately not the case with dogs. Their sexual fluids were reabsorbed and poisoned the body, creating within the canine system the same lethal conditions as those of the inoculated disease.[35]

Unlike humans, dogs could become rabid in more than one way, through the bite of a rabid animal, the efficient cause of rabies in people, or, as was widely believed, through the disease's spontaneous development. On a number of levels, the question of spontaneous rabies dominated debate on the causes of the disease. It was embedded in the question of genesis. It was politicized, and in a curiously French alignment Pasteur, the century's preeminent scientist, found himself arrayed with clergy and monarchists, conservative forces horrified by the claims of freethinkers and positivists. Ready consumers of Darwinian ideas, the latter found the "axiom of physiology," *omne vivum et ovo*, a leaky plank and held not only that "the first representatives of life came into being through spontaneous generation" but that spontaneous generation "has never ceased to occur and that it manifests itself every day in the phenomena of putrefaction and fermentation"—and, they added, within the organism of the dog.[36]

In Paris the Société protectrice des animaux was the forum for much discussion of the matter, and it initiated formal study of the causes of rabies in 1858. During that year considerable interest followed the observations of Jules Lecoeur, professor of veterinary medicine at Caen, member of the departmental council on hygiene, corresponding member and later laureate of the society. Outbreaks of rabies occurred, he insisted, "during the mating season and the more dogs were sequestered and isolated, the more the incidence of rabies rose."[37] François-Joseph Bachelet and C. Froussart's widely approved *Cause de la rage* of 1857 also argued that the sole cause of spontaneous rabies was sexual frustration.[38] Debates on the issue of sex and rabies continued throughout the 1860s and 1870s. In 1866 an obituary by the influential Henri Blatin eulogized Lecoeur in the society's bulletin. Blatin praised Lecoeur for having established that spontaneous rabies "is caused, in the majority of cases, by the constraints imposed on these animals that we confine, that we so recklessly deprive of the freedom to engage in reproduction." Rank-and-file Sociétaires expressed support for these apparently sensible ideas in letters to the editor approving the medals of honor given to these and other works, such as an 1873 study by colonel de Belleville, *La Rage au point de vue physiologique*, which pedantically repackaged this attractive theme.[39]

Blatin and Camille Leblanc were active in committees formed in 1865 and 1872 to study questions relative to rabies, but no agreement was reached within the society as to the best means to prevent the disease. Blatin made a proposal that through the friendly medium of the society's monthly bulletin elicited some support from ordinary members, drawing as it did on common notions of sexuality. Males were more likely than females to feel frustrated and, the syllogism concluded, to contract rabies spontaneously. So owners of bitches were to be given a tax break, in order to increase their popularity as pets. The sexual needs of females were more moderate than those of males, it was argued, and only expressed themselves occasionally, during certain predictable times of year: "They do not allow themselves to be swept away by those seductions males resist only with difficulty."[40]

Rabies was linked with sexuality, and in a world in which gynecologists easily likened menstruation in women to heat in dogs, gender categorization overlay species differentiation—or, rather, gender unpacked into species in the century's synedochic reading of the private lives of animals.[41] Sexual organs described behavior. What mattered in the imagination of contemporaries were degrees of perceived exigencies, accidental to species. Bitch or Parisian bourgeoise, females of each species, canine and human, were docile, more obedient, less demanding and able therefore, as Dr. Blatin puts it, "with less hardship and danger to be confined to the home."[42] One construction mirrored the other.

In 1874 an informal tally of European medical opinion (which heavily favored the French) recorded twelve "partisans de la spontanéité fréquente," staunch believers in spontaneous rabies and its frequent occurrence—Leblanc senior and junior, Tardieu, Vernois, Lecoeur, Lafosse, Huzard, Blatin, Roucher, Toffoli, Grève, and Fleming—and three, more careful, "partisans de la spontanéité rare"—Reynal, Bouley, Renault. Only a few hostile "partisans de la non-spontanéité" were found—Delabere Blaine, Rey, Boudin, and the tally's compiler, Bourrel—and one undecided—Sanson. According to the editors of the *Dictionnaire de médecine*, spontaneous rabies was an established fact, if very rare and without experimental confirmation.[43] Critical to our point, of course, is that discussion of spontaneous rabies was more than just a highbrow affair. Newspapers and monthly journals ran articles on the subject, and paralleling debates in the Académie de médecine and among the governing board of the Société protectrice des animaux were discussions among ordinary people. As we noted, the rank and file of the animal protection society who submitted testimony for publication in the society's bulletin supported this argument, as did pet owners and, generally, the clientele of veterinarians whose case studies formed the bulk of the circumstantial evidence that upheld the theory.

The *Recueil de médecine vétérinaire*, for instance, published just such an account of rabies in October 1873, by M. Leblanc, of an incident that took place in 1864. Monsieur X. (who lived on the chaussée Clignancourt), the owner of an obviously rabid eight-year-old black-and-white Pomeranian dog, came to Leblanc for consultation. According to the owner, the animal was celibate, "had never mounted a bitch." He never left the house unless accompanied by M. X., or M. X. the younger, who each swore that the dog "had never been bitten or attacked by another dog." A case of inoculated rabies therefore was ruled out of the question for this sexually frustrated *loulou*, and the following explanation was offered in support of a diagnosis of spontaneous rabies:

> The person who kept house for M. X. had a bitch in heat toward the end of December 1863, and her clothing was impregnated with the odor of that beast, so much so that M. X.'s dog was continually after the woman, following her and rubbing himself on her. In order to rid herself of his pursuit, the maid brought her bitch to be mounted by the dog. But because the dog was so small, his efforts were unavailing. He had excited himself to no end.[44]

Testimony from dog owners provided the content of other case studies of spontaneous rabies. We learn from Paul Simon, a Parisian veterinarian who published a selection from his case book in 1874, for instance, that a Monsieur G. (a Parisian of comfortable circumstances who lived on the quai d'Anjou) insisted that his rabid "tiny English dog" could not possibly have been bitten by another animal. The dog never went out alone, never was left alone even in the second-floor apartment.[45] Similar anecdotes fill Simon's sometimes salacious but always serious *Observations sur la spontanéité de la rage*. And the clients of the careful Dr. Bourrel were as convinced of the reality of spontaneous rabies as the rest of Parisian dog owners. "If I believed my clients," Bourrel explained, "I would have to accept that four-fifths of the rabid dogs brought to my hospital were suffering from spontaneous rabies."[46]

Bourrel himself, one of the most outspoken critics of the theory among Parisian medical men, was almost persuaded by a client that her dog had become rabid spontaneously. As Bourrel told the story:

> Mme X. (16, rue Portefoin), owned a dog of an exceptionally small breed. . . . He became rabid; she brought him to me. The lady in question never took her *chéri* outside, except in her arms; his little paws had never trod the pavements of Paris. Also, she objected strenuously to my assertion that Toto had been bitten by a rabid dog. Finding the circumstances encouraging, hoping to be close to confirming a case of spontaneous rabies, I made a rigorous investigation, and here is what I found.[47]

What Bourrel discovered was that on returning from an excursion Mme X. habitually left her dog in a courtyard, "to do his duty." "One day, a carter found himself there with his dog, a terrier, who attacked and bit the little darling." Two days later, the terrier was brought to Bourrel's dog hospital, where he died of rabies. Bourrel advised that one should never believe the testimony of pet owners in such circumstances. They lied, sometimes knowingly.[48] A fin-de-siècle veterinarian, a Dr. Richard, agreed, citing in retrospect the case of a colleague, M. Weber, whose client insisted that her apartment-dwelling pet never left her home. What M. Weber discovered, however, was that the maid, although strictly forbidden to do so, had taken the dog for a walk. It was bitten, but the maid had said nothing out of fear of losing her job. Bourrel might have agreed with Richard's conclusions: "An ordinary event then is interpreted as a cause, whereas it is only a matter of simple coincidence."[49]

Bourrel's skepticism was atypical however. And we can go further than Dr. Richard and his observation. In retrospect we can easily see why individuals so persistently arranged reality to support a theory of the spontaneous generation of a disease. Sexuality and violence were foremost in accounts of both the causality and symptomatology of rabies. It is the intersection of these dreaded topics that made rabies into a nightmare expression of nineteenth-century bourgeois culture. A concern with the effects of bourgeois repression went into the articulation of the illness, its symptoms as well as its etiology. Contemporary observations clearly support that argument.

In the secular catechism of disease, the answer to the question, Who created rabies? was, We did (*nous avons créé . . . le chien enragé*). "We ourselves, in short," according to the *Moniteur universel* in May 1875, "are the ones who are often to blame for our dogs' madness and subsequent rabies." Rabies, others explained, "develops in the unwholesome conditions of domesticity," for the more an animal "is brought under our control, the more he is enslaved to our regime, the more he is likely to contract rabies." Rabies, some pointed out, was almost unknown in the East, "*point cardinal* where neither the muzzle nor rabies has made its appearance." In Turkish cities "dogs run riot and live promiscuously, roaming freely, unrestrained"; "they travel in packs, engage in battles, form their own families, and nothing harmful, no accident of disease, ever happens to them." Rabies was rare where dogs ran free: "Constantinople and Africa are rabies-free" was the oft-repeated refrain, and

Eastern freedom contrasted with Western repression, with Paris, where rabies found its refuge, "its home, *un foyer d'élection*, unique in the world."[50]

The pernicious effects of modernity were articulated within a general scheme of human-canine relations. A sweeping vision of a long ancien régime described the history of the world as the history of man and dog marching together toward its conquest. Formerly the partners, it was supposed, had lived close to nature; houses were open to the outside. But modern people lived in apartments, closed off, closed in among themselves—so too the canine companion, the pet being culture's creation. One canine apologist, the author in 1856 of the first French dog-care book, capitalized on the expanding vogue for these pets and viewed the situation sympathetically: "The fashion for little dogs, so in harmony with the limitations of our modern apartments, is today widespread among the comfortable classes of our society."[51]

But other dog lovers were less sanguine. In an 1855 letter to the Chambre des députés, the governing board of the animal protection society expressed concern about the effects of city life on formerly virile hunting and guard dogs who so obviously "lose somewhat in city living the qualities that make them unique. Their constitution weakens; the breeds themselves are distorted beyond recognition by random couplings."[52] One of the most unpopular men in France, Nicolas Fétu, who in 1866 called on dog owners to destroy their pets, described "the modern dog" as the monstrous child of his time, bearing little resemblance to his ancestors; what "we see now in Europe are only grotesque caricatures of the original type."[53]

"In Paris, the dog is becoming almost impossible," concluded Henri Blatin, veterinarian, Freemason, republican, and longtime presiding officer of the animal protection society. The Parisian dog lives in conditions that assault his nature; he, "whose blood runs so hot in his veins, whose penchant for breeding is so marked," was kept "secluded, in celibacy." Many Parisian dogs spent most of their lives inside, in "stuffy apartments," and were leashed and muzzled when walked outside.[54] Dog-care books prescribed inside exercise and birth control, the same conditions that were blamed for the incidence of spontaneous rabies. And Couturier de Vienne, Leblanc, and other representatives of the animal protection society were preaching to the converted in insisting that "the majority of cases of spontaneous rabies occur among apartment dogs." It was among pets, those "*chiens de luxe*, overfed and sometimes forced into unnatural chastity by their mistresses," that this disease of modern times developed.[55]

Petkeeping and rabies phobia were set within coincident discourses in nineteenth-century France. The elaboration of illness, the insistently twisted etiology, formed empathic assumptions between man and beast that within ordinary bourgeois experience found substantiation in the dog. In his dictionary essay on "le chien," Pierre Larousse quoted Buffon: "He takes the tone of the house he inhabits," but Larousse extended the idea to suggest that the dog "has in some way identified himself with us to the point of appropriating from our civilization and our customs a characteristic style, a certain cachet."[56] The point echoed throughout the century, and in 1883 Alfred Barbou developed it in his authoritative work on the French pet: "It is enough for us to note that they have in some way become a part of ourselves, that they are entwined so closely in our society, in our civilization, that if one suddenly did away with them, the appearance of this society and of this civilization would be transformed, changed in a multitude of ways."[57]

Within the canine world, class structure was carefully maintained. To each class, its own compartment was the rule at Bourrel's dog hospital, for instance, where visitors could observe, most tellingly perhaps, "in the first room, little apartment dogs muffled in cotton, wrapped in down."[58] The Parisian dog pound maintained the same distinctions to a no less vital degree, delaying the execution of bourgeois dogs but hanging immediately all other beasts. Products of mixed class "marriages" were aborted (as we noted in chapter five), and any number of other examples support the same point: "As there are social classes, so there are classes of dogs"—so contemporaries expressed it.[59] This is not to say that dogs functioned metaphorically in bourgeois society. Contemporaries spoke, rather, of a special "fifth estate."[60] The human-beastly continuum was so construed as to support an analogy between corset or collar and muzzle, for example, and the construction of household explanations of rabies in the prosaic terms of the bourgeois world. Like "the *coquette* bound in her iron corset, or the *smarteux*, his neck imprisoned in a high collar, rigid as metal," so the canine, our "little brother," suffers in his muzzle.[61]

The many miscellaneous frustrations of city life, of modern life, were blamed for the unacceptable incidence of rabies. One commentator pointed to the typical thirsty summer promenade of a sheepdog, "uneasy and preoccupied, circling the huge fountains in the place de la Concorde, going from one to the other, anxiously looking for an outlet from which he could drink."[62] Like sexual frustration, other restrictions on canine freedom could cause spontaneous rabies: "It seems that constraints of all sorts need to be placed among the first rank of causes of this type." Because they recognized that rabies attacked the central nervous system, theorists believed that "the spontaneous development of rabies is favored by everything that exercises, on the cerebral system of susceptible animals, any excitation whatever."[63] It is significant in this regard therefore that many individuals identified as the central problem of rabies the issue of the muzzle, a disfiguring contraption that inhibited natural impulses, whose function manifestly was to make the beast safe for the city.[64]

A city ordinance had prescribed the use of the muzzle in 1845, but its rigorous enforcement occurred only in 1862. As early as 1858, however, the animal protection society found itself in a difficult position, unsure whether or not to support the use of the contraption. The ordinance was designed to reduce the incidence of rabies by preventing bites, but important opinion suggested that the police measures were misinformed; "If the muzzle is a means of preventing the spread of this terrible disease, some investigators note that the muzzle itself may be a cause of rabies." A selection of letters received by the animal protection society during June 1872 suggests the mixed nature of rank-and-file opinion. The Mlles Chrétien, for instance, wrote asking if statistics could be compiled to demonstrate whether the number of cases of rabies had diminished since the prefecture "enjoined the use of the muzzle over the time when it had shown itself more tolerant." A member from Rouen submitted a journal article in support of his unshakable belief in the "inutility of the muzzle," while M. Davelouis, one of the "small number of muzzle defenders," as the editors noted, pleaded for its consistent use. And although some journals, such as *Le National*, strongly supported measures to muzzle all dogs, other Parisian papers were ambivalent, and the *Journal officiel des théâtres* railed against "this last vestige of the ancien régime."[65]

The government's decision to enforce the muzzle law complicated the position of the Société protectrice des animaux. The minority view held that the society should resist efforts to enforce the law and "subject this animal to such constraint that offends our enlightened civilization."[66] But the society ruled that it could not oppose prefectural authority and decided instead to sponsor a contest for a better, more harmless muzzle (a contradiction in terms, some felt).[67] The *Petit Journal* had the same hopes and for more than twenty years inventors struggled with the very bourgeois problem of creating freedom within bounds.[68]

Rabies was a class-bound disease, deliberately bourgeois in its articulation during the 1860s, 1870s, and 1880s. As in contemporary England, however, rabies was first construed as a working-class disease (or with little obvious regard for logic as retribution for the sins of the rich).[69] In the mental geography of the French, the working class had links to the dangerously natural world, and neither had a place in the bourgeois interior, an environment where the organic world found its negation. In midcentury France poor people's dogs were the ones that spread the disease, and the squalid habits of working-class life were those that caused it. The Société protectrice des animaux and the Conseil d'hygiène publique et de salubrité du département de la Seine worked together in the late 1840s and early 1850s to destroy this noisome weapon of *les classes dangereuses*. The French dog tax of 1855 was a counterattack against poor people's dogs, "usually useless," authorities noted, dirty and diseased. "They foster the insalubrious conditions of poor households. These drawbacks, along with a great many others, and above all the terrifying disease [rabies] whose germ this race carries," argued for the eradication of working-class beasts.[70] (Significantly, the dog tax of 1855 was also conceived in ancien régime terms as a sumptuary tax: only the rich should own pets, luxury articles of consumption.)

In a paradigm shift discussed throughout this book, the pet became referentially bourgeois and bourgeois petkeeping culture became hegemonic in late nineteenth-century France. The objectification of the natural world found its ideal in the bourgeois pet, the denatured and sterilized canine—*le chien de fantaisie*, as it was so aptly termed. But in an astonishing transformation marked by the changing focus of rabies phobia, the fear of nature gave way by degrees to a fear of civilization-as-unnatural. The family dog established itself as a cliché of modern life and, critical to our point, rabies took on a bourgeois complexion, with all its working-class connotations intact. Bourgeois petkeeping developed a tragic cast. Atavistic sexuality and dirt, disorderliness and violence, nature and the working class—all were self-consciously latent in the bourgeois pet: rabies revealed, didactically, the beastly nature of the domesticated beast. "Under the influence of his illness," even the nicest of pets "is overwhelmed by irresistible urges to bite."[71]

The dangerous aspect of the dog may have been part of its appeal; like the beastly nature of its owner, but visibly, tangibly, the pet was the unshakable enemy within. The "staunchest of friends" was, at the same time, the "most treacherous enemy."[72] Rabies was "the dog's fatal and involuntary gift to man," a "terrifying illness that strikes above all at man's best friend, at the dog who lives with us, who, at any given moment becomes, in spite of himself, our mortal enemy."[73] The illness manifested itself, moreover, in a particularly sinister fashion. In the early stages of canine rabies, the only symptoms were an even more pronounced affection on the part of the dog for his master: "The dogs . . . become very affectionate and invariably express an exaggerated attachment and devotion to everyone who approaches them." These symptoms, "far from putting the owner on guard," led typically to dangerously false assurance.[74] "Who could say but at that very instant you see the little King Charles [spaniel] . . . in the arms of his mistress, a fit of the disease of which possibly he is the victim will suddenly cause him to inoculate her with the deadly virus."[75]

A newly rabid dog placed the family in danger, continuing as it did for an indeterminate time "to live with its masters, to sleep on their beds, to play with the children."[76] But the danger to family life, very obviously, was more metaphorical than real. As we suggested above, very few people died of rabies in France, and of them even fewer from bites by their pet dogs. Very rarely did people in France witness a death by rabies. A veterinarian from Nice estimated that only one out of four hundred doctors would happen to "observe a case of rabic hydrophobia." The author, Dr. Portanier, writing in 1886, based his calculations on a

Figure 8.   Musical notation of the "hurlement de la rage." Adapted
from André Sanson, *Le Meilleur Préservatif de la rage* (Paris, 1860) (by
permission of *Representations*).

statistical average of seventy to eighty deaths from rabies per year in
France and a total of thirty-two thousand practicing physicians. Quoting
another authority, he suggested that for every case of rabies a doctor
treated, the doctor saw ten people who needed only reassurance or, more
rarely, cauterization of the wound from a bite, a daunting procedure and
the only true pre-Pasteurian prophylactic. His ambitious arithmetic
allowed him to suggest that for every four thousand Frenchmen who
believed themselves to be in the process of becoming rabid, only one
would have that unhappy success.[77]

Anxious attention, of course, was nonetheless placed on such early
warning signs of lethal canine fits as the "hurlement de la rage," part
bark, part howl and once heard, never forgotten, described in the above
musical notation (figure 8).[78]

Imaginary rabies shattered the myth of the bourgeois interior, folding
nature over culture; in the "hurlement de la rage," human being and
beast became one. There is a cynosural value to the fear of rabies during
the 1860s, 1870s, and 1880s.[79] We have to stop and analyze the widespread belief in spontaneous generation that maintained a tenacious hold
sometimes against (and more often coterminous with) the germ theory
of disease. Uncomfortably and indirectly, bourgeois Parisians admitted
to themselves that wild and uncontrollable sexual desire and fits of
violent rage were the liabilities of a culture that banished lust and anger
and other manifestations of a human being's animal nature from a newly
obsessional, restrictive mental universe. An endogenous model of col-
lective responsibility was pervasive in middle to late nineteenth-century
thinking about the causality of rabies. In the pre-Pasteurian moment, in
a chorus of mea culpa, critics traced the disease to the bourgeois life-style
itself. A Pasteurian perspective allowed the *Grande Encyclopédie*, successor

to the *Grand Dictionnaire* of Larousse, to deplore such literally superficial associations that would link, if loosely, rabies with nymphomania and satyriasis and, by extension, with other imagined illnesses of repression: "When the outward appearance of the disease is the focus of attention, then a series of absurd and unwarranted hypotheses will ensue, producing the grandest confusion."[80] But the logic that grouped rabies together with disorders of the senses, with expressions of the animal nature of humans, drew on insights into societal behavior, not of the microorganic, but of the macrocultural dimension. It described a coherent model of deviance that was ironically prescriptive in its intent.

What disentangled rabies from deviance was the germ theory of disease, a conceptualization that isolated pathogen and pathology and eschewed semiotic categorization. The virus, "a being immeasurably, infinitesimally small, animate, and endowed with life, able to multiply itself, to regenerate," as admiring contemporaries explained,[81] was a modern construction par excellence—neither animal nor plant, organic yet incompletely alive, indeterminate and, like the bourgeois experience itself, knowable only through the traces it leaves.[82] It is not to diminish Pasteur's importance to suggest that the danger rabies posed was as much to mind as to matter. In 1926 Sir William Osler introduced the English translation of René Vallery-Radot's definitive *Life of Pasteur* by suggesting that in the previous century, "before [Pasteur, there was] Egyptian darkness; with his advent a light that brightens more and more as the years give us fuller knowledge."[83] But to decode that darkness is to suggest that the terms of modernism were current both before and after Pasteur. The nineteenth-century construction of rabies was shaped by an anxious awareness of the costs of modern life, by bourgeois' ambivalence toward a world of their own making. Most obviously, the interrogation of bourgeois culture articulated in rabies phobia anticipates Freud, whose work takes up the same themes for a later generation.[84] The strengths of "instinctual passions," of sexuality and aggression, and their potentiality for revolt against an antithetical domesticity are clearly implied in the debate on rabies, an abortive uprising of the beast in the bourgeois.

7

Cats and Categorization

Auguste Renoir's painting of Mme Georges Charpentier and her children (1878) rehearses the major themes of this book. The bourgeois home as cozy retreat, the dog as whimsical signifier of family life, the echo of nature uneasily subdued, these are ideas we easily, even happily, read in a portrait of domestic bliss. If we look very closely at this painting, other themes come to light. As Michael Brenson explains in an article on secondary images in modern art, the "mood of fantasy and enchantment is reinforced by secondary images knitted into or rearing up within the fabric of the painting." A monstrous face within the curtain, skulls in Mme Charpentier's dress, and a cat that seems to rest on the woman's lap and look at her—here are images that intensify the unexpectedly menacing ambiguity in this painting Marcel Proust once called the poetry of the home (figure 9).[1]

In Renoir's painting of the Charpentier family the cat necessarily appears disguised. It was the anti-pet of nineteenth-century bourgeois life, associated with sexuality and marginality, qualities the cat inherited from medieval and early modern times when cats were sometimes burned as witches. Inverted, the tradition persisted in the nineteenth century, since cats were embraced by intellectuals. Baudelaire notably was a lover of cats. Recall that in the poem "The Cat," his mistress and the animal are one:

> Come, superb cat, to my amorous heart;
> Hold back the talons of your paws
>
> . . . .
> When my fingers leisurely caress you,
> Your head and your elastic back,
> And when my hand tingles with the pleasure
> Of feeling your electric body,
>
> . . . .

Figure 9.   Pierre Auguste Renoir, *Madame Georges Charpentier et ses enfants* (by permission of the Metropolitan Museum of Art, Wolfe Fund, 1907; Catharine Lorillard Wolfe collection).

> In spirit I see my woman. Her gaze
> Like your own, amiable beast,
> Profound and cold, cuts and cleaves like a dart,
>
> . . . .
> And, from her head down to her feet,
> A subtle air, a dangerous perfume
> Floats about her dusky body.[2]

The cat was sexually charged, independent, dangerous, egotistical, and cruel. By the end of the century, however, it had become a family pet. It had gained a modern pedigree. Breeds were now important as the cat took its place in bourgeois life alongside the dog. Indeed, it came to act as a dog did, in the determining imagination of pet owners. The cat was neutralized—"rehabilitated," in a telling phrase. Once notoriously faithful to the house, not the person, the cat came to be faithful to its owner even beyond the grave.

Here was an important shift: the rehabilitation of the cat, the inclusion of the feline in bourgeois culture, suggests that by the last decades of the nineteenth century animals had lost some of their power to refract bourgeois life. New metaphors for modernity had developed to link, imaginatively, the symbolism of pets in organic life to the inorganic. The machine now functioned as a new signature for modern times in science fiction beginning with Jules Verne and then, more disturbingly, in futurism and in fascism.

The impulse to categorize that informed nineteenth-century culture remained thematically bound to an organically ordered world. Darwinism, or evolutionism in general, figured minimally in Parisians' thinking about pets. What mattered instead was catachresis, the paradoxical process of inclusion, exclusion, substitution, and completion that powered the postrevolutionary world.[3] Ordinary people used inherited notions of animal behavior to describe something new, something that approximated our understanding of class. For them, the sexuality and independence of the cat, the fidelity and malleability of the dog, were self-reflexive building blocks of culture. And uncertainties in categorizing human being and animal, the working class and the bourgeoisie, which this play with values describes, suggest a "fluid relativism" in Linda Nochlin's phrase about realism that informed scientific and ordinary thinking alike—a pliancy that shifted, sadly, in later modernist thought to a more restrictive mechanical plane.[4]

Buffon is a convenient starting point for our investigation into the place of cats in nineteenth-century culture. The eighteenth century's most widely influential naturalist—Georges Louis Leclerc, le comte de Buffon, whose multivolume *Histoire naturelle* (1749–1788) sold at least twenty thousand copies and whose Petit Buffon had a place in innumerable French homes—remained a touchstone for later debate about feline nature.[5] Buffon hated cats. As Pierre Larousse lamented in his dictionary article on cats, "Buffon has darkened the portrait of the *cat*." In contrast to the dog, the cat was a perfidious animal, an "unfaithful servant," that one kept only out of absolute necessity, as the lesser of two evils, "to control another enemy of domestic life still more discomforting, which we are unable ourselves to hunt."[6]

The cat was a wild animal. "[We find] with the cat," Buffon insisted, "that the shape of its body and its temperament are at one with its nature." Its domesticity was sham. Kittens, especially, could be appealing, even gentle, but "at the same time, they have an innate malice, a falseness of character, a perverse nature, which age augments and education can only mask." Cats were furtive and opportunistic. They feigned devotion and civility for the comfort these might bring. "They take easily to the habits of society, but never to its moral attitudes; they only appear to be affectionate," Buffon added. Unlike the frank and trusting canine, cats were devious; "either out of mistrust or duplicity, they approach us circuitously when looking for caresses that they appreciate only," Buffon insisted, "for the pleasure they [themselves] get from them." Cats were self-indulgent, Larousse reiterated in the kindest of Buffon's comments that he included in his *Dictionnaire*. "The cat is attractive, adroit, clean, and voluptuous; he likes his leisure, he searches out only the softest furniture to sleep and play on."[7]

Buffon based his valuation of cats, he believed, on careful observation of their behavior. For instance, the untrustworthy character of cats is obvious in their demeanor, he explained, "in their shifty eyes; they never look directly at the person they love."[8] A later commentator puzzled out an even more provocative description of Buffon's way of thinking about cats. Henri Lautard, the Belle Epoque author of *Zoophilie ou sympathie envers les animaux: Psychologie du chien, du chat, du cheval*, described in his own overwrought style these disturbing sounds of cats in heat that he thought might have stimulated Buffon's imagination. "Wild nights, parties, disputes and love songs, duels and duets, with little regard for our somewhat disturbed sleep, have told Buffon," Lautard explained, "[that] the cat is very inclined to love." Surprisingly, Buffon's female cat was more driven by her desires than the male was, "and, something rare in animals, the female appears more ardent than the male." Buffon vividly described the female cat's overwhelming need for sex: "she invites it, calls for it, announces her desires by her piercing cries, or rather, the excess of her needs." Driven by sexual desire, the female forced herself on an often reluctant male, "and when the male runs away from her, she pursues him, bites him, and forces him, as it were, to satisfy her," despite the pain of copulation. "Although these approaches are always accompanied by sharp pain," Buffon carefully and delicately explained.[9]

Buffon's stunning association of the cat with rapacious feminine sexuality seems to have been informed by a pre-Enlightenment understanding of the cat. Robert Delort, the medievalist and occasional animal historian, suggests that from the early Middle Ages onward writers have endowed the cat with dangerous feminine qualities. In the image of the cat in Western culture, "One finds woman, sexuality, sensuality, love, mystery, likewise, darkness, evil, and danger." This characterization of the cat as both feminine and sensual was an inheritance from German and Egyptian paganism. Absorbed within Christianity, but uneasily, the cat centered on itself all that was suspect in European life. "One detects a strong hostility for all that [the cat] represents: sexuality, sensuality, femininity, paganism, the moon, darkness, blackness, Diana, treachery, cruelty, demons, that is to say, the greater part of the instruments of witchcraft," Delort explains.[10]

Cats were ritually murdered. They were sacrificed in fertility rites and in rites of purification and protection. At Metz during Lent on "cat Wednesday," at a ceremony first recorded in 1344 and last performed in 1777, thirteen cats were placed in an iron cage and burned (a similar instance was recorded in Lorraine in 1905). Cats were burned also on the festival of Saint-Jean, which marked the end of the sowing season. In Paris this bonfire of felines was performed in the place de Grève.[11]

Roger Chartier warns against a naive assumption that the cat had a fixed meaning in early modern culture.[12] But like canine fidelity, feline perfidy and sexuality were qualities, the tenacious interest in Buffon indicates, that nineteenth-century citizens were ready to appropriate. Writers such as Alphonse Toussenel, the Fourierist and anti-Semite, seized on Buffon's characterization of the cat when looking for a potent analogy for female sexuality. In his *Zoologie passionnelle* of 1855 his chapter on the cat is clearly a point-by-point, and to his mind salutary, exaggeration of Buffon's dissertation. Cats, Buffon had explained, were a necessary evil; without cats, homes would be overrun with mice. As Toussenel more frighteningly elaborated, moving from the domestic to the social realm, the need for cats was like the need for prostitution. "Civilization may no more dispense with the cat than with prostitution," he less charitably continued, this "horrible vampire that it feeds with its flesh and blood and that it dares not do away with for fear of a worse evil."[13]

In Toussenel's logic of symbols, the cat stood for sexuality as the female cat stood for its species; the male was insignificant. Unusually, but instructively, the female was the means of degrading a species. "In all human and animal races," he claimed, "progress works through females." Women married up. Black women married white men, Jewish women married gentlemen, and European women married French men. Only cats, driven by lust, would seek satisfaction among less civilized members of their species. Female cats were interested only in free love. "The [female] cat is essentially antipathetic to marriage," Toussenel explained. "She accepts one, two, three lovers," and if denied by her domesticity the freedom to love, "she goes to reclaim that freedom in the wild."[14]

Like Buffon, Toussenel luridly insisted that cats keenly enjoyed sex, despite its acute attendant pain. "All is not rosy in these shameful affairs that denote the [female] cat," he seemed to warn. "The unfortunate creature confesses this rather strongly by her meows of pain that the brutal caresses of her lovers draw from her, and yet," Toussenel observed with keen interest, "it is not always she who runs in front of her tormenters."[15]

As with Buffon, the cat's sexuality was the element that prompted Toussenel's most extravagant phrases. For Toussenel, however, it also stood for prostitution. Toussenel insisted on the cat's kinship with women of leisure and pleasure: "An animal so keen on maintaining her appearance, so silky, so shiny, so eager for caresses, so ardent and responsive, so graceful and supple . . . ; an animal who makes the night her day, and who shocks decent people with the noise of her orgies, can have only one single analogy in this world, and that analogy is of the feminine kind." Toussenel pressed his point. "Lazy and frivolous and spending entire days in contemplation and sleep, while pretending to be hunting mice . . . incapable of the least effort when it comes to anything repugnant, but indefatigable when it is a matter of pleasure, of play, of sex, lover of the night. Of whom are we writing, of the [female] cat or of the other?" he rhetorically asked.[16]

The cat's outré and irrepressible sexuality was noted by other observers, of course. "When the cat is in heat, its wild nature reveals itself in all its fullness in terrible cries," explained A. L. A. Fée, professor of medicine at Strasbourg and member of the Académie impériale de médecine.[17] Earlier in the century the naturalist Georges Cuvier had described feline courtship as a battle: "The male and the female call each other with sharp high cries, approach each other distrustfully, satisfy their passion in the midst of mutual threats, and then separate, full of fear (each one of the other)," Larousse repeated in his *Dictionnaire*. He also explained (although Larousse was an advocate of cats, as we will see below) that the imperatives of sexual desire in cats were unmitigated by higher needs. Cats were not concerned with the preservation of the species: "But the wildness of their nature is not sweetened by this need, of which the conservation of life is merely the goal," he added. Cats were selfish in love.[18]

As we might expect, notions of feline behavior also informed the century's understanding of rabies. It was widely believed that cats were subject to the spontaneous generation of the disease. The *Dictionnaire de médecine*, for instance, explained that spontaneous rabies was possible in cats, wolves, and foxes, as well as in dogs. Only cats and dogs, however, could become diseased through sexual deprivation.[19]

But cases of feline rabies were very rare. Statistics from the Conseil d'hygiène publique for the years 1850–1876 offered a comparison of feline rabies with the incidence of the disease in dogs. Cats were blamed for twenty-three cases of human rabies, while during the same twenty-six years, 707 cases (still fewer than thirty per year) were the result of bites from dogs.[20] More important, people's perceptions of the disease in cats seem to accord with some of the facts. Tardieu, for instance, public health officer and firm believer in the spontaneous generation of rabies, declared in his 1859 report to the Comité consultatif d'hygiène publique that "the animal whose bite caused rabies" was almost always the dog.[21]

People believed that few cases of rabies occurred among cats because many males were neutered and their sexual drive destroyed. Sexual deprivation was no longer a problem for the sex believed more susceptible to the disease. But that admirable observer of animals and people in nineteenth-century Paris, the veterinarian Dr. Bourrel, pointed out that only one in ten male cats was neutered. And in fifteen years of practice, he had come across only one case of feline rabies in a male. Rather than suggesting that sexual desire in cats was unremarkable, however, Bourrel used the obvious exigent sexuality of female felines as an argument against the theory of the spontaneous generation of disease. "If [the urge for sex] can cause rabies, then cats who have not been neutered would often be struck by the disease, since the cat is, of all animals, the one in which these desires are the most pressing," he argued. He reminded his readers of Buffon's striking description of the cat in heat, repeating Buffon's phrases with a flourish. In such an animal, if in any, sexual frustration would explain the spontaneous generation of this disease, and veterinarians "would very often have to diagnose rabies in (female) cats." Yet they did not.[22]

Bourrel's unwelcome explanation of the rarity of feline rabies fit in with the conventional appreciation of the cat. Cats were hypersexual, independent, and asocial. Cats were devoted to the house, not the person, "The cat is attached to the house," Bourrel noted. "That he belongs to such and such an owner is of little importance to him, provided he is fed." The cat left the house rarely and then only when looking for sex, explained Bourrel. "Ordinarily, he does not stray from home. And it takes all the strength of sexual desire, which in [the cat] is so intense, to compel him to separate himself from his abode." Since the cat left its home only when pressed by desire, periodically, but not habitually, it had only occasional opportunities to catch the disease.[23]

The cat as icon of a sexuality pushed to the margins of bourgeois life was presented with disturbing effect by Edouard Manet in his 1863 painting *Olympia*. As T. J. Clark argues, Manet transformed the conventional nude into a portrait of a working-class prostitute while signaling its prototype with a replacement of signs. Among these signs, the cat figured significantly. *Olympia* revealed its derivation from Titian's *Venus of Urbino*, Clark points out: "The pose of the nude is essentially the same and the nude's accessories seem to be chosen as the modern forms of their Renaissance prototypes; orchid in place of roses, cat for dog, negress and flowers instead of servants bringing dresses from a distant cassone." Clearly part of what made critics judge this painting obscene is the black cat arching its tail at Olympia's feet. Along with Olympia's oversized hands and her dark skin, the cat signaled, in the shorthand of criticism, the painting's distinctive motifs. Cham's caricature of 14 May 1865 in *Le Charivari* offered a good example of this figuration. His "Manet, la naissance du petit ébéniste" exaggerated the size of the cat particularly by elongating the tail and emphasized Olympia's hands by darkening them. *Le Journal amusant* also played with the figure of the black cat in its review of the painting.[24]

Manet echoed Baudelaire's themes. The darkness of Olympia's skin, the evocation of perfume in the bouquet, and the startling image of the cat, of course, rearranged the central and ancillary metaphors of "The Cat," quoted above.[25] A similar image in Zola's *Thérèse Raquin* (1867) reflected the murderous sexuality of the exotic Thérèse in the petit-bourgeois family's cat.[26]

The cat in nineteenth-century culture was distinctly not bourgeois. "If the Parisian cat could choose his own master, it would be the artisan rather than the rich bourgeois he would give himself to," suggested Fée. "Admitted to the honors of the shop or to the pleasures of the salon, he buys these advantages with all the dignity of his sex," Fée continued, "he loses, with the instinct for love, [the instinct] for hunting; and rats and mice might dance round him with impunity, having nothing to fear."[27] The cat was like Thérèse, the bourgeois Raquin's half-Creole relative, who explained to Laurent after he had reawakened her sexuality, "They have so smothered me in their middle-class refinement that I don't know how there can be any blood left in my veins."[28]

But neither was the cat working-class, within the associative terms of petkeeping culture. The cat was linked rather with bohemia, a social space only indirectly concerned with class: intellectuals were elitist, and their affiliation was to the ancien régime's republic of letters rather than to a supposedly Philistine class.[29] "The philosophes of the last century affirmed, on good authority no doubt, that a pronounced taste for cats in certain people was an indication of superior merit," Larousse noted approvingly. "Witness those of our contemporaries whose affection for cats is a matter of notoriety, Théophile Gautier, Albéric Second, Léon Gozlan, Champfleury, Théodore Barrière, Paul de Kock, and several others."[30]

The companionship of a like-minded animal became a trope of intellectuals, the cat a sign for the literary life, a signature. Jules Barbey d'Aurévilly, for example, had a cat named Démonette, "or rather Desdémone—Démonette to close friends," which was given to him in 1884 by Madame Constantin Paul, the famous doctor's wife. The cat "would hardly ever leave the office of her master," his literary executor explained with great exactness, "settling herself comfortably on blank paper or, better yet, when those large pages of foolscap—on which he wrote his articles and novels—were filled with lines, fresh with ink, then, with so many switches of the tail would augment them with cross-hatching!"[31]

Charles Augustin Sainte-Beuve also had a notable feline companion, Polémon, a magnificent tabby, who had the freedom of his master's office. A friend later described him, typically, lounging lazily and deliberately among Sainte-Beuve's mountain of books. Gautier also described the intellectual's ideal companions who purred and performed their toilette as a pleasing background to intellectual work but always discreetly, "as if afraid of distracting or being annoying."[32]

In the realm of the imagination where the myth of the intellectual's life was invented, the cat described the social space to which it was restricted.[33] Looking backward from the twentieth century, we see the cat lazing about the intellectual's study as part of a harmless cliché that described the intellectual and artistic life. But in the nineteenth century the cat intensified, for a caste in formation, its salutary unconventionality. Cats were homologous to intellectuals, their writings suggested. Chateaubriand explained, "What I like about the cat is his character, independent and almost heartless, which prevents him from attaching himself to anyone. . . . The cat lives alone, he has no need of society," Chateaubriand reminded his audience. The cat did what it wanted, obeyed only when it wanted to, and was admirably free of social conventions. Chateaubriand clearly admired "that indifference with which he passes from salon to gutter." Distinctly unlike dogs, the cat was never obsequious. When it socialized, it sought only its own physical pleasure: "one strokes him, he raises his back in pleasure; but it is a physical

pleasure that he experiences, and not, as with the dog, an inane satisfaction in loving and being faithful to a master who thanks him with a
kick."[34]

Like the intellectual, the cat held in limbo, so to speak, values forced
to the margins of bourgeois life.[35] The supreme individualism of genius
that Chateaubriand's comment on the cat described is an instance of this
displacement. So too was the liberty and integrity of an artist who refused
to be sold. The cat defined the way one should behave, the writing of
intellectual cat lovers suggested. "To gain the esteem of a cat is a difficult
thing," explained Gautier. "It's an animal . . . who will not carry affection to the point of foolishness," he stressed. The cat would be your
friend, "if you are worthy [of his friendship]," but never your slave. The
cat maintained his "free will," despite the demands of friendship "and
will not do anything for you that he considers unreasonable," he added.
In the cat, affection was not compromised by convention. As Jules
Michelet explained, cats owned people, not the other way around. "I
have had at least one hundred cats or rather, as Michelet said, one
hundred cats have owned me," noted Paul Morand when the trope was
already a cliché.[36]

Cats refused to accept the constraints of bourgeois life, in the self-
reflexive fictions, perhaps, of intellectuals. Catulle Mendès, for instance,
had a cat that killed itself, he mournfully suspected, after having been
neutered to make him a more agreeable pet. The cat, Mime, was beautiful, but he gave off a very strong odor. Taken to be neutered, he
returned depressed: "Mime fell into a depression blacker than his beautiful velvet coat," we learn. Catulle Mendès lived on the fifth floor, and
the cat was in the habit of walking along the ledge below the windows.
One morning, Mime "deliberately" threw himself off the ledge and onto
the street, where he broke his back. "I have the distinct impression that
Mime committed *suicide*," Mendès asserted.[37]

Significantly, cats rarely allowed themselves to be victims of vivisection. "[A cat] escapes the knife of those experimenters who find the dog,
the rabbit, the pigeon far easier to sacrifice," explained Fée. Cats were
constitutionally difficult to shape to utilitarian ends. "The cat alone [of
all animals] cannot be trained. He is not at all malleable, either physically
or psychologically. He remains obstinately himself, and therein is his

dignity."[38] In another echo of Baudelaire, contemporaries believed that cats could be appreciated solely for their beauty, like art for art's sake. Catulle Mendès, for example, first owned falcons and other birds and then turned to dogs and cats, "the latter which he loved solely for their beauty," we are told.[39]

To understand the cat, wrote Champfleury in an often quoted phrase, "one must be a woman or a poet." The nineteenth century's appreciation of the cat rested for a long time on these two adjunct ideals contained uneasily within bourgeois culture. Within the logic of petkeeping, cats were feminine, philosophical, or both. "He is reserved, a philosophe, closed up within himself," suggested Henri Lautard, a Belle Epoque master at restating the obvious who also traced an affinity between Baudelaire and the cat. Both liked perfume. "Baudelaire loved cats who like himself were such lovers of perfume that a whiff of valerian [garden heliotrope] would throw them into a kind of epileptic fit," he wrote in a frenzy of clichés. Lautard was echoing Larousse who had explained in his *Dictionnaire* that perfume so strongly affected cats that its scent sent them into transports of pleasure.[40]

Cats and courtesans shared a luxurious sexuality, a fantastic sensuality, rather, that was carefully maintained outside the home. "He hides everything that should be hidden," wrote Lautard admiringly about the cat. "At certain times, he will throw off surveillance and escape from the house. . . . But if he cries his love affairs on the rooftops or in the street, it is only during the night that he does so, he never lets us see them," he explained in his work on feline psychology.[41] A utopia of irrepressible sexuality, the world represented by cats and prostitutes in the bourgeois imagination was like the "separate universe," in Pierre Bourdieu's phrase, that intellectuals carved out of bourgeois life. The excessively independent cat lived rather as the intellectual did, an existence of bourgeois individualism freed from the constraints of modern life. In the fictional world of creativity, both set themselves outside of family, society, and state, refusing to be dishonored, as Flaubert felt he would be, by any sense of belonging. The impulse to "affirm oneself as an artist with neither ties nor roots," as Bourdieu reads Flaubert, "'with no boots to lick; homeless, faithless, and lawless'" as Jean-Paul Sartre later expressed the modernist myth, found its animal counterpart in the cat.[42]

This creature intensified decidedly discordant themes within bourgeois culture. Unlike the dog, whose qualities lent themselves to embourgeoisement, the cat seemed resolutely set against incorporation into the mainstream of bourgeois life. Writers often drew unfavorable comparisons between the irascible autonomy of the cat and the fidelity, sociability, and malleability of the dog. "The cat and the dog bear absolutely no resemblance to each other, either in physical being or in educability," Fée said. The dog was our friend, the cat our guest. The cat was useful for chasing mice. But, Fée warned, "do not attribute to him any will to help us, he merely gives in to his instinct to hunt." It would be useless to ask anything more of a cat; "no one has been able to force the cat to render us the least service."[43] Toussenel, predictably, expressed the familiar wisdom with deliberate hostility. "The female cat attaches herself to the dwelling and not to the people who live there, proof of her ingratitude and the aridity of her heart," he concluded. A cat thought only of its comfort, unlike the dog, he insisted, "who attaches himself only to people and who is indifferent to misery provided he is sharing it with the objects of his affections."[44]

Unexpectedly, these same disagreeable feline qualities ensured cats' safety from the disease that dogs were so prone to catch. In his discussion of rabies, the persistently logical Bourrel contrasted admirable canine qualities to feline ones: the dog is a social animal. He is devoted to his master, "to the hand that feeds him," and wherever that master may go, here or there, the dog is happy, "provided he can sleep at the feet of his master, watch over his sleep, and defend him against enemies." A dog's sociability also led it to "fraternize with other dogs." The dog had many more opportunities than cats had to contract the disease.[45]

It is a mark of the strength of these themes that attempts to "rehabilitate" the cat took the form of making a cat seem to behave like a dog. Stories that featured feline fidelity, for instance, began to appear sporadically in the bulletin of the Parisian Société protectrice des animaux in the mid-1860s. In a single bulletin of 1864, Mme Adèle Favre attempted a "rehabilitation of the cat" on page 313 and M. Fournier "a new rehabilitation of the cat" on page 353. In the same year, in the July issue, the society featured another brief story on the "attachment cats are capable of feeling toward us." Cats, like dogs, these stories detailed, could be faithful beyond the grave. An attempted feline suicide, notably, was reported in 1865 under the heading, "Singular attachment of a cat for his master." In this story that purported to be true, observers narrowly prevented a cat whose master had just killed himself from doing the same. Fée, whose work the animal protection society reprinted and publicized in many formats, agreed: "The cat is not loving. However, if one succeeds in gaining his affection, which is not a very easy thing to do," he warned, "he may attach himself to his masters so passionately that sometimes he will die of grief from having lost them."[46]

The theme of feline fidelity was also developed with telling effect outside the bounds of the animal protection society. In children's literature, for instance, we find a polemical story, "Jenny and Minnie," appearing in French about this time. "Jenny and Minnie" tells of the friendship between a kitten, Minnie, and an abused orphan, Jennie. Jennie dies of her mistreatment, of course, and as we might guess Minnie dies on Jenny's grave.[47] So the cat was capable of expressing affection, even if only exceptionally. In a work of animal protection propaganda, Marie-Félicie Testas reluctantly admitted the possibility: "It is said, and truthfully, that the cat does not love his master the way a dog does. He appears to love only his food and lodging. The master leaves and the cat remains. Nevertheless, it is true that there are cats who recognize their master and who love them. I have known one or two of this kind."[48] Ernest Renan was more generous, suggesting that although cats were devoted to the home, they were capable at the same time of affection for people. "With respect to the cat, I believe that there is, indeed, a bit of egoism in him," admitted that positivist admirer of cats. "He likes his comfort above all and attaches himself more to the house than to persons. We have had here, however, striking proofs of that ability cats have to attach themselves to people." Renan warned, collapsing categories with anti-Semitic effect, "Do not charge that animal so much with the sins of Israel."[49]

Occasionally and pointedly a writer might applaud feminine cats for exhibiting masculine canine behavior. Female cats, for instance, could practice "fraternité." The animal protection society printed a letter in its March 1873 bulletin from a M. Heine, "Observation de fraternité comparée." He called readers' attention to "the story of twin cats who had their kittens the same day and in the same basket and who share their affectionate cares."[50]

Larousse, who directly engaged the arguments of Buffon and Toussenel in a premature effort to rehabilitate the cat in bourgeois culture, insisted that the cat could love as the dog did. "Biographers of cats, from the great naturalist [Buffon] to the very witty Toussenel," he explained, "have shown themselves severe on our heroes . . . , and it is a kind of rehabilitation that we are attempting here." Toward this end he whimsically printed a letter to his daughter from a kitten who claimed to be a good pet. The letter ended with the assurance of canine affection: "Which leads me to say to you that I write like a cat but I love like a dog."[51]

Alexandre Dumas, also, had a cat, Mysouff, whom he loved for its canine behavior. As he explained, "that cat missed his vocation, he should have been born a dog." The Dumas family lived on the rue de l'Ouest. Each day Mysouff walked Dumas to work as far as the rue de Vaugirard. On the writer's return, his canine cat would greet Dumas. "He would jump up on my knees as if he were a dog, then run off and return, then take the road home, returning a last time at a gallop," we are told with generous detail.[52]

A defense of the cat that attempted to neutralize feline perfidy by exposing its logic was also sketched out in the 1860s. The "fausseté" of the cat that Buffon had criticized was accidental, merely the result of artificial circumstances, a M. Boitard claimed. Forced to live in close quarters with its worst enemy, the dog, the cat had developed strategies of circumvention. "His natural distrust increased, necessarily, and it is probably to this that we must attribute what Buffon calls his treachery, his insidious gait," Boitard suggested. "He has kept that part of his independence to assure his existence in that position in which we have placed him," he also insisted, with Larousse's approbation.[53] Somewhat paradoxically Fée also tried to distance feline behavior from the morally charged universe to which it had been attached. The cat was not really traitorous when he scratched the hand that caressed him, Fée insisted. The impulse to scratch was a reflex, an instinct, over which he had no control. "When he submits to our caressing, it excites him, and when he appears to enjoy it the most, he will open his claws and scratch the hand that is stroking him. It is this that makes people call him a traitor," he explained. "To my mind, we must understand the thing in a different way and not attribute to treachery what is a simple effect of the nervous system." Furthermore, cat qualities in themselves could be appealing. "For people, in fact, the cat is a friend to talk to and converse with at our ease," Larousse suggested.[54]

By the 1880s, pet owners needed little convincing that cats were good pets. The popularity of cats grew undeniably from the last decades of the nineteenth century until the First World War. Cats continue as a presence in mass culture and today in France are almost as numerous as dogs. According to Theodore Zeldin, in 1983 seven million dogs cohabited officially with six million cats. Unofficial figures put the totals at nine million dogs and seven million cats.[55]

Even before the Belle Epoque, cats had supporters among ordinary people who were neither intellectual nor sexually unconventional. During the Paris Commune, when people had to eat or destroy their pets, some saved their cats.[56] And in the early days of the siege of Paris, when authorities attempted to save dogs from destruction, cats found supporters also. As was explained in the animal protection society's bulletin of 1871, "It took very strong needs to push anyone to destroy that four-footed friend; more than one poor devil shared his last crust of bread with him and in one club when the motion was made to sacrifice, ruthlessly, all of the useless *mouths*, there was a general revolt among the tender-hearted." The reporter was referring to dogs but a small effort was made, less predictably, on behalf of cats. "Several good souls spoke on behalf of cats also, who certainly have their merits, in spite of the lies malicious people make up about them," the writer added.[57]

During the late 1870s the Société protectrice des animaux grew more active in its defense of cats. The 1866 index to the bulletins of that year cites no listings of reports on cats; there were twenty in 1876. These included plain entries entitled "cats" as well as more descriptive ones such as "abandoned," "plans for a shelter," "plans for a pound," "rescued," "bad treatment toward," and other issues that signaled, significantly, cats' canine susceptibilities. In 1873 only six articles on cats were listed under four headings: "cruelties toward," "rescued," "acts of fraternity," and "nursed by a dog"; on dogs, thirty-two headings were needed to organize eighty-one separate entries. Perhaps as important as the increase in articles about cats is a shift in emphasis in the late 1870s from sporadic defenses of the cat's personality and general protection concerns to mainstream pet protection issues. In the 1860s the society was still concerned, for example, with preventing cats from being hunted for their coats in Paris, and with demonstrating that a cat could be loyal. In the late 1870s the dominant cat-related issue was the refuge.[58]

The appearance of cat shows in Paris and an interest in breeding marks an even more significant abandonment of the conventional assessment of the cat. Cat shows, like dog shows earlier, were based on British models. Harriet Ritvo points out in her book on British attitudes toward animals that the first cat show was held in 1871 at the Crystal Palace. And specialist cat clubs "began to spring up at the turn of the century."[59] As Henri Lautard remarked in 1909, cat shows were held yearly in London, adding, somewhat defensively, that Parisians also showed their cats. "We might also note . . . that Paris has also had several fine cat shows during these last few years."[60]

The French interest in cat breeds began in the late 1870s. Robert Delort explains that Abyssinians were brought from Africa in 1869 and first appeared in writings about cats in 1874. Siamese cats, smuggled into Britain in the 1870s and 1880s, were introduced to France by the French ambassador to Siam, Auguste Pavie. In 1885 he presented one to the Jardin des plantes.[61] In 1869, however, A. E. Brehm, "one of the high priests of zoologie," as Delort points out, had listed only eight breeds of cats in *La Vie des animaux illustrée*: "the Angora, the Manx, the Chinese cat, and five other varieties (the Chartreuse, the Persian, the Rumanian, the red cat of Tobolsk, and the red and blue cat of the Cape)." The same edition had described 195 breeds of dogs. Larousse in the 1860s knew only four varieties of domesticated cats: "the domestic tiger, the Chartreuse, the Spanish cat, [and] the Angora."[62]

Cat shows set the standards for breeds. But unlike dogs, where size, gait, shape, even purported function, set one type off from another, cat types differed mainly in color and length of coat.[63] As Lestrange explained in 1937, when the cat show was a set practice, "Cat shows have made us aware of the very special characteristics of the genre 'cat,' according to the color of the coat, which goes from ermine white to black velvet, passing through all the shapes of gray, yellow, and red without counting those of tortoise shell or tabby." The determined exoticism of breeds however—"chats de Perse, de Birmanie, de Siam, chats rouges de Tobolsk, chats nègres de Gambie, chats cypriotes, chats du Canada," as Lestrange detailed[64]—testifies to the impulse to introduce the safely exotic into everyday life, a belated echo of canine structures in catkeeping practice.

Alain Corbin suggests that the cleanliness of the cat played a significant role in its new popularity. "Yet here, too, Pasteur's discoveries changed behavior," he explains in his discussion of the "animal de tendresse" in *The History of Private Life*, the fear of germs "worked in favor of the house cat, which smelled less than its rival and was reputed to take better care of itself."[65] Certainly, the only consistently appealing feline trait, reluctantly conceded by the most hostile of commentators, was its obsessive self-care. Florent Prévost, in one of the few pet-care books to discuss cats, explained that though cats were disagreeably faithful to a house and not to a person, they were, at least, clean. Testas, in the *Contes de l'asile du quai d'Anjou* agreed: "The cat is not lacking in certain qualities. He is clean, glossy, one often notices him performing his toilette. Never has dirt of any kind been seen on his coat."[66]

Even those who celebrated canine qualities of fidelity and affect admitted that the dog's standards of hygiene were low. The Parisian animal protection society made this point in a report on "The dog, the premier domestic animal" published in its early bulletin of 1857. "The feelings he develops for us set him above all others. He loves us and it is because of this, principally, that we are touched." However, left to its own devices, the dog was a glutton, ruled by his stomach. His choice of food was often disgusting: the dog would eat the droppings of other animals—"so lacking in refinement when it comes to food." And the dog was dirty. Unlike the cat, the dog cared little about his appearance, apparently as happy when covered with dirt as when "combed, washed, and perfumed."[67]

The history of the cat, however, addresses the history of the nineteenth century at another level of meaning, one that this book seeks to enclose. The impulse to categorize shaped both scientific and social representations of modern life. Shifting configurations of human and animal, outsider and insider, being and nonbeing, were described at many levels of nineteenth-century culture. Among ordinary people the attempt to catalog concerned primarily the language of class. To speak of the popularization of scientific ideas is to grasp only one of the directions that shaped bourgeois culture, a civilization marked by multiples of self-definition. Like the corporate world it replaced, Pierre Bourdieu reminds us, the universe of class was an attempt, mediated by power, to describe—codify and fix—"a state of the social structure."[68] We could say modernity.

In everyday life the shaping of nineteenth-century modernism was effected in petkeeping culture. Around the dog were clustered qualities that spoke to contemporary feelings of fragmentation and isolation. The faithful and affective dog commented pointedly on the failures of individualism, the perceived lack of community in urban life. At the same time, the dog fixed modernity in notions of class. Bourgeois dogs, contemporaries insisted self-consciously, were distinctly unlike working-class animals. The aseptic pet, denatured in the imagination of pet owners, worked to distinguish culture, or bourgeois ideas of civilization, from nature, a sometimes undifferentiated confusion of categories—animals and the working class, women and the poor, sexuality and violence. It helped describe the norms of everyday life, whose costs were registered in disease.

Natural history per se was less important in petkeeping culture than the bourgeoisie's own understanding of its history. The fidelity of the dog, as well as its opposite value, the perfidy of the cat, were qualities borrowed from, or, rather, renewed with pointed reference to, pre-Enlightenment Europe. Here was a moral zoology that ordered the hierarchy of petkeeping. For Larousse, writing in the 1860s about cats, moral values were intrinsic to species. "First of all, to get a fix on the intrinsic value of a species, a value that is as much moral as physical, we consult proverbs," he noted with true lexicological flair.[69]

The role of the imagination in shaping bourgeois culture was also apparent in the development of the home aquarium. The impulse to collect exotica—in the aquarium, deliberately alienated natural objects—

was paralleled in the development of breeds. Invented histories of other times and places were fixed in types of dogs. Later, Asian and African cats would appeal to the same interest.

The Parisian Société protectrice des animaux shared the view that animals embodied values. The marquess de Montcalm, for example, vice-president of the Parisian society in 1860, could refer to animals as models for human behavior.[70] A more sophisticated view was expressed by Oscar Honoré in *Le Coeur des bêtes*, which a committee of the society's officers praised in 1861. He discussed the relationship of human beings to animals in terms of evolution. More specifically, he posited a moral Lamarckism. Humanity, Honoré argued, had become too complicated to understand: "too complete, too complex to be in itself, and directly, a profitable subject of study. Modified by education," he explained, "disguised by the changing glaze of diverse civilizations, protean human passions . . . sometimes suggest the image of chaos." Animals, however, like children, were easier to read. They expressed human qualities in a simpler form: "Like a child, the animal is without shame or artifice, he opens his heart like a book, where we recover in each line a trait from the human character." The function of zoology was the explication of an otherwise baffling humankind. "Would not the almost impossible analysis of human passions find precious instruction in the observation of these so much simpler combinations of ideas and feelings that the animal presents?" he asked.[71]

Some fifteen years later Sociétaires continued to suggest not only that the function of zoology was moral but that human beings were its determining subject. "What do these anatomical descriptions, these measurements, these analyses, these experiments tell us about the true character of an animal, about those traits that make it a distinct being?" the author of an 1875 article on "la zoologie morale" asked. "Nothing," he answered. Dissected, all animals looked alike. In looking at animals, he suggested astutely, human beings were looking for themselves: "Now, as we know things only by the impression they make on us, it is not in the animal we must search, but in ourselves."[72]

By the end of the nineteenth century, however, canine and feline values had lost the power to reassure or disturb. The excessive individ-ualism and sexuality of the cat, for instance, were no longer sources of

anxiety for the bourgeoisie. Petkeeping grew formulaic, as the participants set the broad strokes of bourgeois culture itself. By the First
World War people knew about the care of pets, just as they intuited the
conventions of bourgeois life; class was an object, knowable and known.

The cat's absorption within bourgeois culture signals not merely the
neutralization of the qualities it represented, but the abandonment in the
late nineteenth century of organic metaphors for modernity. Between
the 1850s and 1880s, scientific and ordinary thinking alike were still
strongly moored to natural models. Nature could still speak to culture,
at least negatively. By the First World War, however, the ambiguities
of bourgeois culture had found other, sadder, resolutions. In art and
technology, in likening human beings to machines, modernism failed.

Epilogue

Petkeeping's importance today is anecdotally obvious even in the pages of the Parisian telephone book. The almost seven hundred thousand dogs currently kept in Paris are supported by anthropomorphic businesses such as Le Home du chien, a canine beauty parlor ironically located on the rue Claude Bernard and the Club vacances des animaux that makes obvious reference to patterns of leisure in today's mass culture. Dozens of other shops advertise haute couture, basic clothing, accessories, and the sale of purebred puppies.[1] And as in many other major Western cities, cats are becoming even more popular than dogs. The ubiquity of pets and the universality of petkeeping culture today should not blind us to the novelty and importance of the system's nineteenth-century beginning.

Petkeeping was so deeply embedded in class as to make the two systems—class and petkeeping—almost indistinguishable to contemporaries. To speak of petkeeping in the nineteenth century was to refer to bourgeois culture. To understand the inventions of petkeeping is for twentieth-century readers to grasp how much class itself was a cultural response to modernity, to the nineteenth century, to the postrevolutionary era.

The experience of modernity—the tangibles of nineteenth-century life—was expressed aesthetically in modernism. In high culture, as Debora Silverman points out with respect to art nouveau in the 1890s, its shift from "technological monumentality" to "organic interiority" was "not an anti-modernist reaction." Modernism in art was deeply informed by the past (as well as by new psychological styles).[2] So too was the modernism that petkeepers inscribed in their ordinary lives. Petkeeping (read bourgeois culture) borrowed freely from supposed ancien régime norms and poignantly set noble values against the individualism of the nineteenth century.

The bourgeoisie adopted aspects of its culture from the eighteenth-century aristocracy. It more dramatically (and appositely) described itself in opposition to the working class, a group that was hovering in mid-century on the point of definition, as Louis Chevalier argues with eccentric brilliance.[3] The working classes were the dangerous classes, violent, sexual, and irrational. Their anti-values were projected onto pets: cleanliness, order, and rationality marked bourgeois petkeeping.

The dichotomy of nineteenth-century class was only apparently fixed, however. Qualities banished from bourgeois life found their way back into the modern personality, strikingly notable in the rabies scare and the anti-vivisection movements. The work of the imagination is key to our understanding of this century. The unstable, complicated transformation of eighteenth-century rationalism to late nineteenth-century modernism was most eloquently articulated, perhaps, by the century's trained elite. But in the private as well as the public spaces of nineteenth-century ideas were the ruins of Enlightenment thought.

Notes

INTRODUCTION

1. Walter Benjamin, "On Some Motifs in Baudelaire," in *Illuminations*, ed. Hannah Arendt, trans. Harry Zorn (New York: Schocken, 1969), 197.

2. "By 1700," Thomas explains, "all the symptoms of obsessive petkeeping were in evidence." Cats were "privileged animals," as well as dogs. "Well fed, doted upon by loving masters, dogs, especially, figured in portraits of country squires and aristocrats" (Keith Thomas, *Man and the Natural World: A History of the Modern Sensibility* [New York: Pantheon, 1983], 117). Harriet Ritvo's work includes *The Animal Estate: The English and Other Creatures in the Victorian Age* (Cambridge, Mass.: Harvard University Press, 1987), and numerous articles on the general subject of animals and British culture.

3. Hester Hastings, *Man and Beast in French Thought of the Eighteenth Century* (Baltimore: Johns Hopkins University Press, 1936), 205–206. See also Sébastien Mercier, *Le Tableau de Paris* (Amsterdam, 1783), 8:133, 337–338.

4. Alain Corbin, *Le Territoire du vide: L'occident et le désir du rivage* (Paris: Aubier, 1988), 321.

CHAPTER 1

1. Société protectrice des animaux, *Bulletin* (hereafter *Bulletin*) 1 (1855): 4–5, 164; *Bulletin* 3 (1857): 57–58. This mix of nobles and professional bourgeoisie was intensified by the addition of *dames patronesses* installed in 1855; in 1860 they included the comtesse de Dino-Talleyrand, Madame Geoffroy Saint-Hilaire, Madame Richelot, and the comtesse Vernède de Corneillan. During the first decades the social composition of the society's membership echoed that of its leadership, with the occasional *mécanicien* buried in a list of architects, lawyers, doctors, professors, men of letters, property owners, and counts. By 1860 the society had three thousand members.

2. In "Le Sang des bêtes: Le problème de la protection des animaux en France au XIXème siècle," *Romantisme: Revue du dix-neuvième siècle* 31 (1981): "From their childhood Domitian and Nero had shown signs of their evil instincts" (92). Agulhon's article surveys research on animal protection in nineteenth-century France; there is as yet no full-length study of the Parisian Société protectrice des animaux. Jacques Léonard discusses the society's for-

mation in *La Médecine entre les pouvoirs et les savoirs: Histoire intellectuelle et politique de la médecine française au XIXème siècle* (Paris: Aubier, 1981).

3. Agulhon, "Sang des bêtes," 92, 91.

4. Quoted by Agulhon, "Sang des bêtes," 90.

5. Agulhon, "Sang des bêtes," 90, 92.

6. A.-J.-B. Parent-Duchâtelet is quoted in the *Bulletin* 2 (1856): 212.

7. Agulhon, "Sang des bêtes," 89, 92.

8. The exposition was discussed in the organization's first published report, *Bulletin* 1 (1855): 111.

9. *Bulletin* 3 (1857): 165; *Bulletin* 2 (1856): 127.

10. *Bulletin* 1 (1855): 66; Henri Richelot, *Bulletin* 1 (1855): 104.

11. As the president remarked, "et nous sommes certains d'être compris en nous adressant à cette ensemble" (*Bulletin* 1 [1855]: 67).

12. Description in *Bulletin* 6 (1860): 177; *Bulletin* 7 (1861): 170.

13. Among the few studies of vivisection in nineteenth-century France are Paul Elliott, "Vivisection and the Emergence of Experimental Physiology in Nineteenth-Century France," in Nicolaas Rupke, ed. *Vivisection in Historical Perspective*, 48–77 (London: Croom Helm, 1987); and John Lesch, *Science and Medicine in France: The Emergence of Experimental Physiology, 1790–1855* (Cambridge, Mass.: Harvard University Press, 1984). See also the many intellectual biographies of Claude Bernard.

14. "The goal that the vivisectionists have in mind—the knowledge of man—the immeasurable achievements they have already achieved along these lines," the chairman argued, ". . . all this allows us no doubt that vivisections are, in principle, an eminently useful thing." He included in his definition of vivisection a defense of science and its benefits: it was "a method of scientific research worthy of the approbation of all those who sincerely love the progress of science, that is to say the good of humanity" (*Bulletin* 6 [1860]: 362); see "Rapport sur les vivisections," 356–364.

15. The "illustrious" François Magendie, as first animal protectionists and later rabid antivivisectionists often noted, destroyed 4,000 dogs in order to verify the results of an experiment performed by the "not less illustrious" Charles Bell. He duly published his results, operated on another 4,000 dogs, and in another *mémoire* "declared with the same assurance that Ch. Bell was wrong." Pierre Flourens then experimented on more thousands of dogs, only to prove Bell right about the distinction between types of nerves (*Sus à la vivisection!* [Paris, 1886], 201). Henri Blatin refers to this incident of medical folly in *Nos Cruautés envers les animaux* (Paris, 1867), 201.

16. First cited by Blatin, *Bulletin* 2 (1856): 217.

17. Quoted in *Bulletin* 5 (1859): 26–27.

18. Blatin, *Nos Cruautés*, 198, 191, 198–199.

19. *Bulletin* 1 (1855): 24. "Vivisection, a new word that will dishonor the nineteenth century," is another remark along these lines (*A Sa Majesté l'Empereur des Français: Humble supplique du caniche Médor* [Paris, 1865], 5).

20. Blatin, *Nos Cruautés*, 193.

21. "Curiosity alone would explain its continuation," as the society's comment on vivisection in the *Bulletin* of 1855 insisted.

22. *Humble supplique du caniche Médor*, 6.

23. Dr. Magne, Sociétaire; see *Bulletin* 7 (1861): 68, 65.

24. Dr. Magne, *Bulletin* 7 (1861): 65; quoted by Blatin, *Nos Cruautés*, 233.

25. Carteaux in *Bulletin* 6 (1860): 382. The animal protection society complained that "the appreciation (*le sentiment*) of scientific curiosity was so powerful as to repress that of intelligent sensibility or to provide its audience with a training of that kind" (*Bulletin* 7 [1861]: 127).

26. The marquis de Montcalm, *Bulletin* 6 (1860): 373.

27. Blatin is citing Joulin in *Bulletin* 2 (1856): 218.

28. Dogs for vivisection were purchased from the pound or stolen directly from the street. The French version of A. E. Brehm's masterpiece of 1869, *The Animals of the World*, one of the most popular nineteenth-century works on natural history, matter-of-factly described for its wide audience the practice of procurement: "Physiologists consume a great number of dogs; and the skill of those hunters who supply scientists with animals for their experiments is so great that when one notifies them the preceding day, the next day one has some hundred of victims chosen among the stray dogs of large cities" (A. E. Brehm, *La Vie des animaux illustrée: Description populaire du règne animal* [Paris, 1869], vol. 1, *Les Mamifères*, 367).

29. Quoted in *Bulletin* 2 (1856): 104; Montcalm in *Bulletin* 6 (1860): 366.

30. Blatin, *Nos Cruautés*, 196.

31. A letter to the press from "the influential anti-vivisectionist" George Hoggan is quoted in William Schupbach, "A Select Iconography of Animal Experiments," in Nicolaas Rupke, ed., *Vivisection in Historical Perspective* (London: Croom Helm, 1987), 351.

32. Victor Meunier is quoted by Blatin, *Nos cruautés*, 212. Meunier was also quoted in *Bulletin* 5 (1859): 27. Magne is quoted in *Bulletin* 7 (1861): 69.

33. So F. A. Couturier de Vienne insisted in *Paris moderne: Plan d'une ville modèle* (Paris, 1860), 219. And as the marquis de Montcalm also explained, the Société protectrice des animaux "must, in our opinion, denounce this infamous and too lucrative business of dog stealing that, at any instant, makes our precious animals liable to being traitorously sold to be tortured; an industry directly stimulated by unlimited vivisection, an industry in every sense immoral" (*Bulletin* 6 [1860]: 377).

34. *Bulletin* 6 (1860): 365; original emphasis.

35. Quoted in D. Metzger, *La Vivisection* (Paris, 1888), 217. The *Bulletin* of March 1876 appears to mention this letter. Cham, of *Le Charivari*, was very active in the cause of animal protection. As the *Bulletin* of February 1876 notes with gratitude, an exposé of the Parisian dog pound was published in *Le Charivari* consisting of Cham's caricatures and an article by Louis Huart that prompted immediate reforms by the Parisian police. The comte de Noé was subsequently

named a member of the committee on the dog pound (*commission de la fourrière*) (*Bulletin* 21 [1876]: 41, 58–59). In August and September 1876 he sent to the Société protectrice des animaux articles from wide-circulation newspapers, the *Petite Presse* and the *Figaro*, on cruelty to dogs in general and at the Fourrière in particular.

36. *Bulletin* 21 (1876): 83; *Bulletin* 23 (1878): 430.

37. Metzger lists the chief animal protection and antivivisection societies in *La Vivisection*, 31–32.

38. See François-Victor Foveau de Courmelles, *La Vivisection: Erreurs et abus*, (Paris, 1912), 15–16, for a sketchy history of the Société française contre la vivisection. Hugo attended meetings rarely, if ever.

39. Maria Deraismes, *Discours contre la vivisection* (Paris, 1884), 21–22.

40. Deraismes, *Discours contre la vivisection*, 24, 27–28.

41. Paul Bert was Bernard's student. He later entered politics and was a member of Gambetta's cabinet in 1881–82, the minister of public instruction. See Jules Besse, "L'Assistance publique des bêtes: Les chats et les chiens de Paris," *La Vie contemporaine* (1895): 248. Francis Ronsin in *La Grève des ventres* (Paris: Aubier, 1980), 44, says that Huot, who "had the taste and talent for brilliant and spectacular gestures," attacked Brown-Séquard during experiments on live *rabbits*.

42. Besse, "Assistance publique des bêtes," 240.

43. *Bulletin* 20 (1875): 316–317, 211.

44. Alain Corbin, *Le Miasme et la jonquille: L'odorat et l'imaginaire social, 18ème–19ème siècle* (Paris: Aubier, 1982), 311.

45. Besse, "Assistance publique des bêtes," 255.

46. A version of this story appears in Robert Lestrange, *Les Animaux dans la littérature et dans l'histoire* (Gap: Ophrys, 1937), 156–157. Besse also discusses Mlle Bernard in "Assistance publique des bêtes." No biography or biographical sketch of Bernard mentions the Fanny Bernard story although Agulhon explains that Claude Bernard's wife, from whom he was later divorced, "reproached her husband equally strongly for being a freethinker and for being cruel, and it was she, *la dévote*, who sent in each year their two francs' membership dues to the Société protectrice des animaux" (Agulhon, "Sang des bêtes," 100). The standard biographies also discuss (unsympathetically) the wife's hostility to Bernard's work: see J. M. D. Olmsted and E. Harris Olmsted, *Claude Bernard and the Experimental Method in Medicine* (New York: Henry Achuman, 1952), 112; and Reino Virtanen, *Claude Bernard and His Place in the History of Ideas* (Lincoln: University of Nebraska Press, 1960). Virtanen notes (119) that it was believed that Mme Bernard turned her daughters against their father and that she herself ran a home for dogs in order to make amends for the supposed crimes of her husband. Much of the information about the marital problems of the Bernards comes from Anatole de Monzie, *Les Veuves abusives* (Paris: Grasset, 1936).

47. Besse, "Assistance publique des bêtes," 245.

48. Besse, "Assistance publique des bêtes," 245.

49. *Bulletin* 20 (1875): 435, 433.

50. Valentin Magnan described the limits of female participation in the public sphere, redefining a trope for feeling as illness (Valentin Magnan, *De la folie des antivivisectionists*, from the *Comptes rendus hebdomadaires de la Société de biologie* [Paris, n.d.], 3–4).

51. For a review of the problem in England see Mary Ann Elston, "Women and Anti-vivisection in Victorian England, 1870–1900," in Nicolaas Rupke, ed., *Vivisection in Historical Perspective* (London: Croom Helm, 1987), 259–294.

52. Theodore Zeldin, *France 1848–1945: Anxiety and Hypocrisy* (Oxford: Oxford University Press, 1981), 5:156.

53. Coral Lansbury, *The Old Brown Dog: Women, Workers, and Vivisection in Edwardian England* (Madison: University of Wisconsin Press, 1985), 162–163.

54. Cleyre Yvelin, *De la vivisection: Etude psychologique* (Paris, 1910), 53, 77.

55. *Bulletin* 20 (1875): 437; *Bulletin* 21 (1876): 128, 314.

56. Besse, "Assistance publique des bêtes," 241. See also Pierre Mégnin, "Un Asile pour les chiens près de Paris," *La Nature* (1893): 325–327.

57. *Bulletin* 21 (1876): 275; *Bulletin* 19 (1874): 118. For other appeals to Bourrel see *Bulletin* 18 (1873): 246, 371; *Bulletin* 20 (1875): 321; *Bulletin* 21 (1876): 283, 357.

58. *Bulletin* 21 (1876): 83; "La Fourrière de Paris," *Revue Britannique* 5 (Paris, 1873): 343–354. This article was originally published in *Fraser's Magazine* and came to the attention of the Société protectrice des animaux in 1876 after Cham published an exposé of the pound in *Le Charivari*; see *Bulletin* 21 (1876): 58–59.

59. *Bulletin* 18 (1873): 244. See also comments in the *Bulletin* 17 (1872): 191, 379 and discussion at the May 1873 meeting as well as *Bulletin* 18 (1873): 131. Bernard and Magendie, for example, had to work in their rooms during the early stages of their careers; see Schupbach, "A Select Iconography," 349, who quotes Bernard's *Leçons de physiologie opératoire* to this effect.

60. *Bulletin* 21 (1876): 283.

61. "Les Chiens de la Sorbonne," from the *Gaulois*, 24 July 1879 (London: Office of the Society for the Protection of Animals from Vivisection, 1882). Gélyot won her case on appeal. The trial process became a forum for presenting positions on vivisection. Gélyot's lawyer explained how, exactly, Paul Bert operated on dogs. A handbook for vivisectors was presented as evidence. The government defended French science. A petition was sent in May 1879 to the prefect of police asking for restrictions on Bert's operations: "alongside the signatures of the most modest concierges, tailors, workers, [were] those from neighboring *hôtels*, those of several lawyers, that of L'Hermite, member of the Institut de France, those of engineers, of professors, of a [director of taxes], and, the most serious thing! that of the prefect of police's secretary!" The only

neighborhood resident not to sign the petition supposedly was the pharmacist, who made money selling sleeping potions ("Les Chiens de la Sorbonne," 17; the testimony of the officer and attorney appears on 4).

62. In January 1873, for instance, a Mlle Delorme prevented a butcher from putting a wounded dog out of its misery. As the organization more attractively reported the incident: "A helpless (*infirme*) dog had just been run over and a butcher was going to dispatch it with his knife, when a young lady, twenty-two years old, picked it up in her arms and carried it home to her mother" (*Bulletin* 18 [1873]: 41). Mlle Delorme was a friend of the society's president.

CHAPTER 2

1. Quoted in Robert Lestrange, *Les Animaux dans la littérature et dans l'histoire* (Gap: Ophrys, 1937), 135–136. Told to Gaston Picard, "for the readers of *Nouvelles littéraires*," by Georges Payele, the first honorary president of the Cour des Comptes and one of the six young men selected as Hugo's pallbearers at the national funeral on 1 June 1885 (Lestrange, *Les Animaux*, 135).

2. For M. Cheval's statement see *Bulletin* 19 (1874): 397, and on 386 one by a cemetery keeper, which first appeared in *Le Figaro*. For a discussion of the governing council, see the *Bulletin* 20 (1875): 7, 13, and a member's comment on 277–278. For Chéri's death see *Bulletin* 21 (1876): 53–54.

3. See Michael W. Fox, *Understanding Your Dog* (New York: Bantam, 1981). Konrad Lorenz, *King Solomon's Ring*, trans. M. K. Wilson (New York: Harper, 1979), 118–119.

4. Quoted in Lestrange, *Les Animaux*, 137.

5. *Bulletin* 17 (1872): 349; A. Mahé de la Bourdonnais, *Le Chien: L'ami de l'homme* (Paris, 1893), 6; Jean Robert, *Le Chien d'appartement et d'utilité: Education, dressage, hygiène, maladies* (Paris, 1888), 122. See also Jean Robert and L. Fortin, *Les Chiens: Chiens de luxe et d'utilité, chiens de chasse, nomenclature, description, élevage, hygiène, et maladies* (Paris, 1898); Henri Lautard, *Zoophilie ou sympathie envers les animaux: Psychologie du chien, du chat, du cheval* (Paris, 1909), 114; le baron de Vaux, *Notre Ami le chien* (Paris, 1897), 4.

6. "Car l'oeil a sa langue, surtout quand il s'éteint" (*Bulletin* 1 [1855]: 236). The poem "Mon Dernier Coup de fusil," also known as "La Mort d'un chevreuil," was recited by Lamartine at the society's annual meeting and reported in *Bulletin* 21 (1876); the quote is from 236.

7. Lestrange, *Les Animaux*, 137; Robert, *Chien d'appartement*, 61.

8. Lestrange, *Les Animaux*, 129; Aurélien Scholl, preface to Vaux, *Notre Ami le chien*, xviii, xix.

9. Vaux, *Notre Ami le chien*, 196–198.

10. For French hunting laws in the nineteenth century see *La Grande Encyclopédie* (Paris, 1886–1902), s.v. "chasse."

11. Jean-Claude Schmitt, *The Holy Greyhound: Guinefort, Healer of Children since the Thirteenth Century*, trans. M. Thom (Cambridge: Cambridge University Press, 1983), 138.

12. For the enduring importance of the aristocracy in the nineteenth century see Arno Mayer, *The Persistence of the Old Regime: Europe to the Great War* (New York: Pantheon, 1981).

13. Scholl, preface, *Notre Ami le chien*, xvii, xviii; le comte de Bony de la Vergne, *Les Chiens* (Metz, 1858), 13.

14. Lestrange, *Les Animaux*, 123.

15. Oscar Honoré, *Le Coeur des bêtes* (Paris, 1863), 40; Honoré's summary of the story is on 36–37.

16. See, for instance, *Bulletin* 9 (1863): 365: "he who stays when the others depart, he who by his tenderness in the face of all life's trials consoles the man who is unhappy and who would have precluded the cry of the afflicted Ovid, '*solus eris*, you will be alone,' if Ovid had had a dog near him, when he wrote his *Tristia* in exile." Also see the *Bulletin* 12 (1866): 231.

17. The most famous faithful British dog may be Bobby of Greyfriars' churchyard who for fourteen years after his master's death until his own in 1872 spent his days and nights mourning on his master's grave, leaving only for brief periods to satisfy his hunger.

18. *Bulletin* 20 (1875): 435–436.

19. For examples see *Bulletin* 2 (1856): 227, which describes a dog who dies on his owner's grave; *Bulletin* 24 (1879): 346, which describes a dog who attempts to dig his owner out of the grave; *Bulletin* 17 (1872): 72, a dog who dies on the doorstep of the hospital; and *Bulletin* 7 (1861): 175, a dog who, after "paying his last respects to his master," returns home to die. Henri Blatin in *Nos Cruautés envers les animaux* (Paris, 1867), 105–106, describes how the vigil of a starving dog on the banks of the Seine near where his master committed suicide is broken when the dog is taken to the pound. The Société protectrice des animaux decides to rescue the faithful dog from the pound where he would certainly be destroyed. When representatives of the society arrive there, however, they discover that they are too late: "[he] has gone to rejoin his master."

20. On the importance of Larousse's *Grand Dictionnaire* see Pascal Ory, "Le 'Grand Dictionnaire' de Pierre Larousse," in Pierre Nora, ed., *La République*, vol. 1 of *Les Lieux de Mémoire* (Paris: Gallimard, 1984). For the chien du Louvre see Pierre Larousse, *Le Grand Dictionnaire universel* (Paris, 1865–1890), s.v. "chien." John Russell mentions Médor, le chien du Louvre, in his *Paris* (New York: Abrams, 1983), 98.

21. *Bulletin* 21 (1876): 53–54. For comments on other canine suicides see *Bulletin* 21 (1876): 128; and Mme Charles Boeswillwald, *Le Chien de luxe: Comment élever, dresser, et soigner nos chiens* (Paris, 1907), 65, which illustrates the prototypical faithful dog who "threw himself in despair from the third floor during a long absence of his master."

22. "So many times superior to humanity itself," for example, as an anonymous contributor noted in a society journal, *La Vie élégante* 1 (1880); Vaux, *Notre Ami le chien*, 2.

23. Reprinted in *Bulletin* 20 (1875): 344–345. *Bateaux-mouches* were introduced during the 1867 exposition.

24. *Bulletin* 20 (1875): 345.

25. Version one is in Oscar Honoré, *Le Coeur des bêtes* (Paris, 1863), 59–60. Version two appears in A. L. A. Fée, *Les Misères des animaux* (Paris, 1863), 67. For variations see *Bulletin* 19 (1874): 212; in this version the nearly drowned dog returns home to the master who tried to kill him.

26. Mme F. H. Jobert, trans., *Jocelyn: An Episode, Journal Found at the House of a Village Curé* (Paris and London, 1837), 347. The excerpt from *Jocelyn* is quoted also in Lestrange, *Les Animaux*, 139–140.

27. *Bulletin* 20 (1875): 391. On Argus see also Société du jardin zoologique d'acclimatation du bois de Boulogne, *Exposition universelle des races canines de 1865: Catalogue des chiens exposés* (Paris, 1865), 5. See also Lautard, *Zoophilie*, 90.

28. Quoted in Lestrange, *Les Animaux*, 136. Dated 12 July 1855, no. 18 from book 3 of *Le Livre lyrique: La destinée*.

29. Lestrange, *Les Animaux*, 140.

30. Dossier Durand, le cimetière des chiens, Bibliothèque Marguerite Durand.

31. Dossier Durand, le cimetière des chiens; Lucien Richard, *Annuaire Richard pour 1898: Chiens célèbres et chiens de célébrités* (Paris, 1898), 70.

32. Lautard, *Zoophilie*, 105; Richard Thomson also notes the prevalence of this theme ("'Les Quat' Pattes': The Image of the Dog in Late Nineteenth-Century French Art," *Art History* 5, no. 3 [September 1982]: 323–337).

33. Blatin, *Nos Cruautés*, 95.

34. *Bulletin* 10 (1864): 295–296.

35. Charles Baudelaire, *The Parisian Prowler: Le spleen de Paris, petits poèmes en prose*, trans. Edward K. Kaplan (Athens: University of Georgia Press, 1989), 126.

36. Walter Benjamin, "Paris, Capital of the Nineteenth Century," in *Reflections: Essays, Aphorisms, Autobiographical Writings*, trans. Edmund Jephcott, ed. Peter Demetz (New York: Harvest, 1978).

37. The *barbet* is a type of poodle from which the French poodle developed in the nineteenth century; see chapter five. The story ends with the comment, "A complete recovery is expected" (*Bulletin* 5 [1859]: 340). Honoré also notes the story (*Le Coeur des bêtes*, 18).

38. The event was reported in *Le Figaro* of 15 April 1872; see *Bulletin* 17 (1872): 165.

39. Aaron H. Katcher, "Are Companion Animals Good for Your Health?" *Aging Magazine*, September–October 1982, 7.

40. E. Leroy, *L'Enfance du chien* (Paris, 1896).

41. In *La Curée*, for example, Zola presents the villainous Saccard enjoying the prospect of modernization (Emile Zola, *Les Romans d'Emile Zola: La Curée* [Lausanne: Henri Guillermin, 1961], 4:125–126).

42. Edmond and Jules de Goncourt, *Pages from The Goncourt Journal*, ed. and trans. Robert Baldick (Oxford: Oxford University Press, 1978), 18–19:

> After reading Edgar Allan Poe. Something the critics have not noticed: a new literary world, pointing to the literature of the twentieth century. . . . Something monomaniacal. Things playing a more important part than people; love giving way to deductions and other sources of ideas, style, subject, and interest . . .
>
> 16 July 1856

CHAPTER 3

1. "La Journée du célibataire," *Le Charivari*, April–September 1839. The series is reproduced in Loys Delteil, *Honoré Daumier* (Paris, 1925–1930), vol. 21, plates 607–618. Delteil says (mistakenly, I believe) that the series begins in February 1839.

2. I refer to the reading Clifford Geertz might adopt (as in "The Balinese Cockfight," in *The Interpretation of Cultures* [New York: Basic Books, 1973], 412–453).

3. Alfred Barbou, *Le Chien: Son histoire, ses exploits, ses aventures* (Paris, 1883), 262–263; Archives parlementaires, 1787–1860: Table générale alphabétique et analytique (Paris: Dupont, 1879), 113.

4. Des Essarts is quoted in Solange Belin, "Une Vie de chien sous l'ancien régime," *Historia* 456 (December 1984): 59; Sébastien Mercier, *Le Tableau de Paris* (Amsterdam, 1783), 8:337–338.

5. On the eighteenth century as a golden age for dogs see Donald Posner, *Watteau: A Lady at Her Toilet* (New York: Viking, 1973), 77, and, concerning dogs as possible sexual partners, see 81; Mercier, *Tableau de Paris*, 133.

6. For the dog as a sexual symbol see Richard Thomson, "'Les Quat' Pattes': The Image of the Dog in Late Nineteenth-Century French Art," *Art History* 5, no. 3 (September 1982): 323–337. On the execution of little dogs during the Revolution see *L'Almanach des honnêtes femmes pour l'année 1790*, according to A. Girodie in his *Jean-Frédéric Schall: Un peintre de fêtes galantes* (Strasbourg, 1927), 20. Posner also mentions the incident and refers the reader to Girodie (Posner, *Watteau*, 82, 104).

7. Eugène Compans, "La Taxe sur les chiens" (Ph.D. thesis, faculté de droit, Université de Toulouse, 1907), 22–23.

8. *Bulletin* 1 (1855): 61.

9. The tax was obligatory—"The law does not simply give communes the right to tax dogs: it makes it imperative"—and insistently universal—"and demands that all these animals without exception be taxed." Regulation issued from the Ministère de l'Intérieur 5 August 1855 is cited in Henry Delaporte, *Guide manuel de la taxe sur les chiens* (Paris, 1887), 5. See Compans's "Taxe sur les chiens" also for a list of all documents pertaining to the tax on dogs.

10. Many sources describe the administration of the dog tax. In addition to Compans, "Taxe sur les chiens"; and Delaporte, *Guide manuel*; see Pierre La-

rousse, *Grand Dictionnaire universel*, s.v. "chien"; and *Grande Encyclopédie*, s.v. "chien" for authoritative discussions. For the *état-matrice* see Ministère des Finances, *Bulletin des contributions directes et du cadastre* (Paris, 1855), 217 and 220–221.

11. Ministère des Finances, *Bulletin des contributions directes*, 219.

12. Archives du département de la Seine, sous-série V.D.⁶, 101, no. 11, Taxe municipale sur les chiens: Instructions, circulaires, arrêts, 1856 à 1878. See the letter of 30 September 1855 from the prefect to the city hall of the 1st arrondissement informing tax officials of this decision. See also the letter to the city hall of the 6th arrondissement in Archives du département de la Seine, fonds des maires, sous-série V.D.⁴, An VIII à 1859, no. 4441–4461; Taxes municipales et revenus mobiliers, C: Taxe sur les chiens, 1855–1859, no. 4441.

13. See Archives du département de la Seine, V.D.⁴, no. 4445, for instance, where the tariff for Parisian dogs is explained: "As a result in Paris . . . hunting dogs and luxury dogs will be taxed at a rate of *10 francs* and guard dogs and dogs who lead the blind will be taxed at a rate of *5 francs*" (original emphasis).

14. Archives du département de la Seine, V.D.⁴. For example see no. 4459, a memo dated 25 September 1859. Compare this memo with earlier directives on the matter. See, for instance, memo no. 4441 on the tax, dated 30 September 1855, which included the following warning: "It is important that all these details be carefully noted." The letter goes on to note that such information notwithstanding, only one category of dogs, luxury dogs, would be set for Paris.

15. See Archives du département de la Seine, V.D.⁴, no. 4456, memo of 27 September 1859, Etablissement de la taxe sur les chiens, which included the following new directions to city halls: "The Conseil d'Etat recognizes as guard dogs only those who are leashed during the day: the law accepts, however, that dogs guarding shops, workshops, and stores may also be ranked in the second class. The nature and breed of dogs as well as the profession of taxpayers may serve then to understand the use to which the dogs are put and consequently the class in which they must be ranked."

16. See Compans, "Taxe sur les chiens," 50–57, for judgments and interpretations issued by the Conseil d'Etat; Delaporte, *Guide manuel*, 13.

17. Delaporte, *Guide manuel*, 12, 13.

18. Compans, "Taxe sur les chiens," 50.

19. Haussmann, the most powerful politician in Paris, quite unsurprisingly was granted his request for this move by the minister of finance (Archives du département de la Seine, V.D.⁴, no. 4443, 28 December 1855: Clôture du registre des déclarations, addressed to the city hall of the 6th arrondissement). For Haussmann's memo about the classification of dogs see Archives du département de la Seine, V.D.⁴, no. 4445, 28 January 1856, addressed to the city hall of the 1st arrondissement in reference to Application du décret du 9 janvier 1856.

20. Author's collection, signed Cham [Amadée de Noé], n.d.

21. Many commentators insisted on this point. *Le Petit Moniteur universel*, for instance, noted in September 1876: "The census of dogs has ended. There are

112,000 dogs paying tax in Paris. One may well estimate at 38,000 the number of [those not declared]. That makes, therefore, a total of 150,000 dogs in Paris, or around one for each 12 inhabitants" (quoted in *Bulletin* 21 [1876]: 355). For Haussmann's comment see Archives du département de la Seine, V.D.⁴, no. 4452: Etablissement de la taxe pour 1858, addressed to the city hall of the 6th arrondissement.

22. Jean Robert, *Le Chien d'appartement et d'utilité: Education, dressage, hygiène, maladies* (Paris, 1888), 114, 115; J. R. Ackerley, *My Dog Tulip* (1965; New York: Poseidon, 1987).

23. Robert, *Chien d'appartement*, 157, 158.

24. Alexis Godin, *Le Protecteur, le législateur, et l'ami des animaux* (Paris, 1855), 1:300 (original emphasis); Robert, *Chien d'appartement*, 10, 9.

25. Laure Desvernays, *Les Animaux d'agrément* (Paris, 1913), 35; Henri Lautard, *Zoophilie ou sympathie envers les animaux: Psychologie du chien, du chat, du cheval* (Paris, 1909), 98.

26. See Michael Ignatieff's review of *The City as a Work of Art: London, Paris, Vienna*, by Donald Olsen (*Times Literary Supplement*, 2 January 1987, 3).

27. Lautard, *Zoophilie*, 105.

28. Jules Maret-Leriche, *Les Chiens* (Paris, 1864), 10.

29. Portanier, "Le Chien à travers les âges": excerpt from report to the Société protectrice des animaux, Nice, 1889, 9.

30. Barbou, *Le Chien*, 190; emphasis added.

31. *Times Literary Supplement*, 2 January 1987, 3. See chapters seven and eight of Olsen's *The City as a Work of Art* (New Haven: Yale University Press, 1986).

32. Desvernays, *Animaux d'agrément*, i.

33. Le comte de Bony de la Vergne, *Les Chiens* (Metz, 1858), 21.

34. *Le Chien primitif: Aperçus nouveau sur l'origine du culte des animaux, du langage, du pouvoir représentatif, et de la musique* (Nantes, 1846), i.

35. Portanier, "Le Chien à travers les âges," 3, 4, 5.

36. Oscar Honoré, *Le Coeur des bêtes* (Paris, 1863), 9–10.

37. Portanier, "Le Chien à travers les âges," 5; Aurélien Scholl, preface to le baron de Vaux, *Notre Ami le chien* (Paris, 1897), xvi.

38. Lautard, *Zoophilie*, 91.

39. Pierre Mégnin, *Le Chien: Histoire, hygiène, médecine* (Paris, 1877), 19, 22.

40. Fétu, *Requête à mes concitoyens pour l'extinction de la race canine à Dijon* (n.p., 1866), 8.

41. Fétu, *Requête à mes concitoyens*, 15, 19, 20.

42. *Lettres de son excellence le maréchal Vaillant à M. Nicolas Fétu sur l'extinction de la race canine à Dijon et réponse de M. Nicolas Fétu à son excellence* (n.p., 8 and 10 June 1866), 16.

43. *Bulletin* 12 (1866): 274–275.

44. Scholl in Vaux, *Notre Ami le chien*, 2, 3.

45. A. L. A. Fée, *Les Misères des animaux* (Paris, 1863), front cover.

46. Fée, *Misères des animaux*, 52, 59.

47. Barbou, *Le Chien*, 262.

48. Robert, *Chien d'appartement*, 7; see *Bulletin* 21 (1876): 355.

49. *Bulletin* 21 (1876): 355. See also Barbou, *Le Chien*, 204. Barbou quotes from an article in *Le Temps* in 1879 to the effect that statistics of the Parisian dog tax accounted for 65,782 dogs in Paris. Actually, there were more than 70,000 Parisian dogs. See also Larbalétrier, *Manuel pratique de l'amateur de chiens* (Paris, 1907), i. Larbalétrier suggests that although officially there were 2,690,00 dogs in France, many eluded the tax. At the very least we can assume that in 1885 there were 3,000,00 dogs in France. For France overall see Compans, "Taxe sur les chiens", 22.

50. For figures from 1856 see Maret-Leriche, *Les Chiens*, 7. He also claims there were 2,500,00 dogs for which a tax was paid in that same year. For 1872 and 1885, see *Grande Encyclopédie*, s.v. "chien." Lucien Richard's *Annuaire Richard pour 1898: Chiens célèbres et chiens de célébrités* (Paris, 1898) cites an official figure of 2,500,000 dogs in France in 1885, and 2,000,000 for 1878, and for 1898, 2,960,000 in France and 134,000 in Paris. For other figures see Ministère des Finances, *Annuaire de l'administration des contributions directes et du cadastre*. Tables for the tax on dogs begin in 1890 for the year 1888.

51. V. Galtier, *La Rage à Lyon* (Lyons, 1890), 1.

52. Paul Charpentier, *La Rage, comment M. Pasteur empêche les chiens de devenir enragés* (Meux, 1886), 10.

53. Reproduced in Delteil, *Honoré Daumier*, vol. 26, plates 2737–2740.

54. Compans, "Taxe sur les chiens," 29.

55. Vaux, *Notre Ami le chien*, 1.

CHAPTER 4

1. Florent Prévost, *Des animaux d'appartement et de jardin: Oiseaux, poissons, chiens, chats* (Paris, 1861), 108; it is reviewed in *Bulletin* 7 (1861): 150–152.

2. Prévost, *Animaux d'appartement*, 108–109.

3. Prévost, *Animaux d'appartement*, 109–110.

4. J. J. Grandville's anthropomorphic illustrations of animals were popular in nineteenth-century France; see P. J. Hetzel, ed., *The Public and Private Life of Animals* (1877; reprint, London: Paddington, 1977); and Jean de La Fontaine, *Les Fables de La Fontaine* (Paris: Dominique Leroy, 1982).

5. Prévost, *Animaux d'appartement*, 122.

6. Prévost, *Animaux d'appartement*, 122.

7. Tom Adams and Keith Banister, *Aquarial Fish* (New York: Crescent, 1977), 19, make the point about aquarium keeping in general: "By 1890, unnatural aquarium decorations were on sale. In a book published in that year we read: 'rockwork . . . ruins . . . for no one with any taste at all would care to see a fish, for instance, swimming through the window of a house or a triton wriggling through the loophole of a castle.'"

8. For definition of the aquarium see Adams and Banister, *Aquarial Fish*, 15.

9. *La Grande Encyclopédie* (Paris, 1886–1902), s.v. "aquarium."

10. David Elliston Allen, *The Naturalist in Britain: A Social History* (London:

Allen Lane, 1976), 133–134. Shirley Hibberd is the fern enthusiast Lynn Barber quotes (*The Heyday of Natural History 1820–1870* [New York: Doubleday, 1980], 113). Ward is discussed in Barber, *Heyday of Natural History*, 115.

11. Barber, *Heyday of Natural History*, 116, 117. *Grande Encyclopédie*, s.v. "aquarium."

12. Prévost, *Animaux d'appartement*, 119. Aquariums are discussed in *Bulletin* 8 (1862): 121; *Grande Encyclopédie*, s.v. "aquarium."

13. *Grande Encyclopédie*, s.v. "aquarium." Prévost, *Animaux d'appartement*, 118, 119.

14. Quotes are in Barber, *Heyday of Natural History*, 117, and her comments are on 118; Prévost, *Animaux d'appartement*, 123.

15. Adams and Bannister, *Aquarial Fish*, 15. See *Grande Encyclopédie*, s.v. "aquarium," for Gosse's private collection and for an illustration of the aquarium at the Trocadéro.

16. Barber, *Heyday of Natural History*, 122–123.

17. *Grande Encyclopédie*, s.v. "aquarium."

18. Barber, *Heyday of Natural History*, 14, 122. Wood is quoted in Adams and Banister, *Aquarial Fish*, 12; and in Barber, *Heyday of Natural History*, 122.

19. *Grande Encyclopédie*, s.v. "aquarium."

20. Quoted in Adams and Banister, *Aquarial Fish*, 21.

21. Barber, *Heyday of Natural History*, 124.

22. Allen, *Naturalist in Britain*, 137.

23. Allen, *Naturalist in Britain*, 137.

24. George B. Sowerby, *Popular History of the Aquarium of Marine and Fresh-Water Animals and Plants* (London, 1857), 2, 3. Sowerby is recommended in the *Grande Encyclopédie*, s.v. "aquarium."

25. G. H. Lewes is quoted in Barber, *Heyday of Natural History*, 121.

26. Prévost, *Animaux d'appartement*, 117–118.

27. Prévost, *Animaux d'appartement*, 117.

28. Yves-Alain Bois refers to Hildebrand's abhorrence of the "mixing of real space and the space of art . . . in the panorama" in his essay "Kahnweiler's Lesson," *Representations*, no. 18 (Spring 1987): 33–68.

29. Prévost, *Animaux d'appartement*, 84. On the importance of flowers see Alain Corbin, *Le Miasme et la jonquille: L'odorat et l'imaginaire social, 18ème–19ème siècles* (Paris: Aubier, 1982), 220–229. Zola's *La Curée* includes a typically over-wrought description of a greenhouse and its exotic power. Although Prévost devotes several chapters of his *Animaux d'appartement* to birds, he discusses types such as wagtails and swallows that do not survive in captivity in the section where he discusses the needs of starlings and nightingales, types that he recommends for cages.

30. Gustave Flaubert, included in *Three Tales*, trans. Arthur McDowall (Norfolk, Ct.: New Directions, 1947).

31. See Harriet Ritvo, *The Animal Estate: The English and Other Creatures in the Victorian Age* (Cambridge, Mass.: Harvard University Press, 1987), especially the chapter "Prize Pets," 82–121.

32. According to Pierre Mégnin, *Les Races de chiens: Histoire, origine, description* (Vincennes, 1889–1901), 1:23, where the British author appears as Delabère-Blaine.

33. Pierre Larousse, *Le Grand Dictionnaire universel* (Paris, 1865–1890), s.v. "chien."

34. Pierre Mégnin, *Les Races de chiens,* 1:23.

35. *Grande Encyclopédie,* s.v. "anthropologie."

36. Joseph Boyer, *Recherches sur les races humaines de l'Auvergne* (Paris, 1876).

37. Larousse, *Grand Dictionnaire,* s.v. "chien."

38. Pierre Mégnin, *Les Races de chiens,* 1:33; original emphasis.

39. Ritvo, *The Animal Estate,* 111, 113, 102, 104.

40. Ritvo, *The Animal Estate,* 104, 106, 115.

41. Archives nationales, série F^{12}, no. 6784, Compagnie du jardin zoologique et d'acclimatation: Concessions de terrains par la ville de Paris, 1857–1858 (acte constitutif, 1858–1859).

42. Paul Mégnin, *Nos Chiens: Races, dressage, élevage, hygiène, maladies* (Paris: 1909), 375–376.

43. Larousse, *Grand Dictionnaire,* s.v. "chien." The "establishment of the state" is the Grignon Imperial Farm, whose director gave Larousse the dog, but perhaps the committee meant Larousse himself.

44. Inexplicably, Moustache also appears in the 1865 exposition: "Moustache, belonging to Pierre Larousse," is number 391 in the *catalogue des chiens exposés*; Larousse may have confused the dates (Société du jardin zoologique d'acclimatation du bois de Boulogne, *Exposition universelle des races canines de 1865: Catalogue des chiens exposés* [Paris, 1865]).

45. Société impériale zoologique d'acclimatation, *Exposition des races canines de 1865: Discours prononcé à l'occasion des récompenses le 17 mai 1865 par M. de Quatrefages* (Paris, 1865), 2.

46. Le baron de Vaux, *Notre Ami le chien* (Paris, 1897), 175.

47. Paul Mégnin, *Nos Chiens,* 376.

48. All these clubs appeared in the *Annuaire-Almanach du commerce et de l'industrie: Didot-Bottin* (hereafter Didot-Bottin), 1910, "Paris: adresses et professions," 1:2860. See also Paul Mégnin, *Nos Chiens,* 376.

49. Ritvo, *The Animal Estate,* 98.

50. Paul Mégnin, *Nos Chiens,* 380.

51. Société centrale pour l'amélioration des races de chiens en France, *Bulletin mensuel* (Paris, 1887–1888): 49–52.

52. Société centrale pour l'amélioration des races de chiens en France, *Catalogue officiel illustré: 9ème exposition canine du 21 au 28 mai 1890 sur la terrasse de l'Orangerie du jardin des Tuileries,* 101–113.

53. *La Vie élégante* 2 [1882]: 61.

54. Prévost, *Animaux d'appartement,* 143.

55. Peter Brooks, *Reading for the Plot: Design and Intention in Narrative* (New York: Vintage, 1985), 22.

56. Jean Robert, *Le Chien d'appartement et d'utilité: Education, dressage, hygiène, maladies* (Paris, 1888), 11; Paul Mégnin, *Nos Chiens*, 40 (first edition in 1903).

57. Société centrale pour l'amélioration des races de chiens, *Catalogue officiel de l'exposition internationale de chiens à Paris 1885*, 43–51.

58. Prévost, *Animaux d'appartement*, 152, 153, 146.

59. Paul Mégnin, *Nos Chiens*, 88.

60. Robert, *Chien d'appartement*, 24. Paul Mégnin explained that not the monks of mont Saint-Bernard but members of Saint Bernard dog clubs in Europe and America were responsible for making the modern breed; the monks' concern was training large mountain dogs to rescue travelers, and visitors to the monastery were often shocked by how straggly and generally unappealing those dogs looked (*Nos Chiens*, 50).

61. Vero Shaw, *The Classic Encyclopedia of the Dog* (New York: Bonanza, 1984), 488–492; it was published in 1879–1880 in London.

62. Paul Mégnin, *Nos Chiens*, 46.

63. Alphonse Toussenel, *L'Esprit des bêtes: Zoologie passionnelle. Mammifères de France* (Paris, 1855), 187–188.

64. Prévost, *Animaux d'appartement*, 147.

65. And Robert asserted they have been crying since (*Chien d'appartement*, 94).

66. Robert, *Chien d'appartement*, 61.

67. Pierre Mégnin, *Les Races de chiens: Les lévriers, les chiens courants, les bassets*, 2:76–166. The *Guide Marabout* traces all French hunting dogs to the four sixteenth-century breeds defined by their color (Jacques Freydiger, *Le Guide Marabout des chiens* [Verviers, Belgium: Marabout, 1978], 65).

68. Robert, *Chien d'appartement*, 34, 90.

69. Lucien Richard, *Annuaire Richard pour 1898: Chiens célèbres et chiens de célébrités* (Paris, 1898), 32–40.

70. See Pierre Mégnin, *Les Races de chiens: Les chiens de montagne, les dogues, les bouledogues, les terriers, et les chiens d'appartement*, 3:192, 149. See also Paul Mégnin, *Nos Chiens*, 250.

71. See Georg Simmel's 1904 essay on fashion in *On Individuality and Social Forms: Selected Writings*, ed. D. Levine (Chicago: University of Chicago Press, 1971), 302ff.

72. Brooks uses the phrase "escape from narrative" in his *Reading for the Plot*, 32. Benjamin speaks of "dialectics seen at a standstill" in his essay "Paris, Capital of the Nineteenth Century" in *Reflections: Essays, Aphorisms, Autobiographical Writings*, trans. Edmund Jephcott, ed. Peter Demetz (New York: Harvest, 1978), 157. Benjamin's essay has strongly influenced the argument of this chapter.

CHAPTER 5

1. Odile Marcel, *Une Education française* (Paris: Presses universitaires de France, 1984), 28, 13, 14; her grandfather was the Christian existentialist philosopher Gabriel Marcel.

2. Marcel, *Education française*, 17, 15, 18, 16.

3. Marcel, *Education française*, 29, 16–17; Marcel's reference to a "univers de précautions" is on 19. For a recent encyclopedic instance, see the formidably documented *From the Fires of Revolution to the Great War*, ed. Michelle Perrot, vol. 4 of Philippe Ariès and Georges Duby, eds., *History of Private Life* (Cambridge, Mass.: Harvard University Press, 1990).

4. Paul Mégnin, *Nos Chiens: Races, dressage, élevage, hygiène, maladies*, 2d ed. (Paris, 1909), 327. For dogs as eternal children see Alfred Bonnardot, *Des petits chiens de dames, spécialement de l'épagneul nain* (Paris, 1856), 37, 38, 61; ex-chef d'institution, *Chat et chien, ou les enfants volontaires* (Rouen, 1858); A. L. A. Fée, *Les Misères des animaux* (Paris, 1863), xiii: "With respect to intelligence, they remain in a never-ending childhood, it's a minority without end."

5. Alfred Barbou, *Le Chien: Son histoire, ses exploits, ses aventures* (Paris, 1883), 272. Guides to Paris also discuss the dog market: Alb. [Richard Whiteing], *Living Paris and France: A Guide to Manners, Monuments, Institutions, and the Life of the People* (London, 1886), 293.

6. Didot-Bottin (1863, 1873, 1883, 1910), s.v. "le chien."

7. Terry Eagleton speaks of the aesthetic but his remark holds equally true for domesticity and its crystallization in pets ("The Ideology of the Aesthetic," *Times Literary Supplement*, 22–28 January 1988; see also *The Ideology of the Aesthetic* [Oxford: Basil Blackwell, 1990]).

8. Marcel, *Education française*, 29.

9. Edward of Norwich (second duke of York), *The Master of Game* (1406–1413; reprint 1909).

10. Jacques du Fouilloux, *La Vénerie de Jacques du Fouilloux: Avec plusieurs receptes et remèdes pour guerir les chiens de diverses maladies. Plus l'adolescence de l'auteur* (1562; cardinal de Rohan's copy, 1566; reprint, Anger, 1844): "Prenez deux tests d'aulx et un demy couillon d'une beste qui se nomme *Castor*, avec de ius de cresson alenois, et une douxaine de mouches cantharides [*sic*]," 7.

11. Pierre Mégnin, *Le Chien: Histoire, hygiène, médecine* (Paris, 1877), 17, 18.

12. Solange Bélin, "Une Vie de chien sous l'ancien régime," *Historia* 456 (December 1984): 54–59. On the care of noble dogs, she explains that Henry III maintained a baker for his little dogs. The counts of Artois in the sixteenth century collected a special manorial due in oats, for dog feed.

13. See Caroline Hannaway, "Veterinary Medicine and Rural Health Care in Pre-Revolutionary France," *Bulletin of the History of Medicine* 51 (1977): 431–447.

14. On British dog breeding see Harriet Ritvo, *The Animal Estate: The English and Other Creatures in the Victorian Age* (Cambridge, Mass.: Harvard University Press, 1987), 82–115.

15. Jean Robert, *Le Chien d'appartement et d'utilité: Education, dressage, hygiène, maladies* (Paris, 1888), 96, 97.

16. Bonnardot, *Des petits chiens de dames*, 3–4. The book by Delabere Pritchett Blaine, *Canine Pathology* (London, 1817), was published in Paris by Raynal in 1828.

17. Ritvo, *The Animal Estate*, 87.

18. Bonnardot, *Des petits chiens de dames*, 4.

19. Laure Desvernays, *Les Animaux d'agrément* (Paris, 1913), ii.

20. Robert, *Chien d'appartement*, 7–8.

21. Pierre Mégnin, *Le Chien*, i.

22. Paul Mégnin, *Nos Chiens*, 8.

23. In Nelson Goodman's terms in *Ways of Worldmaking* (Indianapolis: Hackett, 1978).

24. Bonnardot, *Des petits chiens de dames*, 3, 25.

25. Mme Charles Boeswillwald, *Le Chien de luxe: Comment élever, dresser, et soigner nos chiens* (Paris, 1907), 204. This chapter is informed by Wolfgang Iser, *The Act of Reading: A Theory of Aesthetic Response* (Baltimore: Johns Hopkins University Press, 1978), 98ff.

26. Fée, *Les Misères des animaux*, xiii.

27. Ex-chef d'institution, *Chat et chien*.

28. See his illustration, "children playing." E. Leroy, *L'Enfance du chien* (Paris, 1896), 31. See also postcards in Cabinet des estampes, Bibliothèque Nationale, Jb mat 1—les chiens.

29. Bonnardot, *Des petits chiens de dames*, 69.

30. Boeswillwald, *Chien de luxe*, 193.

31. Robert, *Chien d'appartement*, 99, 106.

32. Desvernays, *Animaux d'agrément*, 37.

33. Boeswillwald, *Chien de luxe*, 203; Leroy, *Enfance du chien*, 34–35. For Jean Robert's prosaic description of "Fais le beau!" see *Chien d'appartement*, 108.

34. Boeswillwald, *Chien de luxe*, 201–202. See also her illustrations of obedience lessons, 200–221.

35. Boeswillwald, *Chien de luxe*, 199; she pointed out that the size of apartment dogs could vary: "Certain greyhounds and terriers are not at all small yet are *chiens d'appartement* by virtue of their cleanliness and beauty" (212). Leroy, *Enfance du chien*, 21–22.

36. Robert, *Chien d'appartement*, 109, 110.

37. Paul Mégnin, *Nos Chiens*, 327; Robert, *Chien d'appartement*, 71, 72; on the miniature greyhound, 70–73. Mallarmé gave Julie Manet a miniature greyhound around 1893: see *Berthe Morisot: Impressionist*, exhibition catalog by Charles Stuckey and William P. Scott assisted by Suzanne Lindsay (Mount Holyoke College Art Museum and National Gallery of Art, 1987), 164.

38. For the elegant *toutou* see Paul Mégnin, *Nos Chiens*, 325: "The *toutou élégant* must have a complete wardrobe that will differ according to breed"; Barbou, *Le Chien*, 257; Didot-Bottin (1910), s.v. "colliers, muselières, et articles pour chiens"; Robert, *Chien d'appartement*, back page.

39. Paul Mégnin, *Nos Chiens*, 325, 326; Boeswillwald, *Chien de luxe*, 236.

40. This comment is based on Said's paraphrase of Lévi-Strauss (Edward Said, *Orientalism* [New York: Vintage, 1978], 53).

41. Note the detail, for instance, in the costume of this elegant beast dressed for evening by its mistress "in marvelous black with a flared stand-up collar and

over all, three strands of Isigny lace, ruffles interlaced with black satin, its lining in old-rose colored fabric" (Paul Mégnin, *Nos Chiens*, 326).

42. See Philippe Perrot's chapter on women's clothing in Jean-Paul Aron, ed., *La Femme du XIXème siècle* (Brussels: Editions Complexe, 1984). For a fuller treatment of clothing in the nineteenth century see Philippe Perrot, *Les Dessus et les dessous de la bourgeoisie* (Paris: Fayard, 1981).

43. Boeswillwald, *Chien de luxe*, 232; she gave sewing directions on 231. For the well-connected pet, the practice of wearing livery was current (Paul Mégnin, *Nos Chiens*, 188; Barbou, *Le Chien*, 257–258).

44. Paul Mégnin describes poodle hairstyles and their popularity in *Nos Chiens*, 322. The Empress Eugénie wore her hair in the coil shape (*tonte en macarons*), which grew fashionable during the Second Empire.

45. Desvernays, *Animaux d'agrément*, 14.

46. Paul Mégnin, *Nos Chiens*, 322–323; his description of the *tonte à la zoave* is detailed: "In place of cuffs and sides, pantaloons of fur, blunt cut . . . the middle of the body is completely shaved, the eyes are left free, open to view, and a very prominent mustache [is given him]. . . . And of course, a pompom on the tail, more or less long, more or less puffed, according to taste" (323); *La Vie élégante* [1880], 377.

47. Paul Mégnin, *Nos Chiens*, 257, 323, 324.

48. The poodle was "le meilleur client du coiffeur" (Paul Mégnin, *Nos Chiens*, 257); on the importance of hairstyling see 249–250.

49. Boeswillwald, *Chien de luxe*, 45. See also Leroy, *Enfance du chien*, 13–14. Barbou in *Le Chien* and Robert in *Chien d'appartement* also discuss the *barbet* and the poodle in their sections on the poodle.

50. Barbou, *Le Chien*, 259.

51. Bélin, "Vie de chien," 58.

52. Gaston Bachelard, *The Poetics of Space*, trans. M. Jolas (New York: Orion, 1964), 211ff.

53. Bonnardot, *Des petits chiens de dames*, 76, 77.

54. Robert, *Chien d'appartement*, 97.

55. Bonnardot, *Des petits chiens de dames*, 78. Photographers advertised in dog show catalogs; see, for instance, Société centrale pour l'amélioration des races de chiens, *Catalogue officiel illustré: 9ème Exposition canine du 21 au 28 mai 1890 sur la terrasse de l'Orangerie du jardin des Tuileries* (Paris, 1890).

56. Boeswillwald, *Chien de luxe*, 239; she also recommended the pet cemetery and included a photograph of the monument to "chère Emma" on 177 (see figure 2).

57. The fate of dogs' bodies is explained in a pamphlet of the 1920s on the pet cemetery: L. Durfalc, "Une curiosité: Le cimetière des chiens d'Asnières" [n.d], 6–7, in Bibliothèque Marguerite Durand, dossier Durand—cimetière des chiens. Proposals for a dog cemetery are discussed in an article by L. Dubois, in the otherwise unidentified journal, *L'Ami des chiens* (Bibliothèque Marguerite Durand, dossier Durand—cimetière des chiens).

58. Dossier Durand—cimetière des chiens. See also an advertisement in *La Fronde*, 13 July 1899.

59. As the Michelin guide accurately notes, "The monuments are surprising and the epitaphs often quaint" (*Guide vert Michelin: Paris*, 5th ed., s.v. "Curiosités de banlieu: Asnières"). See also Boeswillwald, *Chien de luxe*, 177, for a good illustration of one of these monuments.

60. Henri Blatin, *Nos Cruautés envers les animaux* (Paris, 1867), 298.

61. Pierre Mégnin, *Le Chien*, 124.

62. Ritvo, *The Animal Estate*, 86. In Paris their outlet was at 38, rue Caumartin; see Pathfinder and Dalziel, *Dressage et élevage des chiens*, appendix to the French edition, whose title page reads: "Conseils pratiques sur l'hygiène et l'alimentation des chiens, communiqués par Spratts Patent" (Paris: Dumoulin, 1906); appendix, 4–5.

63. See Pierre Mégnin, *Le Chien*, 123.

64. Maret-Leriche, *A bas la muselière: Pétition de messieurs les chiens et leurs maîtres adressée à M. le préfet de police* (Paris, 1861), 7.

65. Pathfinder and Dalziel, appendix, 1.

66. *La Grande Encyclopédie* (Paris, 1886–1902), s.v. "le chien."

67. Pierre Mégnin, *Le Chien: Elevage, hygiène, médecine* (hereafter *Elevage, hygiène, médecine*) (Paris, 1899–1901), 1:72.

68. Robert, *Chien d'appartement*, 151, 152.

69. Desvernays, *Animaux d'agrément*, 26–27; P. J. Cadiot et F. Breton, *Médecine canine* (Paris, 1901), 111: "When satyriasis and nymphomania occur independently of any infection of the genitals (tumours, vaginitis), reduce feed to the bare minimun and eliminate meat from the diet."

70. "It is too generally forgotten that the systems of animals—above all of those that live with people—have the same requirements (*exigences*) as the human system" (Boeswillwald, *Chien de luxe*, 95); Robert, *Chien d'appartement*, 152; Leroy, *Enfance du chien*, 21–22; Bonnardot, *Des petits chiens de dames*, 31.

71. [Desvignes], *Les Chiens par un de leurs amis* (Dijon, 1869), 13; Bonnardot, *Des petits chiens de dames*, 62; Boeswillwald, *Chien de luxe*, 61.

72. See Pierre Mégnin's chapter 10, "Mals nerveuses," in vol. 2 of *Elevage, hygiène, médecine*; for the ataxic terrier see 332.

73. Bonnardot, "Mariage des épagneuls," *Des petits chiens de dames*, 61; and 326–327.

74. Bonnardot, "Mariage des épagneuls," *Des petits chiens de dames*, especially 61–63.

75. Harriet Ritvo, "Sex and the Single Animal," *Grand Street* 7, no. 3 (Spring 1988): 131.

76. Boeswillwald, *Chien de luxe*, 61, 56–57.

77. Joanny Pertus, *Le Chien: Races, hygiène, et maladies* (Paris, 1893), 16.

78. Boeswillwald, *Chien de luxe*, 62; Mme H. Ducret-Baumann, *L'Education et l'hygiène du chien: Ses maladies, ses misères, reproduction, élevage des chiots* (Paris, 1913), 11. Ducret-Baumann is mostly concerned about the size of the unwanted puppies and their effect on the health of the bitch.

79. Boeswillwald, *Chien de luxe*, 155. See also Leroy, *Enfance du chien*, 128.

80. Robert, *Chien d'appartement*, 152.

81. Robert, *Chien d'appartement*, 152; Desvernays, *Animaux d'agrément*, 19; Bonnardot, *Des petits chiens de dames*, 40–41; Boeswillwald, *Chien de luxe*, 99; Desvernays, *Animaux d'agrément*, 19. On women and illness in the nineteenth century see Elaine Showalter, *The Female Malady: Women, Madness, and English Culture, 1830–1980* (New York: Penguin, 1985). See also Helena Michie, *The Flesh Made Word: Female Figures and Women's Bodies* (Oxford: Oxford University Press, 1987). Boeswillwald's solution was a doggy litter box, "le plateau de sciure de bois" (*Chien de luxe*, 72–75).

82. *Catalogue officiel illustré: 9ème exposition canine du 21 au 28 mai 1890 sur la terrasse de l'Orangerie du jardin des Tuileries* (Paris, 1890).

83. Mme Roseline de Cazis, *Plaintes des chiens à Sir Richard Wallace* (Paris, 1877), 63.

CHAPTER 6

1. Robert G. Petersdorf et al., eds., *Harrison's Principles of Internal Medicine*, 10th ed. (New York: McGraw Hill, 1983), 1136–1138. See also the chapter on rabies virus in Bernard Davis and Renato Dulbecco, eds., *Microbiology*, 2d ed. (Hagerstown, Md.: Harper and Row, 1973), 1368–1375.

2. Guy-Raoul, *La Rage: Son meilleur préservatif, d'après MM. Tardieu, Sanson, Hertwig, Youatt* (Paris, 1862), 1–2.

3. These figures may well be an underestimation. About the same number of deaths were occasionally reported for Paris—twenty-one in 1881, twenty-two in 1885. See Georges Dujardin-Beaumetz, *Rapport sur les cas de rage humaine constatés dans le département de la Seine de 1881 à 1891* (Paris, 1892), 5. And only forty-nine departments are known to have submitted figures during the period 1863–1868. See Constantin James, *M. Pasteur, sa nouvelle méthode dite intensive: Peut-elle communiquer la rage?* (Paris, 1887), 16. Nonetheless, even if actual deaths were five, ten, or even one hundred times the number of reported ones—and the highly publicized and public nature of known deaths militates against this last supposition—the figure is still small when measured against a population of some thirty-six million. The public health officer responsible for the first set of reports to the Comité consultatif—Ambroise Tardieu, first member and then president of the Conseil d'hygiène publique et de salubrité du département de la Seine and also of the Académie de médecine—hoped in vain however when he suggested in 1863 that his statistics would be reassuring: "The figure of twenty-five cases must be set against numbers six or eight times higher that must no longer be allowed to strike fear in people's hearts"; Tardieu's *Rapport sur la rage* appeared in 1863. Portanier estimates seventy to eighty deaths in 1886 (*La Rage* [Nice, 1886], 43). Xavier Raspail estimates nineteen deaths each year (*Les Inoculations de M. Pasteur contre la rage* [Paris, 1886], 6); an anonymous work cites twelve to fifteen deaths per year before Pasteur (*La Rage: Questions à M. Pasteur par un médecin* [Paris, 1886], 10). J. Bourrel cites an average of two deaths per annum in Paris-Seine 1853–1858 (*Traité complet de la rage, chez le chien et chez le chat: Moyen*

de s'en préserver [Paris, 1874], 90). For statistics see also R. Repiquet, *Méthode de M. Pasteur pour prévenir la rage après morsure* (Saint-Etienne, 1891), 14; and Auguste-Adrien Ollivier, *Rapport sur la rage chez les enfants* (Paris, 1887), 14.

4. Jean Robert, *Le Chien d'appartement et d'utilité* (Paris, 1888), 149.

5. Portanier, *La Rage*, 36.

6. As described by Renaud Suzor in his *Hydrophobia* (London, 1887), 3: "Those who escaped death still had to live for years with a feeling as if the sword of Damocles was ever hanging over their heads, an uncertainty of life which led not a few to commit suicide." For obsessive fears among Parisian veterinarians see Bourrel, *Traité complet*, 48: "Vatel, Barthélémy, Leblanc senior each have experienced the most painful emotions after having been bitten either by a rabid dog or by one suspected of being rabid"; and André Sanson, in his work *Le Meilleur Préservatif de la rage* (Paris, 1860), 76, cites the case of Dr. Barthélémy who from that time on displayed an obsessive fear of rabies. Robert, *Chien d'appartement*, 149, discusses the fear of dogs, "when they do not drink and when they do drink, when they bite and when they caress, when they hide themselves, and when they do anything at all." Bourrel, *Traité complet*, 47–48, gives an example: "Mme X., rue Dauphine, was bitten by a six-month-old dog who only had convulsions but who she believed was rabid. For a long time she remained gripped by fear, not being able to sleep, for instance, and her mind was relieved only after I demonstrated to her in my office how little basis there was for her apprehensions."

7. See for example the warning of Guy-Raoul in *La Rage*, 145: "It is therefore always a bad habit, often a risk, to let these animals lick one's face and hands. Without a doubt, this is one of the ways rabies is most frequently transmitted to man." Guy-Raoul also cites Tardieu: "In the case of two of the victims, the disease had been transmitted by little pet dogs that, trained to lick the face of their master, had impregnated the master's slightly peeling lips with the virus. This mode of contagion, observed already more than once, cannot be signaled too strongly as an example of the danger of such habits." See also Sanson, *Le Meilleur Préservatif*, 24, 77; and Paul Levasseur, *Observation d'un cas de rage* (Rouen, 1882), 8.

8. Bourrel, *Traité complet*, 50: "And that idea had so strongly possessed him that he took to his bed and was manifestly wasting away."

9. See the case described by Henri Sabarthez, *Un Cas de rage atténuée produite très probablement par les inoculations pasteuriennes* (Perpignan, 1901), 5–6. Attending doctors seek Pasteur's advice. Pasteur is uncertain whether it is a case of rabies or hysteria.

10. Jules Lecoeur, *Etudes sur la rage* (Caen, 1856), 46. Aside from respiratory problems that most experts identified uniquely in rabies, only a longer incubation period distinguished the true from the false. In hysterical rabies, symptoms invariably followed on the heels of a bite.

11. A. Larché, *Un Village enragé* (Avignon, 1895). For panics triggered by the press see Guy-Raoul, *La Rage*, inside front cover; Félix Bron, *La Muselière et la*

vaccination rabique (Lyons, 1892), 5–6; Lecoeur, *Etudes*, vii, 3, 21; and Sanson, *Le Meilleur Préservatif,* 1.

12. In 1879 in Paris, 9,479 dogs were slaughtered (Levasseur, *Observation,* 10). Terms are those of Levasseur, Bron, and Jules Maret-Leriche (*Les Chiens* [Paris, 1864], 7).

13. See also René Vallery-Radot, *Life of Pasteur,* translated by Mrs. R. L. Devonshire (New York: Doubleday, 1926), 390.

14. For a statement of the case against Pasteur see Edouard Potin, *Observation d'un cas de rage mortelle après le traitement Pasteur* (Paris, 1890), 4.

15. See Arthur Kleinman's letter to the editor, *Times Literary Supplement,* 31 January 1986, 114, on the meaning of illness. Useful works on this subject include Kleinman, *Patients and Healers in the Context of Culture: An Exploration of the Borderland between Anthropology, Medicine, and Psychiatry* (Berkeley: University of California Press, 1980); J. B. Loudon, ed., *Social Anthropology and Medicine* (London: Academic Press, 1976); and Eliot Freidson, *Profession of Medicine: A Study of the Sociology of Applied Knowledge* (New York: Harper and Row, 1970).

16. G. E. Fredet, *La Rage: Deux jours chez M. Pasteur* (Clermont-Ferrand, 1861), 12.

17. Emile Littré and Charles Robin, *Dictionnaire de médecine* (Paris, 1865, 1878, 1884), s.v. "la rage."

18. Ollivier, *Rapport sur la rage,* 8.

19. Bourrel, *Traité complet,* 48.

20. Lecoeur, *Etudes,* 34.

21. Albert Charrin, "Les récents travaux sur la rage," *Archives générales de médecine* (Paris, 1887), 3; Fredet, *La Rage,* 12.

22. J. Amédée Arnaud de Fabre, "Une observation de rage" (Paper read at the Société de médecine de Vaucluse, 13 December 1882), 1, 3–5.

23. Portanier, *La Rage,* 189.

24. Fredet, *La Rage,* 4. The victim "remains rational, appreciating fully the gravity of his condition and, while suffering the most horrible torments, sees the hour of his death approach."

25. Levasseur, *Observation,* 7.

26. Lecoeur, *Etudes,* 34.

27. Lucien Richard, *Annuaire Richard pour 1898: Chiens célèbres et chiens de célébrités* (Paris, 1898), 121.

28. For instance Lecoeur, *Etudes*; and François-Joseph Bachelet and C. Froussart, *Cause de la rage et moyen d'en préserver l'humanité* (Valenciennes, 1857).

29. Bachelet and Froussart, *Cause de la rage,* 78–79, 113 (original emphasis); on 81 they cite cases of nymphomaniacs who try to have sex with dogs.

30. Bachelet and Froussart, *Cause de la rage,* 82.

31. Albrecht von Haller is the authority quoted in Littré and Robin, *Dictionnaire,* s.v. "la rage." Lecoeur (*Etudes,* 34) notes the connection with satyriasis; Bachelet and Froussart (*Cause de la rage,* 82) refer to Antoine Portal's observations of "la fureur utérine" and discuss findings of such autopsies.

32. Bachelet and Froussart, *Cause de la rage*, 113–114.

33. Levasseur, *Observation*, 8–9. In the nineteenth century, the term *virus* could be used in a nonspecific sense to describe any pathogen, as *Le Petit Robert* (1984) concisely notes.

34. Lecoeur, *Etudes*, 72.

35. Bachelet and Froussart, *Cause de la rage*, 110 (original emphasis); Lecoeur, *Etudes*, 73.

36. Portanier, *La Rage*, 16–18. See also John Farley and Gerald Geison, "Science, Politics, and Spontaneous Generation in Nineteenth-Century France: The Pasteur-Pouchet Debate," *Bulletin of the History of Medicine* 48 (Summer 1974): 161–198.

37. *Bulletin* 16 (1870–71): 221ff. for the history of the Société protectrice des animaux and the problem of rabies; on 221 Sociétaires refer to Lecoeur's *Etudes*.

38. Their work is noted in Littré and Robin, *Dictionnaire*, s.v. "la rage."

39. *Bulletin* 8 (1862): 405; *Bulletin* 12 (1866): 180; *Bulletin* 18 (1873): 276, which also summarizes Belleville's argument.

40. *Bulletin* 16 (1870–71): 221. The quote is from Henri Blatin, *Nos Cruautés envers les animaux* (Paris, 1867), 111.

41. See Thomas Laqueur, "Orgasm, Generation, and the Politics of Reproductive Biology," *Representations*, no. 14 (Spring 1986), esp. on menstruation and heat, 26–32; Laqueur quotes a phrase Jean Borie applies to nineteenth-century medical writers, "une gynécologie militante."

42. Blatin, *Nos Cruautés*, 111. For Blatin's proposal see also *Bulletin* 16 (1870–71): 221; for members' response, 18 (1873): 275.

43. Bourrel, *Traité complet*, 33; Littré and Robin, *Dictionnaire*, s.v. "la rage."

44. Quoted in Bourrel, *Traité complet*, 23.

45. Paul Simon, *Observations sur la spontanéité de la rage dans la race canine* (Paris, 1874), 9.

46. Bourrel, *Traité complet*, 25.

47. Bourrel, *Traité complet*, 25.

48. Bourrel, *Traité complet*, 25: "Often the information they give is intentionally false, and even when offered in good faith, their reports are always inadequate."

49. Richard, *Annuaire Richard*, 120–121.

50. Oscar Honoré, *Le Coeur des bêtes* (Paris, 1863), 17. The *Moniteur universel* is quoted in *Bulletin* 20 (Paris, 1875): 254–255. For the unwholesome conditions of domesticity and Turkish dogs see Maret-Leriche, *Les Chiens*, 23. *Bulletin* 19 (1874): 155; *Bulletin* 6 (1860): 39; *Bulletin* 21 (1876): 43–44. Dujardin-Beaumetz, *Rapport sur les cas de rage*, 31.

51. Alfred Bonnardot, *Des petits chiens de dames, spécialement de l'épagneul nain* (Paris, 1856), 5. More exactly, Bonnardot's is the first French dog-care book about pets.

52. *Bulletin* 1 (Paris, 1855): 62.

53. Nicholas Fétu, *Requête à mes concitoyens pour l'extinction de la race canine à Dijon* (Dijon, 1866), 8.

54. Blatin, *Nos Cruautés*, 108; Pierre Mégnin, *Le Chien: Histoire, hygiène, médecine* (Paris, 1877), 120.

55. *Bulletin* 10 (1864): 254, 383.

56. Pierre Larousse, *Le Grand Dictionnaire universel* (Paris, 1869), s.v. "le chien."

57. Alfred Barbou, *Le Chien: Son histoire, ses exploits, ses aventures* (Paris, 1883), 203.

58. Barbou, *Le Chien*, 260.

59. The quote is from Henri Lautard, *Zoophilie ou sympathie envers les animaux: Psychologie du chien, du chat, du cheval* (Paris, 1909), 105. See "La Fourrière de Paris," *Revue Britannique* 5 (1873): 343–54, for a good description of the Parisian dog pound. Richard Thomson discusses class in dogdom in " 'Les Quat' Pattes': The Image of the Dog in Late Nineteenth-Century French Art," *Art History* 5, no. 3 (September 1982): 323–325.

60. *Bulletin* 12 (1866): 333.

61. Paul-Juvénal Richard, *Notice sur la rage de chien* (Saumur, 1899), 30.

62. *Bulletin* 10 (1864): 311.

63. Sanson, *Le Meilleur Préservatif*, 64–65.

64. Bourrel, *Traité complet*, 100.

65. *Bulletin* 16 (1870–71): 220; *Bulletin* 17 (1872): 306–307, 323; *Bulletin* 18 (1873): 313, 373.

66. Bourrel, *Traité complet*, 100.

67. *Bulletin* 11 (1865): 78–79 and 17 (1872): 300.

68. Richard, *Notice sur la rage*, 30.

69. Rabies in Britain is discussed by Harriet Ritvo in her book on animals in Victorian culture, *The Animal Estate: The English and Other Creatures in the Victorian Age* (Cambridge, Mass.: Harvard University Press, 1987).

70. *Bulletin* 1 (1855): 61. Note that in eighteenth-century France, rabies was perceived as a problem of policing. Des Essarts (Nicolas Toussaint Le Moyne), the author of the *Dictionnaire universel de police* (Paris, 1786–1789) called for measures prohibiting poor people from owning dogs. Jean-Pierre Lenoir, the indefatigable lieutenant general of police in Paris from 1776 to 1785, offered a gold medal for possible rabies antidote. A plethora of folk remedies was still popular in nineteenth-century rural France.

71. *La Grande Encyclopédie* (Paris, 1886–1902), s.v. "la rage."

72. Fredet, *La Rage*, 6.

73. *Bulletin* 9 (1863): 365.

74. Fredet, *La Rage*, 6; Richard, *Annuaire Richard*, 119.

75. Sanson, *Le Meilleur Préservatif*, 2.

76. *Grande Encyclopédie*, s.v. "la rage."

77. Portanier, *La Rage*, 44.

78. For Sociétaires' discussion of the "hurlement de la rage," see the *Bulletin* 20 (1875): 57; Suzor, *Hydrophobia*, 111; *Grande Encyclopédie*, s.v. "la rage"; and Fredet, *La Rage*, 6. Its musical notation appears in Sanson, *Le Meilleur Préservatif*,

34, who describes the three most common types of rabic howls. A more elaborate musical notation representing the "hurlement de la rage" is offered by the Parisian veterinarian Alexandre Landrin, in a supplement to Barbou, *Le Chien*, 306.

79. Kleinman refers to cynosural illnesses in his *Times Literary Supplement* letter on the meaning of illness.

80. *La Grande Encyclopédie*, s.v. "la rage."

81. Portanier, *La Rage*, 10.

82. Walter Benjamin makes this suggestion throughout his writings.

83. Vallery-Radot, *Life of Pasteur*, vi.

84. See especially Sigmund Freud, *Civilization and Its Discontents*, trans. and ed. James Strachey (New York: Norton, 1961). It should also be remembered that Anna O's hysterical symptoms, to which Freud ascribed a sexual basis, included hydrophobia.

CHAPTER 7

1. Michael Brenson, "Art View: Faces in the Shadows: What Do They Mean?" *New York Times*, 24 July 1988. *Renoir*, Exhibition catalog by Annie Distel and John House; as Distel explains (214), at the beginning of *Le Temps retrouvé* Proust described Madame Charpentier as "ridiculously petty bourgeois" but also suggested that "posterity will learn more about the poetry of an elegant home and the beautiful dresses of our day from Renoir's painting of the *salon* of the publisher Charpentier than from Cot's portrait of the Princesse de Sagan or Chaplin's portrait of the Comtesse de la Rochefoucauld."

2. Charles Baudelaire, *The Flowers of Evil*, trans. William Aggeler (Fresno, Ca.: Academy Library Guild, 1954), 119. On this poem, see Roman Jakobson and Claude Lévi-Strauss, "*Les Chats* de Charles Baudelaire," *L'Homme: Revue française d'anthropologie* 2 (1962): 21. Enid Starkie explains that Baudelaire's mistress, Jeanne Duval, sent away his cat, which he loved, and replaced it with dogs "because she knew that he hated them" (*Baudelaire* [1958; New York: Paragon House, 1988], 240). But Paul Keegan in discussing translations of Baudelaire's prose poems notes: "Among the many transformations that Belgium worked upon Baudelaire, one of the most telling was the shift in his loyalties away from cats and towards dogs ('The Negroes of Belgium')." It was "most telling" because he was moved to write "Les bons chiens," which Keegan argues is "one of the great occasional poems of the nineteenth century" (*Times Literary Supplement*, 30 November–6 December 1990).

3. The central study on Darwinism in France is Yvette Conry's *L'Intro-duction du darwinisme en France au XIXème siècle* (Paris: Vrin, 1974). For the nineteenth century's use of catachresis see Paul Ricoeur, *The Rule of Metaphor*, trans. Robert Czerny, Kathleen McLaughlin, and John Costello (Toronto: University of Toronto Press, 1977), 82. Ricoeur discusses Pierre Fontanier's distinction (*Figures du discours*, 1830) between the figurative and the catachretic:

"The difference has to do first with a fact of language, namely that certain ideas *lack* signs: 'In general, catachresis refers to a situation in which the sign, already assigned to a first idea, is assigned also to a new idea, this latter idea having no sign at all or no other proper sign within the language'" (emphasis added).

4. Linda Nochlin, *Realism* (London: Penguin, 1987), 25. Nochlin's discussion of realism—and of its problematic relation to "reality" and its relation to science and social theory—has influenced the argument of this chapter.

5. For a discussion of Buffon's work in the context of eighteenth-century thinking about animals see Hester Hastings's classic study, *Man and Beast in French Thought of the Eighteenth Century* (Baltimore: Johns Hopkins University Press, 1936). For the nineteenth century, see Emile Revel, *Leconte de Lisle animalier et le goût de la zoologie en France au XIXème siècle* (Marseilles, 1942). The publishing history of Buffon's *Histoire* appears in Revel, *Leconte de Lisle*, 41.

6. Pierre Larousse, *Le Grand Dictionnaire universel* (Paris, 1865–1890), s.v. "chat"; original emphasis.

7. Larousse, *Grand Dictionnaire*, s.v. "chat."

8. Larousse, *Grand Dictionnaire*, s.v. "chat."

9. Henri Lautard, *Zoophile ou sympathie envers les animaux: Psychologie du chien, du chat, du cheval* (Paris, 1909), 133; he quotes Buffon on 133–134.

10. Robert Delort, *Les Animaux ont une histoire* (Paris: Editions du Seuil, 1984), 336, 333.

11. Delort, *Les Animaux ont une histoire*, 341–342. See his full discussion of the cat in medieval and early modern culture, 336–346.

12. Chartier's comments appear in his review of Robert Darnton, *The Great Cat Massacre and Other Episodes in French Cultural History*. See "Text, Symbols, and Frenchness" in his recent and brilliant *Cultural History: Between Practices and Representations*, trans. Lydia G. Cochrane (Ithaca: Cornell University Press, 1988), especially 109–110. Chartier's concept of appropriation that informs the argument of this chapter is rightly seen by Patrick Curry as a brilliant solution "to the conundrum of how to relate social practices to cultural (mental, ideological) representations" (review of Chartier's *Cultural History* in *Times Literary Supplement*, 17–23 February 1989).

13. Alphonse Toussenel, as the title page to the second edition of *L'Esprit des bêtes: Zoologie passionnelle* (Paris, 1855) informed his readers, was the author also of *Juifs, rois de l'époque*. The fourth edition (1884) omitted this information. Toussenel explained what he meant by *zoologie passionnelle* in the preface to the second edition: "This is a treatise on 'passionate' zoology, in other words on the kind of zoology that is not taught at the Sorbonne. Many have written about animals (*la bête*), but no historian has yet envisaged the subject from the particular point of view of its analogy with the passions, that is to say from the point of view of their moral, intellectual, and physical resemblance to humans. So many studies of zoology are, therefore, incomplete. The animal is the mirror of man, as man is the mirror of God." For Toussenel's comments about cats and prostitution see *L'Esprit des bêtes*, 240.

14. Toussenel, *L'Esprit des bêtes*, 239, 241.

15. Toussenel, *L'Esprit des bêtes*, 240.

16. Toussenel, *L'Esprit des bêtes*, 240, 242.

17. A. L. A. Fée, *Les Misères des animaux* (Paris, 1863), 84. Fée was also *officier de la Légion d'honneur*.

18. Cuvier quoted in Larousse, *Grand Dictionnaire*, s.v. "chat."

19. E. Littré and Charles Robin, *Dictionnaire de médecine* (Paris, 1878), s.v. "la rage."

20. Cited in Auguste Marie, *La Rage*, vol. 266B of *Encyclopédie scientifique des aide-mémoires* (Paris, 1901), 147.

21. Quoted by Guy-Raoul in *La Rage: Son meilleur préservatif, d'après MM. Tardieu, Sanson, Hertwig, Youatt* (Paris, 1862).

22. J. Bourrel, *Traité complet de la rage, chez le chien et chez le chat: Moyen de s'en préserver* (Paris, 1874), 128, 129.

23. Bourrel, *Traité complet*, 124.

24. Most contemporaries did not pick up these clues to Olympia's social status; see T. J. Clark's chapter on the work in *The Painting of Modern Life: Paris in the Art of Manet and His Followers* (New York: Knopf, 1985), 79–146. For Clark's comments on the cat in the painting discussed here see 93, 92 figure 30, 97 figure 33.

25. Clark also points to the resemblance between "Olympia's hopeless, disabused nobility" and the "kind described—and recommended to the modern artist—in *Le Peintre de la vie moderne*" (*Painting of Modern Life*, 85).

26. For the identification of Thérèse and the cat, note the following passage: "Thérèse joked like a child, putting on catlike movements, poking out her fingers like claws, and doing feline undulations with her shoulders. François remained as still as a statue and contemplated her. Only his eyes seemed alive, and two deep wrinkles at the corners of his mouth made him look like a stuffed animal suddenly grinning" (Emile Zola, *Thérèse Raquin*, trans. Leonard Tancock [London: Folio Society, 1969], 52).

27. Fée, *Les Misères des animaux*, 88.

28. Zola, *Thérèse Raquin*, 48.

29. In bohemia, as Jerrold Seigel shows, the ambiguities of bourgeois life were projected and resolved (*Bohemian Paris: Culture, Politics, and the Boundaries of Bourgeois Life, 1830–1930* [New York: Viking, 1986], 3–30 especially). Seigel's argument has influenced the themes of this chapter.

30. Think of the widow of Helvétius, the comtesse de Ligniville d'Autricourt, who, Simon Schama explains, "ran the most brilliant salon in Paris surrounded by a vast troop of Angora cats, each answering to a different name and dressed in silk ribbon" (*Citizens: A Chronicle of the French Revolution* [New York: Knopf, 1989], 76); Larousse, *Grand Dictionnaire*, s.v. "chat."

31. Robert Lestrange, *Les Animaux dans la littérature et dans l'histoire* (Gap: Ophrys, 1937), 95–96.

32. Lestrange, *Les Animaux*, 72; Lautard, *Zoophilie*, 125–126.

33. On the "invention" of the intellectual, see Pierre Bourdieu, "The Invention of the Artist's Life," in *Everyday Life*, ed. Alice Kaplan and Kristin Ross (New Haven: Yale University Press, 1987), 75–103.

34. Quoted in Lestrange, *Les Animaux*, 65.

35. Bohemia, as Seigel suggests, is exactly those margins of bourgeois life (*Bohemian Paris*, 3–30).

36. Quoted in Lestrange, *Les Animaux*, 78, 89.

37. Quoted in Lestrange, *Les Animaux*, 71–72.

38. Fée, *Les Misères*, 87, 86.

39. Lestrange, *Les Animaux*, 71.

40. Quoted in Lautard, *Zoophilie*, 120, with Lautard's comments on 134, 125; Larousse, *Grand Dictionnaire*, s.v. "chat."

41. Lautard, *Zoophilie*, 133.

42. Bourdieu, "The Invention of the Artist's Life," 79, 78; quote from Sartre is on 79.

43. Fée, *Les Misères*, 85.

44. Toussenel, *L'Esprit des bêtes*, 241–242.

45. Bourrel, *Traité complet*, 124.

46. See *Bulletin* 10 (1864): contents and 258; *Bulletin* 11 (1865): 392; Fée, *Les Misères*, 86.

47. "Jenny et Minnie" appeared in a book by Mme W. de Coninck, *Le Coeur et l'esprit des bêtes* (Paris, n.d.); the death scene is on 116.

48. Marie-Félicie Testas, *Contes de l'asile du quai d'Anjou* (Paris, 1867), 102.

49. Quoted in Lestrange, *Les Animaux*, 98.

50. M. Heine's letter appears in the correspondence section of the February issue (*Bulletin* 18 [1873]: 44–45).

51. Larousse, *Grand Dictionnaire*, s.v. "chat."

52. Lestrange, *Les Animaux*, 73–74.

53. Larousse offered Boitard's evaluation of the cat as a corrective for Buffon's: "To this portrait sketched by [Buffon], but a little overblown, we posit the following, which has the merit of coming closer to the truth" (Larousse, *Grand Dictionnaire*, s.v. "chat").

54. Fée, *Les Misères*, 86; Larousse, *Grand Dictionnaire*, s.v. "chat."

55. Theodore Zeldin, *The French* (New York: Vintage, 1984), 337.

56. See Alistair Horne, *The Terrible Year: The Paris Commune 1871* (New York: Viking, 1971) for a description of dog and cat butchers.

57. *Bulletin* 16 (1870–1871): 480.

58. *Bulletin* 12 (1866): contents; *Bulletin* 21 (1876): 504; *Bulletin* 18 (1873): contents; *Bulletin* 12 (1866): 186–187. In the *Bulletin* 11 (1865), "chat . . . son attachement pour son maître" is a typical entry. Demands for a refuge begin to appear frequently in 1876, along with commentary on the "cat ladies" of Paris.

59. Harriet Ritvo, *The Animal Estate: The English and Other Creatures in the Victorian Age* (Cambridge, Mass.: Harvard University Press, 1987), 116, 118.

60. Lautard, *Zoophilie*, 125.

61. Delort, *Les Animaux ont une histoire*, 348. Ritvo explains that "Victorian legend held that the animals were the special property of the King of Siam." Ritvo, *The Animal Estate*, 119.

62. Delort, *Les Animaux ont une histoire*, 348; Larousse, *Grand Dictionnaire*, s.v. "chat."

63. Ritvo, *The Animal Estate*, 117.

64. Lestrange, *Les Animaux*, 60.

65. Alain Corbin, "Backstage," in *From the Fires of Revolution to the Great War*, ed. Michelle Perrot and trans. Arthur Goldhammer, vol. 4 of *A History of Private Life*, ed. Philippe Ariès and Georges Duby (Cambridge, Mass.: Harvard University Press, 1990), 530.

66. See Florent Prévost, *Des animaux d'appartement et de jardin* (Paris, 1861); Testas, *Contes de l'asile*, 101.

67. *Bulletin* 3 (1857): 89–90.

68. Bourdieu briefly discusses Georges Duby in the conclusion to *Distinction: A Social Critique of the Judgment of Taste*, trans. Richard Nice (Cambridge, Mass.: Harvard University Press, 1984), 477.

69. Larousse, *Grand Dictionnaire*, s.v. "chat."

70. A discussion on the goals of animal protection defended the vice-president for this suggestion (*Bulletin* 6 [1860]: 197).

71. The committee included Blatin, Bourguin, Hervieux, and Lobligeois (*Bulletin* 7 [1861]: 143); review of Honoré's book, and quotations from it, are on 143–144.

72. *Bulletin* 20 (1875): 415.

EPILOGUE

1. 1985 Paris telephone book, s.vv. "chiens et chats (toilettage)" and "chenils." Ben Sherwood, "Of the Pampered Paris Dog and His Sacred Right to Pollute," *International Herald Tribune*, 3 April 1985. Sherwood notes that there are "almost 700,000 dogs in Paris, one for every three humans."

2. "First, the shift from an art nouveau of technological monumentality to an art nouveau of organic interiority is not an antimodernist reaction. Rather, modernity, privacy, and interiority were deeply linked in France, informed both by an aristocratic tradition that had joined modern style to private retreat in the eighteenth century and by the new knowledge of psychological interior in the late nineteenth century" (Debora L. Silverman, *Art Nouveau in Fin-de-Siècle France: Politics, Psychology, and Style* [Berkeley: University of California Press, 1989], 10).

3. In *Laboring Classes and Dangerous Classes*, trans. Frank Jellinek (Princeton: Princeton University Press, 1973). For a discussion of midcentury developing class consciousness from the workers' point of view see William H. Sewell, *Work and Revolution in France: The Language of Labor from the Old Regime to 1848* (Cambridge: Cambridge University Press, 1982).

Bibliography

PRIMARY SOURCES

ARCHIVAL MATERIALS

Archives du Département de la Seine

Fonds des maires. Sous-série V.D.⁴, no. 4441–4461—Taxe municipale sur les chiens, 1856–1859.
———. Sous-série V.D.⁶ 101, no. 11—Taxe sur les chiens: Instructions, circulaires, et arrêts, 1856–1878.

Archives Nationales

Série F¹⁷ 11696 and 11697—Protection des animaux: Encouragements, demandes par la société protectrice des animaux, diffusion de la loi Grammont (circulaire du 10 mars 1894), 1863–1900.
Série F¹² 6784—Compagnie du jardin zoologique et d'acclimatation: Concessions de terrains par la ville de Paris, 1857–1858 (acte constitutif, 1858–1859).

Bibliothèque Nationale

Cabinet des estampes, Jb mat 1—les chiens.

Bibliothèque Marguerite Durand

Dossier Durand—le cimetière des chiens.
Roger-Viollet: Agence photographique de presse, documentation générale: Expositions, animaux-protection.

BULLETINS, ANNUALS, AND OTHER PERIODICALS

Almanach du commerce de la ville de Paris. 1805–1856.
Almanach du commerce de Paris contenant plus de 50,000 adresses. Paris, 1840, 1843.
Annuaire-Almanach du commerce et de l'industrie: Didot-Bottin. Paris, 1863, 1873, 1883, 1910.

Annuaire des vétérinaires. Paris, 1895.

L'Antivivisection. 1913.

Archives parlementaires 1787–1860: Table générale alphabétique et analytique. Paris: Dupont, 1879.

Le Charivari. 1832–1872.

Ministère des Finances. *Annuaire de l'administration des contributions directes et du cadastre*. Paris, 1883–1910.

————. *Bulletin des contributions directes et du cadastre*. Paris, 1855, 1856.

Société centrale pour l'amélioration des races de chiens en France. *Bulletin mensuel*. Paris, 1887, 1888.

————. *Bulletin trimestriel*. Paris, 1898.

Société française contre la vivisection. *Bulletin*. 1894–1898.

Société protectrice des animaux. *Almanach*. Paris, 1869–1870.

————. *Bulletin*. Paris, 1855–1910.

La Vie élégante. Paris, 1880, 1882.

BOOKS AND PAMPHLETS

A Sa Majesté l'Empereur des Français: Humble supplique du caniche Médor. Paris, 1865.

Alb. [Richard Whiteing]. *Living Paris and France: A Guide to Manners, Monuments, Institutions, and the Life of the People*. London, 1886.

Alexandre, A. *Rapport sur la rage des animaux*. Conseil d'hygiène publique et de salubrité du département de la Seine. Paris, 1888.

Arnaud de Fabre, J. Amédée. "Une observation de rage." Paper read at the Société de médecine de Vaucluse, 13 December 1882. N.p., n.d.

Audron, H. M. "Le Chien: Races, éducation, hygiène, dressage." *Encyclopédie A. L. Guyot*. Paris, n.d.

Bachelet, François-Joseph, and C. Froussart. *Cause de la rage et moyen d'en préserver l'humanité*. Valenciennes, 1857.

Balvet, L., and Cleyre Yvelin. *Les Torquemadas de la science*. Paris, 1910.

Barbou, Alfred. *Le Chien: Son histoire, ses exploits, ses aventures*. Paris, 1883.

Baudelaire, Charles. *The Flowers of Evil*. Translated by William Aggeler. Fresno, Ca.: Academy Library Guild, 1954.

————. *The Painter of Modern Life and Other Essays*. Translated by Jonathan Mayne. London: Phaidon, 1964.

————. *The Parisian Prowler: Le spleen de Paris, petits poèmes en prose*. Translated by Edward K. Kaplan. Athens: University of Georgia Press, 1989.

Bernard, Claude. *An Introduction to the Study of Experimental Medicine*. Translated by Henry Copley Greene. New York: Macmillan, 1927.

Besse, Jules. "L'Assistance publique des bêtes: Les chats et les chiens de Paris." *La Vie contemporaine et Revue parisienne réunies* (November 1895): 239–256.

Blatin, Henri. *Nos Cruautés envers les animaux*. Paris, 1867.

Bochefontaine, Louis-Théodore. *Expériences pour servir à l'étude de la prophylaxie et du traitement de la rage*. Paris, 1885.

Boeswillwald, Mme Charles. *Le Chien de luxe: Comment élever, dresser, et soigner nos chiens*. Paris, 1907.

Bonnardot, Alfred. *Des petits chiens de dames, spécialement de l'épagneul nain*. Paris, 1856.

Bony de la Vergne, le comte de. *Les Chiens*. Metz, 1858.

Borel, F. *Sur le vif: Considérations sur la vivisection*. Paris, 1883.

Bosc, Ernest. *De la vivisection: Etude physiologique, psychologique, et philosophique*. Paris, 1894.

Bourrel, J. *Traité complet de la rage, chez le chien et chez le chat: Moyen de s'en préserver*. Paris, 1874.

Boyer, Joseph. *Recherches sur les races humaines de l'Auvergne*. Paris, 1876.

Brehm, A. E. *Les Mamifères*. Vol. 1 of *La Vie des animaux illustrée: Description populaire du règne animal*. Paris, 1869.

Bron, Félix. *La Muselière et la vaccination rabique*. Lyons, 1892.

Buffon [Georges Louis Leclerc, comte de]. *Histoire naturelle*. 1749–1788.

Cadiot, P. J., and F. Breton. *Médecine canine*. Paris, 1901.

Cazis, Mme Roseline de. *Plaintes des chiens à Sir Richard Wallace*. Paris, 1877.

Charpentier, Paul. *La Rage: Comment M. Pasteur empêche les chiens de devenir enragés*. Meux, 1886.

Charrin, Albert. "Les récents travaux sur la rage." Excerpt from *Archives générales de médecine*. Paris, 1887.

Le Chien. Bibliothèque de renseignements et conseils pratiques. Paris, n.d.

"Le Chien." *Recueil choisi de romances et ariettes*. Falaise, 1822.

Le Chien primitif: Aperçus nouveaux sur l'origine du culte des animaux, du langage, du pouvoir représentatif, et de la musique. Nantes, 1846.

"Les Chiens de la Sorbonne." Excerpt from *Le Gaulois*, 24 July 1879. London: Office of the Society for the Protection of Animals from Vivisection, 1882.

Compans, Eugène. "La Taxe sur les chiens." Ph.D. dissertation, faculté de droit, Université de Toulouse, 1907.

Coninck, W. de. *Le Coeur et l'esprit des bêtes*. Paris, n.d.

———. *Enfants et animaux*. Paris, n.d.

Coote, C. D. *Histoire de trois chiens, d'une jument et de trois oiseaux*. Paris, 1877.

Couturier de Vienne, F. A. *Paris moderne: Plan d'une ville modèle*. Paris, 1860.

Darwin, Charles. *The Expression of the Emotions in Man and Animals*. Chicago: University of Chicago Press, 1965.

———. *The Origin of Species*. London: Penguin, 1988.

Delaporte, Henry. *Guide manuel de la taxe sur les chiens*. Paris, 1887.

Delteil, Loys. *Honoré Daumier*. 29 vols. Paris, 1925–1930.

Deraismes, Maria. *Discours contre la vivisection*. Paris, 1884.

Desvernays, Laure. *Les Animaux d'agrément*. Paris, 1913.

[Desvignes.] *Les Chiens par un de leurs amis*. Dijon, 1869.

Donnadieu, A. L. "La vivisection." Excerpt from *La Controversie et "Le Contemporain."* Lyons, 1888.

Dostoyevsky, Fyodor. *Crime and Punishment*. Translated by Sidney Monas. New York: Signet, 1968.

Doublet, Georges. *La Rage en Provence et la clef miraculeuse de Saint Marcuphie*. N.p, n.d.

Ducret-Baumann, Mme H. *L'Education et l'hygiène du chien: Ses maladies, ses misères, reproduction, élevage des chiots*. Paris, 1913.

Dujardin-Beaumetz, Georges. *Rapport sur les cas de rage humaine constatés dans le département de la Seine de 1881 à 1891*. Conseil d'hygiène publique et de salubrité du département de la Seine. Paris, 1892.

Edward of Norwich. *The Master of Game*. [1406–1413]. Reprint. New York: Duffield, 1909.

Ex-chef d'institution. *Chat et chien, ou les enfants volontaires*. Bibliothèque morale de la jeunesse. Rouen, 1858.

Exposition canine du bois de Boulogne. *Journal des chasseurs*. Paris, 1863.

Fée, A. L. A. *Les Misères des animaux*. Paris, 1863.

Fétu, Nicolas. *Lettre à Fortunio sur l'extinction de la race canine à Dijon*. 14 June 1866.

———. *Lettres de son excellence le maréchal Vaillant à M. Nicolas Fétu sur l'extinction de la race canine à Dijon et réponse de M. Nicolas Fétu à son excellence*. 8 and 10 June 1866.

———. *Requête à mes concitoyens pour l'extinction de la race canine à Dijon*. 1866.

Flaubert, Gustave. *The First Sentimental Education*. Translated by Douglas Garman. Berkeley: University of California, 1972.

———. *Sentimental Education*. Translated by Robert Baldick. London: Penguin, 1984.

———. *Three Tales*. Translated by Arthur McDowall. Norfolk, Ct.: New Directions, 1947.

"La Fourrière de Paris." *Revue Britannique* 5 (1873): 343–354.

Foveau de Courmelles, F. V. *La Vivisection: Erreurs et abus*. Paris, 1912.

Fredet, G. E. *La Rage: Deux jours chez M. Pasteur*. Clermont-Ferrand, 1861.

Galtier, V. *La Rage à Lyon et dans le département du Rhône: Mesures que la situation comporte*. Lyons, 1890.

———. *La Rage à Lyon: Mesures propres à diminuer le nombre des chiens errants*. Lyons, 1891.

———. *La Rage envisagée chez les animaux et chez l'homme*. Lyons, 1886.

Gauvin, J. *Bon ami le chien*. Paris, n.d.

Girard, Maurice. *Animaux utiles*. Vol. 1 of *Catalogue raisonné des animaux utiles et nuisibles de la France*. Paris, 1878.

Godin, Alexis. *Le Protecteur, le législateur, et l'ami des animaux*. 2 vols. Paris, 1855–1856.

Goncourt, Edmond de, and Jules de Goncourt. *Pages from the Goncourt Journal*. Edited and translated by Robert Baldick. Oxford: Oxford University Press, 1978.

Gosse, Philip Henry. *A Naturalist's Rambles on the Devonshire Coast*. London, 1853.

Grandville, J. J. Illustrations for *The Public and Private Life of Animals*. Edited by P. J. Hetzel. 1877. Reprint. London: Paddington, 1977.

———. Illustrations for *Les Fables de La Fontaine*. Paris: Dominique Leroy, 1982.

Guide du promeneur au jardin zoologique d'acclimatation du bois de Boulogne. Paris, 1903.

Guy-Raoul. *La Rage: Son meilleur préservatif, d'après MM. Tardieu, Sanson, Hertwig, Youatt*. Hygiène populaire. Paris, 1862.

Honoré, Oscar. *Le Coeur des bêtes*. Paris, 1863.

Innes, William T. *Goldfish Varieties and Tropical Aquarium Fishes: A Guide to Aquaria and Related Subjects*. 9th ed. Philadelphia, 1926.

Jacques du Fouilloux. *La Vénerie de Jacques du Fouilloux: Avec plusieurs receptes et remèdes pour guerir les chiens de diverses maladies. Plus l'adolescence de l'auteur*. 1562. Reprint. Anger, 1844.

Jaffe, John. *Notes sur les moyens de prévenir la rage chez les chiens et l'hydrophobie chez l'homme*. Nice, 1891.

James, Constantin. M. *Pasteur, sa nouvelle méthode dite intensive: Peut-elle communiquer la rage? Réponse à cette question*. Paris, 1887.

Joly, N. "Etudes de psychologie comparée sur l'intelligence et l'instinct des animaux." Excerpt from *Mémoires de l'Académie des sciences, inscriptions, et belles-lettres de Toulouse*. N.d.

Lange, J. *Contributions à l'étude de la rage*. Paris, 1886.

Larbalétrier, Albert. *Manuel pratique de l'amateur de chiens*. Paris, 1907.

Larché, A. *Un Village enragé*. Avignon, 1895.

Larousse, Pierre. *Le Grand Dictionnaire universel*. 17 vols. Paris, 1865–1890.

Lautard, Henri. *Zoophilie ou sympathie envers les animaux: Psychologie du chien, du chat, du cheval*. Paris, 1909.

Lecoeur, Jules. *Etudes sur la rage*. Caen, 1856.

Leroy, E. *L'Enfance du chien*. Paris, 1896.

Lesèble, Louis. *Exposition de la Société centrale pour l'amélioration des races canines: Compte rendu*. Paris [1883].

Levasseur, Paul. *Observation d'un cas de rage*. Rouen, 1882.

Lichy, Lucien-André, and G. R. Laurent. *Qu'est-ce que la vivisection?* Paris, 1912.

Littré, Emile, and Charles Robin. *Dictionnaire de médecine*. Paris, 1865, 1878, 1884.

Livon, Charles. *Manuel de vivisection*. Paris, 1882.

Magnam, T. *Considérations sur la rage canine*. Nice, 1895.

Magnan, Valentin. "De la folie des antivivisectionnistes." Excerpt from *Comptes rendus hebdomadaires de la Société de biologie*. Paris, n.d.

Mahé de la Bourdonnais, A. *Le Chien: L'ami de l'homme*. Paris, 1893.

Maindron, Maurice. *Les Hôtes d'une maison parisienne: Animaux domestiques, commensaux, et parasites vivant dans nos maisons*. Paris, 1891.

Mallet, Mrs. Charles. *The Growth of the Vivisection Evil*. London, 1899.

Maret-Leriche, Jules. *Les Chiens*. Paris, 1864.

———. *A bas la muselière: Pétition de messieurs les chiens et leurs maîtres adressée à M. le préfet de police.* Paris, 1861.

Marie, Auguste. *La Rage.* Vol. 266B of *Encyclopédie scientifique des aide-mémoires.* Paris, 1901.

Marx, Karl. *Capital.* Vol. 1. Translated by Ben Fowkes. New York: Vintage, 1977.

———. *The Economic and Philosophic Manuscripts of 1844.* Translated by Martin Milligan, edited by Dirk Struik. New York: International Publishers, 1964.

Marx, Karl, and Frederick Engels. *The German Ideology.* Edited by C. J. Arthur. New York: International Publishers, 1985.

———. *The Communist Manifesto.* Translated by Paul M. Sweezy. New York: Monthly Review Press, 1964.

Mégnin, Paul. *Nos Chiens: Races, dressage, élevage, hygiène, maladies.* 2d ed. Paris, 1909.

Mégnin, Pierre. "Un Asile pour les chiens près de Paris." *La Nature* 1 (1893): 325–327.

———. *Le Chien: Elevage, hygiène, médecine.* 2 vols. Paris, 1899–1901.

———. *Le Chien: Histoire, hygiène, médecine.* Paris, 1877.

———. *Les Races de chiens.* 3 vols. Vincennes, 1889–1891.

Menard, Saint-Yves. *Note sur la maladie des chiens.* Versailles, n.d.

Mercier, Sébastien. *Tableau de Paris.* Vols. 3 and 8. Amsterdam, 1782, 1783.

Metzger, D. *La Vivisection.* Paris, 1888.

———. *La Vivisection: Ses dangers et ses crimes.* 1891. 2d ed. Paris, 1906.

Meunier, Eugène. *La Liberté pour le chien.* Paris, 1863.

Michelet, Jules. *L'Oiseau.* Paris, 1867.

Montferrier, le marquis de. *Les Femmes, la danse, la politesse.* Paris, 1930.

Moynier, Louis. *Lettres d'un chien errant sur la protection des animaux.* Paris, 1888.

Ollivier, Auguste-Adrien. *Rapport sur la rage chez les enfants.* Conseil d'hygiène publique et de salubrité du département de la Seine. Paris, 1887.

Pape-Carpentier, Mme. *Les Animaux domestiques.* Paris, 1872.

Pasteur, Louis. *Correspondance de Pasteur.* Edited by Pasteur Vallery-Radot. 4 vols. Paris: Flammarion, 1940–1951.

Pathfinder [pseud.], and Hugh Dalziel. *Dressage et élevage des chiens de chasse, de garde, et d'agrément.* Paris, 1906. Originally published as *Of Breaking and Training Dogs* (London, 1885).

Pertus, Joanny. *Le Chien: Races, hygiène, et maladies.* Paris, 1893.

———. *Traité des maladies du chien: Précédé d'une description des races et de l'âge.* Paris, 1885.

Poe, Edgar Allan. *The Portable Poe.* Edited by Philip Van Doren Stern. New York: Viking, 1985.

Portanier, Marius. "Le Chien à travers les âges." Excerpt from report to the Société protectrice des animaux. Nice, 1889.

———. *La Rage.* Nice, 1886.

Potin, E. *Observation d'un cas de rage mortelle après le traitement Pasteur*. Paris, 1890.

Pourtale, V. *La Rage: Considérations au point de vue de sa genèse, sa nature, son traitement*. Paris, 1889.

Prévost, Florent. *Des animaux d'appartement et de jardin: Oiseaux, poissons, chiens, chats*. Paris, 1861.

La Rage: Questions à M. Pasteur par un médecin. Paris, 1886.

Raspail, Xavier. *Les Inoculations de M. Pasteur contre la rage*. Paris, 1886.

Repiquet, R. *Méthode de M. Pasteur pour prévenir la rage après morsure*. Saint-Etienne, 1891.

Richard, Lucien. *Annuaire Richard pour 1898: Chiens célèbres et chiens de célébrités*. Paris, 1898.

Richard, Paul-Juvénal. *Notice sur la rage de chien*. Saumur, 1899.

Robert, Jean. *Le Chien d'appartement et d'utilité: Education, dressage, hygiène, maladies*. Paris, 1888.

Robert, Jean, and L. Fortin. *Les Chiens: Chiens de luxe et d'utilité, chiens de chasse, nomenclature, description, élevage, hygiène, et maladies*. Paris, 1898.

Sabarthez, H. *Un Cas de rage atténuée produite très probablement par les inoculations pasteuriennes*. Perpignan, 1901.

Saint-Loup, Rémy. *Les Animaux auxiliaires de la science*. Paris, 1892.

Sanson, André. *Le Meilleur Préservatif de la rage*. Paris, 1860.

Scholl, Aurélien. Preface to *Notre Ami le chien*, by le baron de Vaux. Paris, 1897.

Shaw, Vero. *The Classic Encyclopedia of the Dog*. New York: Bonanza, 1984. Originally published as *The Illustrated Book of the Dog* (London, 1879–1880).

Simon, Paul. *Observations sur la spontanéité de la rage dans la race canine*. Paris, 1874.

Société anonyme de la grande encyclopédie. *La Grande Encyclopédie*. 31 vols. Paris, 1886–1902.

Société centrale pour l'amélioration des races de chiens. *Catalogue officiel de l'exposition internationale de chiens à Paris 1885, Cours-la-Reine, Champs-Elysées*. Paris, 1885.

————. *Catalogue officiel de l'exposition internationale de chiens à Paris 1887, Cours-la-Reine, Champs-Elysées*. Paris, 1887.

————. *Catalogue officiel illustré: 9ème exposition canine du 21 au 28 mai 1890 sur la terrasse de l'Orangerie du jardin des Tuileries*. Paris, 1890.

————. *Exposition internationale 1883 à Paris, jardin des Tuileries, terrasse de l'Orangerie*. Paris, 1883.

————. *Liste officielle des récompenses de l'exposition internationale de chiens à Paris 1885, Cours-la-Reine, Champs-Elysées*. Paris, 1885.

Société de chien sanitaire et des chiens de guerre. *Le Chien sanitaire et des chiens de guerre*. Paris, n.d.

Société impériale zoologique d'acclimatation. *Exposition des races canines de 1865: Discours prononcé à l'occasion des récompenses le 17 mai 1865 par M. de Quatrefages*. Paris, 1865.

Société du jardin zoologique d'acclimatation du bois de Boulogne. *Exposition universelle des races canines de 1865: Catalogue des chiens exposés.* Paris, 1865.

Sowerby, George B. *Popular History of the Aquarium of Marine and Fresh-Water Animals and Plants.* London, 1857.

Sus à la vivisection! Paris, 1886.

Suzor, Renaud. *Hydrophobia: An Account of M. Pasteur's System Containing a Translation of All His Communications on the Subject, the Technique of His Method, and the Latest Statistical Results.* London, 1887.

Testas, Marie-Félicie. *Contes de l'asile du quai d'Anjou.* Paris, 1867.

Tocqueville, Alexis de. *Recollections.* Translated by George Lawrence. New York: Doubleday, 1970.

Toussenel, Alphonse. *L'Esprit des bêtes: Zoologie passionnelle. Mammifères de France.* 2d ed. Paris, 1855.

Vaux, le baron de. *Notre Ami le chien.* Paris, 1897.

Verne, Jules. *Twenty Thousand Leagues Under the Sea.* Translated by Mercier Lewis and Walter James Miller and edited by Walter James Miller. New York: Meridian, 1977.

Vulpian, Alfred. *Statistique générale des personnes qui ont été traitées à l'institut Pasteur.* Paris, 1887.

Wernert, Auguste. *Origine végétale de la rage.* Paris, 1899.

Wickersheimer, Ernest. "Rage et bains de mer." Excerpt from *Bulletin de la Société française d'histoire de la médecine.* Paris, 1909.

Yvelin, Cleyre. *De la vivisection: Etude psychologique.* Paris, 1910.

Zola, Emile. *L'Assommoir.* Translated by Leonard Tancock. London: Penguin, 1986.

———. *La Curée.* Vol. 4 of *Les Romans d'Emile Zola.* Lausanne: Henri Guillemin, 1961.

———. *The Debacle.* Translated by Leonard Tancock. London: Penguin, 1980.

———. *Doctor Pascal.* Translated by Mary J. Serrano. New York: Macmillan, 1898.

———. *Nana.* Translated by George Holden. New York: Penguin, 1983.

———. *Thérèse Raquin.* Translated by Leonard Tancock. London: Folio Society, 1969.

SECONDARY SOURCES

Ackerley, J. R. *My Dog Tulip.* New York: Poseidon, 1987.

Adams, Tom, and Keith Banister. *Aquarial Fish.* New York: Crescent, 1977.

Adorno, Theodor. *Prisms.* Translated by Samuel and Shierry Weber. Cambridge, Mass.: MIT Press, 1986.

Agulhon, Maurice. *1848, ou l'apprentissage de la république, 1848–1852.* Vol. 8 of *Nouvelle Histoire de la France contemporaine.* Paris: Seuil, 1973.

———. "Le Sang des bêtes: Le problème de la protection des animaux en France au XIXème siècle." *Romantisme: Revue du dix-neuvième siècle* 31 (1981): 81–109.

Allen, David Elliston. *The Naturalist in Britain: A Social History*. London: Allen Lane, 1976.

Allen, James Smith. *Popular French Romanticism: Authors, Readers, and Books in the 19th Century*. Syracuse: Syracuse University Press, 1981.

Aron, Jean-Paul, ed. *La Femme du XIXème siècle*. Brussels: Editions Complexe, 1984.

Aron, Jean-Paul, and Roger Kempf. *La Bourgeoisie, le sexe, et l'honneur*. Brussels: Editions Complexe, 1984.

Eugène Atget, 1857–1927: Intérieurs parisiens, photographies. Exhibition catalog, Musée Carnavalet, 19 October–21 November 1982.

Autin, Jean. *L'Impératrice Eugénie ou l'empire d'une femme*. Paris: Fayard, 1990.

Avineri, Shlomo. *The Social and Political Thought of Karl Marx*. Cambridge: Cambridge University Press, 1968.

Azéma, Jean-Pierre, and Michel Winock. *La Troisième République*. Paris: Pluriel, 1976.

Bachelard, Gaston. *On Poetic Imagination and Reverie*. Translated by Colette Gaudin. Dallas, Tex.: Spring Publications, 1987.

———. *The Poetics of Space*. Translated by Maria Jolas. New York: Orion, 1964.

Bakhtin, Mikhail. *The Dialogic Imagination: Four Essays*. Translated by Caryl Emerson and Michael Holquist. Austin: University of Texas Press, 1981.

Barber, Lynn. *The Heyday of Natural History, 1820–1870*. New York: Doubleday, 1980.

Barnes, Julian. *Flaubert's Parrot*. New York: Vintage, 1990.

Beer, Gillian. *Darwin's Plots: Evolutionary Narrative in Darwin, George Eliot and Nineteenth-Century Fiction*. London: Ark, 1985.

Bélin, Solange. "Une Vie de chien sous l'ancien régime." *Historia* 456 (December 1984): 54–59.

Benjamin, Walter. *Illuminations*. Translated by Harry Zorn and edited by Hannah Arendt. New York: Schocken, 1969.

———. *Reflections: Essays, Aphorisms, Autobiographical Writings*. Translated by Edmund Jephcott and edited by Peter Demetz. New York: Harvest, 1978.

Bois, Yves-Alain. "Kahnweiler's Lesson." Translated by Katherine Streip. *Representations*, no. 18 (Spring 1987): 33–68.

Bourdieu, Pierre. *Distinction: A Social Critique of the Judgment of Taste*. Translated by Richard Nice. Cambridge, Mass.: Harvard University Press, 1984.

———. "The Invention of the Artist's Life." In *Everyday Life*, edited by Alice Kaplan and Kristin Ross, 75–103. New Haven: Yale University Press, 1987.

Brenson, Michael. "Art View: Faces in the Shadows: What Do They Mean?" *New York Times*, 24 July 1988.

Briggs, Asa. *Victorian Things*. Chicago: University of Chicago Press, 1988.

Brooks, Peter. *Reading for the Plot: Design and Intention in Narrative*. New York: Vintage, 1985.

Bruner, Jerome. *Actual Minds, Possible Worlds*. Cambridge, Mass.: Harvard University Press, 1986.

Buci-Glucksmann, Christine. "Catastrophic Utopia: The Feminine as Allegory of the Modern." *Representations*, no. 14 (Spring 1986): 220–229.

Buck-Morss, Susan. *The Dialectics of Seeing: Walter Benjamin and the Arcades Project*. Cambridge, Mass.: MIT Press, 1989.

Bürger, Peter. *Theory of the Avant-Garde*. Translated by Michael Shaw. Vol. 4 of *Theory and History of Literature*. Minneapolis: University of Minnesota, 1984.

Burke, Peter. *Popular Culture in Early Modern Europe*. London: Maurice Temple Smith, 1978.

Calinescu, Matei. *Five Faces of Modernity: Modernism, Avant-Garde, Decadence, Kitsch, Postmodernism*. Durham, N.C.: Duke University Press, 1987.

Cassirer, Ernst. *The Philosophy of the Enlightenment*. Translated by Fritz Koelln and James Pettegrove. Princeton: Princeton University Press, 1951.

———. *The Problem of Knowledge: Philosophy, Science and History Since Hegel*. Translated by William Woglam and Charles Hendel. New Haven: Yale University Press, 1978.

Cavell, Stanley. *In Quest of the Ordinary: Lines of Skepticism and Romanticism*. Chicago: University of Chicago Press, 1988.

———. "Postscript (1989): To Whom It May Concern." *Critical Inquiry* 16 (Winter 1990): 248–289.

Centre national de documentation pédagogue. *Les Animaux dans les romans: Guide documentaire*. Paris, 1979.

Certeau, Michel de. *The Practice of Everyday Life*. Berkeley: University of California Press, 1984.

Chartier, Roger. *Cultural History: Between Practices and Representations*. Ithaca: Cornell University Press, 1988.

Chesnais, Jean-Claude. *Histoire de la violence*. Paris: Laffont, 1981.

Chevalier, Louis. *Laboring Classes and Dangerous Classes*. Translated by Frank Jellinek. Princeton: Princeton University Press, 1973.

Clark, T. J. *The Absolute Bourgeois: Artists and Politics in France, 1848–1851*. Princeton: Princeton University Press, 1982.

———. *The Painting of Modern Life: Paris in the Art of Manet and His Followers*. New York: Knopf, 1985.

Connor, Steven. *Postmodernist Culture: An Introduction to Theories of the Contemporary*. Oxford: Basil Blackwell, 1989.

Conry, Yvette. *L'Introduction du darwinisme en France au XIXème siècle*. Paris: Vrin, 1974.

Corbin, Alain. *Les Filles de noce*. Paris: Flammarion, 1978.

———. *Le Miasme et la jonquille: L'odorat et l'imaginaire social, 18ème–19ème siècles*. Paris: Aubier, 1982.

———. *Le Territoire du vide: L'occident et le désir du rivage, 1750–1840*. Paris: Aubier, 1988.

Corson, Samuel, and Elizabeth Corson. "Pet Animals as Nonverbal Communication Mediators in Psychotherapy in Institutional Settings." In *Ethology and Nonverbal Communication in Mental Health*, edited by Corson and Corson. Oxford: Pergamon, 1980.

Culler, Jonathan. *On Deconstruction: Theory and Criticism After Structuralism*. Ithaca: Cornell University Press, 1982.

Curry, Patrick. Review of *Cultural History: Between Practices and Representations*, by Roger Chartier. *Times Literary Supplement*, 17–23 February 1989.

Darnton, Robert. *The Great Cat Massacre and Other Episodes in French Cultural History*. New York: Vintage, 1985.

Daumard, Adeline. *Les Bourgeois et la bourgeoisie en France depuis 1815*. Paris: Aubier, 1987.

———. *La Bourgeoisie parisienne de 1815 à 1848*. Ecole pratique des hautes études—VIe section, Centre de recherches historiques, démographie, et sociétés, no. 8. Paris, 1963.

Daumard, Adeline, ed. *Oisiveté et loisirs dans les sociétés occidentales au XIXème siècle*. Centre de recherche d'histoire sociale de l'université de Picardie. 1983.

Davidoff, Leonore. *The Best Circles*. London: Hutchinson, 1986.

Davis, Bernard, and Renato Dulbecco, eds. *Microbiology*. 2d ed. Hagerstown, Md.: Harper and Row, 1973.

Delaporte, François. *Disease and Civilization: The Cholera in Paris, 1832*. Cambridge, Mass.: MIT Press, 1986.

Delort, Robert. *Les Animaux ont une histoire*. Paris: Seuil, 1984.

De Man, Paul. *Allegories of Reading: Figural Language in Rousseau, Nietzsche, Rilke, and Proust*. New Haven: Yale University Press, 1979.

Dijkstra, Bram. *Idols of Perversity: Fantasies of Feminine Evil in Fin-de-Siècle Culture*. New York: Oxford University Press, 1986.

Douglas, Mary. *Purity and Danger: An Analysis of the Concepts of Pollution and Taboo*. London: Ark, 1985.

Dubos, René. *Louis Pasteur: Freelance of Science*. London: Victor Gollancz, 1951.

Eagleton, Terry. "The Ideology of the Aesthetic." *Times Literary Supplement*, 22–28 January 1988.

———. *The Ideology of the Aesthetic*. Oxford: Basil Blackwell, 1990.

———. *Walter Benjamin, or Towards a Revolutionary Criticism*. London: Verso, 1981.

Elliot, Paul. "Vivisection and the Emergence of Experimental Physiology in Nineteenth-Century France." In *Vivisection in Historical Perspective*, edited by Nicolaas Rupke, 48–77. London: Croom Helm, 1987.

Elston, Mary Ann. "Women and Anti-vivisection in Victorian England, 1870–1900." In *Vivisection in Historical Perspective*, edited by Nicolaas Rupke, 259–294. London: Croom Helm, 1987.

Eros, John. "The Positivist Generation of French Republicanism." *Sociological Review* (1955): 255–277.

Farley, John, and Gerald Geison. "Science, Politics, and Spontaneous Generation in Nineteenth-Century France: The Pasteur-Pouchet Debate." *Bulletin of the History of Medicine* 48 (Summer 1974): 161–198.

Feenberg, Andrew. *Lukacs, Marx, and the Sources of Critical Theory*. New York: Oxford University Press, 1986.

Foucault, Michel. *The Archaeology of Knowledge and the Discourse on Language*. Translated by A. M. Sheridan Smith. New York: Pantheon, 1972.

———. *An Introduction*. Vol. 1 of *The History of Sexuality*. Translated from the French by Robert Hurley. New York: Vintage, 1980.

———. *The Order of Things: An Archaeology of the Human Sciences*. 1971. Reprint. New York: Vintage, 1973.

Fox, Michael Allen. *The Case for Animal Experimentation: An Evolutionary and Ethical Perspective*. Berkeley: University of California Press, 1986.

Fox, Michael W. *Understanding Your Dog*. New York: Bantam, 1981.

Freidson, Eliot. *Profession of Medicine: A Study of the Sociology of Applied Knowledge*. New York: Harper and Row, 1970.

French, Richard D. *Antivivisection and Medical Science in Victorian Society*. Princeton: Princeton University Press, 1975.

Freud, Sigmund. *Civilization and Its Discontents*. Translated and edited by James Strachey. New York: Norton, 1961.

Freydiger, Jacques. *Le Guide Marabout des chiens*. Verviers, Belgium: Marabout, 1978.

Frykman, Jonas, and Orvar Löfgren. *Culture Builders: A Historical Anthropology of Middle-Class Life*. Translated by Alan Crozier. New Brunswick, N.J.: Rutgers University Press, 1987.

Gallagher, Catherine, and Thomas Laqueur. *The Making of the Modern Body: Sexuality and Society in the Nineteenth Century*. Berkeley: University of California Press, 1987.

Gay, Peter. *Education of the Senses*. Vol. 1 of *The Bourgeois Experience: Victoria to Freud*. New York: Oxford University Press, 1984.

Geertz, Clifford. *The Interpretation of Cultures*. New York: Basic Books, 1973.

Girodie, A. *Jean-Frédéric Schall: Un peintre de fêtes galantes*. Strasbourg, 1927.

Girouard, Mark. *The Return to Camelot: Chivalry and the English Gentleman*. New Haven: Yale University Press, 1981.

Gluck, Mary. *Georg Lukacs and His Generation, 1900–1918*. Cambridge, Mass.: Harvard University Press, 1985.

Goodman, Nelson. *Ways of Worldmaking*. Indianapolis: Hackett, 1978.

Les Grands Boulevards. Exhibition catalog, Musée Carnavalet, 25 June–20 October 1985.

Griffin, Donald. *Animal Thinking*. Cambridge, Mass.: Harvard University Press, 1984.

Guerrand, Roger-Henri. *Les Lieux: Histoire des commodités*. Paris: La Découverte, 1985.

Guiral, Pierre. *La Vie quotidienne en France à l'âge d'or du capitalisme, 1852–1879*. Paris: Hachette, 1976.

Habermas, Jürgen. *The Structural Transformation of the Public Sphere: An Inquiry into a Category of Bourgeois Society*. Translated by Thomas Burger with the assistance of Frederick Lawrence. Cambridge, Mass.: MIT Press, 1989.

Hamilton, George Heard. *Manet and His Critics*. New Haven: Yale University Press, 1986.

Hannaway, Caroline. "Veterinary Medicine and Rural Health Care in Pre-Revolutionary France." *Bulletin of the History of Medicine* 51 (1977): 431–447.

Harris, Ruth. *Murders and Madness: Medicine, Law, and Society in the Fin-de-Siècle*. Oxford: Clarendon Press, 1989.

Harrison, Brian. "Animals and the State in Nineteenth-Century England." In *Peaceable Kingdom: Stability and Change in Modern Britain*, 82–122. Oxford: Oxford University Press, 1982.

Harvey, David. *The Condition of Postmodernity: An Inquiry into the Origins of Cultural Change*. Oxford: Basil Blackwell, 1989.

Hastings, Hester. *Man and Beast in French Thought of the Eighteenth Century*. Baltimore: Johns Hopkins University Press, 1936.

Hause, Steven C. with Anne R. Kenney. *Women's Suffrage and Social Politics in the French Third Republic*. Princeton: Princeton University Press, 1984.

Hearne, Vicki. *Adam's Task: Calling Animals by Name*. New York: Vintage, 1986.

Higonnet, Anne. "Secluded Vision: Images of Feminine Experience in Nineteenth-Century Europe." *Radical History Review* 38 (Spring 1987): 16–36.

Higonnet, Anne, Margaret Higonnet, and Patrice Higonnet. "Facades: Walter Benjamin's Paris." *Critical Inquiry* 10 (March 1984): 391–419.

Higonnet, Patrice. *Sister Republics: The Origins of French and American Republicanism*. Cambridge, Mass.: Harvard University Press, 1988.

Hobsbawm, Eric. *The Age of Capital, 1848–1875*. New York: Mentor, 1979.

Hobsbawm, Eric, and Terence Ranger, eds. *The Invention of Tradition*. Cambridge: Cambridge University Press, 1987.

Holmes, Frederic Lawrence. *Claude Bernard and Animal Chemistry: The Emergence of a Scientist*. Cambridge, Mass.: Harvard University Press, 1974.

Horkheimer, Max, and Theodor Adorno. *Dialectic of Enlightenment*. Translated by John Cumming. New York: Continuum, 1988.

Horne, Alistair. *The Terrible Year: The Paris Commune 1871*. New York: Viking, 1971.

Hughes, H. Stuart. *Consciousness and Society: The Reorientation of European Social Thought, 1890–1930*. New York: Knopf, 1958.

Hunt, Lynn. *Politics, Culture, and Class in the French Revolution*. Berkeley: University of California Press, 1984.

Hunt, Lynn, ed. *The New Cultural History*. Berkeley: University of California Press, 1989.

Ignatieff, Michael. Review of *The City as a Work of Art: London, Paris, Vienna*, by Donald Olsen. *Times Literary Supplement*, 2 January 1987.

Iser, Wolfgang. *The Act of Reading: A Theory of Aesthetic Response*. Baltimore: Johns Hopkins University Press, 1978.

Jakobson, Roman, and Claude Lévi-Strauss. "Les Chats de Charles Baudelaire." *L'Homme: Revue française d'anthropologie* 2 (1962): 5–21.

Jameson, Fredric. Afterword to *Aesthetics and Politics: Theodor Adorno, Walter Benjamin, Ernst Bloch, Bertolt Brecht, Georg Lukacs.* Translation editor, Ronald Tayler. London: Verso, 1986.

Jay, Martin. *Marxism and Totality: The Adventures of a Concept from Lukacs to Habermas.* Berkeley, University of California Press, 1984.

Jelavich, Peter. *Munich and Theatrical Modernism: Politics, Playwriting, and Performance, 1890–1914.* Cambridge, Mass.: Harvard University Press, 1985.

Johnson-Laird, Philip. *Mental Models.* Cambridge, Mass.: Harvard University Press, 1983.

Jones, Gareth Stedman. *Languages of Class: Studies in English Working Class History, 1932–1982.* Cambridge: Cambridge University Press, 1983.

Kaplan, Alice, and Kristin Ross, eds. *Everyday Life.* New Haven: Yale University Press, 1987.

Katcher, Aaron H. "Are Companion Animals Good for Your Health?" *Aging Magazine,* September–October 1982.

Katcher, Aaron H., and A. Beck. *New Perspectives on Our Lives with Companion Animals.* Philadelphia: University of Pennsylvania Press, 1982.

Kaufmann, Walter. *Nietzsche: Philosopher, Psychologist, Antichrist.* 4th ed. Princeton: Princeton University Press, 1974.

Kern, Stephen. *The Culture of Time and Space, 1880–1918.* Cambridge, Mass.: Harvard University Press, 1983.

Kleinman, Arthur. *Patients and Healers in the Context of Culture: An Exploration of the Borderland Between Anthropology, Medicine, and Psychiatry.* Berkeley: University of California Press, 1980.

———. Letter to the editor. *Times Literary Supplement,* 31 January 1986.

Kracauer, Sidney. *Orpheus in Paris: Offenbach and the Paris of His Time.* Translated by Gwenda David and Eric Mosbacher. New York: Vienna House, 1972.

Kudo, Yoko. "La Première *Education sentimentale* de Flaubert: L'épisode du chien." *Etudes de langue et littérature française* 25–26 (1975): 34–49.

Kuhn, Thomas. *The Structure of Scientific Revolutions.* 2d ed. Chicago: University of Chicago Press, 1970.

LaBerge, Ann Fowler. "The Paris Health Council, 1802–1848." *Bulletin of the History of Medicine* 49 (1975): 339–352.

LaCapra, Dominick. *Rethinking Intellectual History: Texts, Contexts, Language.* Ithaca: Cornell University Press, 1983.

LaCapra, Dominick, and Steven L. Kaplan, eds. *Modern European Intellectual History: Reappraisals and New Perspectives.* Ithaca: Cornell University Press, 1982.

Landes, Joan. *Women and the Public Sphere in the Age of the French Revolution.* Ithaca: Cornell University Press, 1988.

Lansbury, Coral. *The Old Brown Dog: Women, Workers, and Vivisection in Edwardian England.* Madison: University of Wisconsin Press, 1985.

Laporte, Dominique. *Histoire de la merde.* Paris: Christian Bourgeois, 1978.

Laqueur, Thomas. *Making Sex: Body and Gender from the Greeks to Freud.* Cambridge, Mass.: Harvard University Press, 1990.

————. "Orgasm, Generation, and the Politics of Reproductive Biology." *Representations*, no. 14 (Spring 1986): 1–41.

Latour, Bruno. *The Pasteurization of France*. Translated by Alan Sheridan and John Law. Cambridge, Mass.: Harvard University Press, 1988.

Latzarus, Marie-Thérèse. *La Littérature enfantine en France dans la seconde moitié du XIXème siècle*. Paris: Presses universitaires de France, 1923.

Leach, Edmund. "Anthropological Aspects of Language: Animal Categories and Verbal Abuse." In *New Directions in the Study of Language*, edited by Eric H. Lenneberg. Cambridge, Mass.: MIT Press, 1966.

Lebreton de Montry, Annie, and Françoise Lepeuve. *Cartes postales de chats*. Paris: Pierre Horoy, 1984.

Léonard, Jacques. *La Médecine entre les pouvoirs et les savoirs: Histoire intellectuelle et politique de la médecine française au XIXème siècle*. Paris: Aubier, 1981.

Lesch, John. *Science and Medicine in France: The Emergence of Experimental Physiology, 1790–1855*. Cambridge, Mass.: Harvard University Press, 1984.

Lestrange, Robert. *Les Animaux dans la littérature et dans l'histoire*. Gap: Ophrys, 1937.

Lévi-Strauss, Claude. *The Savage Mind*. Chicago: University of Chicago Press, 1966.

Levinson, Boris. "The Child and His Pet: A World of Nonverbal Communication in Mental Health." In *Ethology and Nonverbal Communication in Mental Health*, edited by Samuel Corson and Elizabeth Corson. Oxford: Pergamon, 1980.

Lorenz, Konrad. *King Solomon's Ring*. Translated by Marjorie Kerr Wilson. New York: Harper, 1979.

————. *Man Meets Dog*. Translated by Marjorie Kerr Wilson. London: Penguin, 1973.

Loudon, J. B., ed. *Social Anthropology and Medicine*. Association of Social Anthropologists Monograph 13. London: Academic Press, 1976.

Lowe, Donald. *History of Bourgeois Perception*. Chicago: University of Chicago Press, 1982.

Lowenthal, David. *The Past Is a Foreign Country*. Cambridge: Cambridge University Press, 1985.

Lukacs, Georg. *The Historical Novel*. Translated by Hannah and Stanley Mitchell. London: Penguin, 1981.

————. *History and Class Consciousness: Studies in Marxist Dialectics*. Translated by Rodney Livingstone. Cambridge, Mass.: MIT Press, 1971.

————. *The Theory of the Novel*. Translated by Anna Bostock. Cambridge, Mass.: MIT Press, 1985.

McLaren, Angus. *Sexuality and Social Order: The Debate over the Fertility of Women and Workers in France, 1770–1920*. New York: Holmes and Meier, 1983.

Mainardi, Patricia. *Art and Politics of the Second Empire: The Universal Expositions of 1855 and 1867*. New Haven: Yale University Press, 1987.

Marcel, Odile. *Une Éducation française*. Paris: Presses universitaires de France, 1984.

Martin-Fugier, Anne. *La Bourgeoise: Femme au temps de Paul Bourget*. Paris: Grasset, 1983.

————. *La Place des bonnes: La Domesticité féminine en 1900*. Paris: Grasset, 1979.

————. *La Vie élégante ou la formation du Tout-Paris, 1815–1848*. Paris: Fayard, 1990.

Mason, Stephen. *A History of the Sciences*. New York: Collier, 1962.

Mayer, Arno. *The Persistence of the Old Regime: Europe to the Great War*. New York: Pantheon, 1981.

Merriman, John, ed. *Consciousness and Class Experience in Nineteenth-Century Europe*. New York: Holmes and Meier, 1979.

Michie, Helena. *The Flesh Made Word: Female Figures and Women's Bodies*. Oxford: Oxford University Press, 1987.

Miller, Michael. *The Bon Marché: Bourgeois Culture and the Department Store, 1869–1920*. London: George Allen and Unwin, 1981.

Monzie, Anatole de. *Les Veuves abusives*. Paris: Grasset, 1936.

Berthe Morisot: Impressionist. Exhibition catalog by Charles Stuckey and William P. Scott with the assistance of Suzanne Lindsay. Mount Holyoke College Art Museum in association with the National Gallery of Art, 1987.

Moses, Claire Goldberg. *French Feminism in the Nineteenth Century*. Albany: State University of New York Press, 1984.

Mugford, Roger. "The Social Significance of Pet Ownership." In *Ethology and Nonverbal Communication in Mental Health*, edited by Samuel Corson and Elizabeth Corson. Oxford: Pergamon, 1980.

Muller, John, and William Richardson, eds. *The Purloined Poe: Lacan, Derrida, and Psychoanalytic Reading*. Baltimore: Johns Hopkins University Press, 1988.

Nicolle, Jacques. *Louis Pasteur: The Story of His Major Discoveries*. New York: Basic Books, 1961.

Nochlin, Linda. *Realism*. London: Penguin, 1987.

Nolan, Mary. "The *Historikerstreit* and Social History." *New German Critique* 44 (Spring–Summer 1988): 51–80.

Nora, Pierre, ed. *La République*. Vol. 1 of *Les Lieux de mémoire*. Paris: Gallimard, 1984.

Nord, Philip. *Paris Shopkeepers and the Politics of Resentment*. Princeton: Princeton University Press, 1986.

Nye, Robert. *Crime, Madness, and Politics in Modern France: The Medical Concept of National Decline*. Princeton: Princeton University Press, 1984.

Offen, Karen. "Defining Feminism: A Comparative Historical Approach." *Signs* 14 (1988): 119–157.

Olmsted, J. M. D., and E. Harris Olmsted. *Claude Bernard and the Experimental Method in Medicine*. New York: Henry Schuman, 1952.

Olsen, Donald. *The City as a Work of Art: London, Paris, Vienna*. New Haven: Yale University Press, 1986.

Osler, William. Introduction to *The Life of Pasteur*, by René Vallery-Radot. Translated by Mrs. R. L. Devonshire. New York: Doubleday, 1926.

Palmer, Michael. *Des petits journaux aux grandes agences: Naissance du journalisme moderne, 1863–1914*. Paris: Aubier, 1983.

Paradis, James, and Thomas Postlewait, eds. *Victorian Science and Victorian Values: Literary Perspectives*. New Brunswick, N.J.: Rutgers University Press, 1985.

Patterson, James T. *The Dread Disease: Cancer and Modern American Culture*. Cambridge, Mass.: Harvard University Press, 1987.

Pernoud, Régine. *Les Temps modernes*. Vol. 2 of *Histoire de la bourgeoisie en France*. Paris, Seuil, 1982.

Perrot, Marguerite. *La Mode de vie des familles bourgeoises 1873–1953*. 2d ed. Paris: Presses de la Fondation nationale des sciences politiques, 1982.

Perrot, Michelle, ed. *From the Fires of Revolution to the Great War*. Vol. 4 of *A History of Private Life*, edited by Philippe Ariès and Georges Duby. Translated by Arthur Goldhammer. Cambridge, Mass.: Harvard University Press, 1990.

———. *Une Histoire des femmes: Est-elle possible?* Marseilles: Rivages, 1984.

Perrot, Philippe. *Les Dessus et les dessous de la bourgeoisie*. Paris: Fayard, 1981.

———. "Le Jardin des modes." In *La Femme du XIXe siècle*. Edited by Jean-Paul Aron, 101–134. Brussels: Editions Complexe, 1984.

———. *Le Travail des apparences, ou les transformations du corps féminin, XVIIIème–XIXème siècles*. Paris: Seuil, 1984.

Petersdorf, Robert G., Raymond D. Adams, Eugene Braunwald, Kurt J. Isselbacher, Joseph B. Martin, and Jean D. Wilson, eds. *Harrison's Principles of Internal Medicine*. 10th ed. New York: McGraw Hill, 1983.

Pinkney, David. *Napoleon III and the Rebuilding of Paris*. Princeton: Princeton University Press, 1972.

Pippin, Robert. *Modernism as a Philosophical Problem: On the Dissatisfactions of European High Culture*. Oxford: Basil Blackwell, 1991.

Porter, Roy. "Man, Animals, and Nature." *The Historical Journal* 28, no. 1 (1985): 225–229.

Posner, Donald. *Watteau: A Lady at Her Toilet*. New York: Viking, 1973.

Price, Roger. *A Social History of Nineteenth-Century France*. New York: Holmes and Meier, 1987.

Rabout, Jean. *Féministes à la "Belle Epoque."* Paris: France-Empire, 1985.

Reid, Robert. *Microbes and Men*. London: British Broadcasting Corporation, 1974.

Renoir. Exhibition catalog by Anne Distel and John House. Hayward Gallery, London; Galeries nationales du Grand Palais, Paris; and Museum of Fine Arts, Boston, 1985–1986.

Revel, Emile. *Leconte de Lisle animalier et le goût de la zoologie en France au XIXème siècle*. Marseilles: Sémaphore, 1942.

Rewald, John. *The History of Impressionism*. 4th rev. ed. New York: Museum of Modern Art, 1973.

Ricoeur, Paul. *The Rule of Metaphor*. Translated by Robert Czerny, Kathleen McLaughlin, and John Costello. Toronto: University of Toronto Press, 1977.

Ritvo, Harriet. *The Animal Estate: The English and Other Creatures in the Victorian Age*. Cambridge, Mass.: Harvard University Press, 1987.

―――. "The Emergence of Modern Pet-Keeping." In *Animals and People Sharing the World*, edited by Andrew Rowan. Hanover, N.H.: University Press of New England, 1988.

―――. "Sex and the Single Animal." *Grand Street* 7, no. 3 (Spring 1988): 124–139.

Ronsin, Francis. *La Grève des ventres: Propagande néo-malthusienne et baisse de la natalité française, XIXème–XXème siècles*. Paris: Aubier, 1980.

Rosenblum, Robert. *The Dog in Art: From Rococo to Post-Modernism*. New York: Abrams, 1988.

Rupke, Nicolaas, ed. *Vivisection in Historical Perspective*. London: Croom Helm, 1987.

Russell, John. *Paris*. New York: Abrams, 1983.

Rybczynski, Witold. *Home: A Short History of an Idea*. New York: Penguin, 1987.

Said, Edward. *Orientalism*. New York: Vintage, 1979.

Sainte-Marie, Marc. *Le Chien dans la littérature*. Paris: Dansel, 1984.

Saisselin, Rémy. *The Bourgeois and the Bibelot*. New Brunswick, N.J.: Rutgers University Press, 1984.

Sayre, Robert, and Michael Löwy. "Figures of Romantic Anti-Capitalism." *New German Critique* 32 (Spring–Summer 1984): 42–93.

Schama, Simon. *Citizens: A Chronicle of the French Revolution*. New York: Knopf, 1989.

Schmitt, Jean-Claude. *The Holy Greyhound: Guinefort, Healer of Children since the Thirteenth Century*. Translated by Martin Thom. Cambridge: Cambridge University Press, 1979.

Schor, Naomi. "*Cartes Postales*: Representing Paris 1900." *Critical Inquiry* 18 (1992): 188–244.

Schorske, Carl. *Fin-de-Siècle Vienna: Politics and Culture*. New York: Vintage, 1981.

Schupbach, William. "A Select Iconography of Animal Experiments." In *Vivisection in Historical Perspective*, edited by Nicolaas Rupke, 340–360. London: Croom Helm, 1987.

Seigel, Jerrold. *Bohemian Paris: Culture, Politics, and the Boundaries of Bourgeois Life, 1830–1930*. New York: Viking, 1986.

Sewell, William H. *Work and Revolution in France: The Language of Labor from the Old Regime to 1848*. Cambridge: Cambridge University Press, 1982.

Shell, Marc. "The Family Pet." *Representations*, no. 15 (1986): 121–153.

Sherwood, Ben. "Of the Pampered Paris Dog and His Sacred Right to Pollute." *International Herald Tribune*, 3 April 1985.

Showalter, Elaine. *The Female Malady: Women, Madness, and English Culture, 1830–1980*. New York: Penguin, 1985.

Silverman, Debora L. *Art Nouveau in Fin-de-Siècle France: Politics, Psychology and Style*. Berkeley: University of California Press, 1989.

Silverman, Ruth. *The Dog Observed: Photographs, 1844–1988*. San Francisco: Chronicle Publications, 1988.

Simmel, Georg. *On Individuality and Social Forms: Selected Writings*. Edited by D. Levine. Chicago: University of Chicago Press, 1971.

Singer, Peter. *Animal Liberation: A New Ethics for Our Treatment of Animals*. New York: New York Review of Books, 1975.

————, ed. *In Defence of Animals*. Oxford: Basil Blackwell, 1985.

Smith, Bonnie. *Ladies of the Leisure Class: The Bourgeoises of Northern France in the Nineteenth Century*. Princeton: Princeton University Press, 1981.

Sontag, Susan. *Illness as Metaphor*. New York: Vintage, 1979.

Starkie, Enid. *Baudelaire*. 1958. Reprint. New York: Paragon House, 1988.

Suleiman, Susan Rubin, ed. *The Female Body in Western Culture: Contemporary Perspectives*. Cambridge, Mass.: Harvard University Press, 1986.

Terdiman, Richard. *Discourse/Counter-Discourse: The Theory and Practice of Symbolic Resistance in Nineteenth-Century France*. Ithaca: Cornell University Press, 1985.

Théodoridès, Jean. *Histoire de la rage: Cave canem*. Paris: Masson, 1986.

Thomas, Keith. *Man and the Natural World: A History of the Modern Sensibility*. New York: Pantheon, 1983.

Thomson, Richard. *Seurat*. Oxford: Phaidon, 1985.

————. " 'Les Quat' Pattes': The Image of the Dog in Late Nineteenth-Century French Art." *Art History* 5, no. 3 (September 1982): 323–337.

Toulmin, Stephen. *Cosmopolis: The Hidden Agenda of Modernity*. New York: Free Press, 1990.

Tuan, Yi-Fu. *Dominance and Affection: The Making of Pets*. New Haven: Yale University Press, 1984.

Turner, James. *Reckoning With the Beast: Animals, Pain, and Humanity in the Victorian Age*. Baltimore: Johns Hopkins University Press, 1980.

Unwin, Timothy. "The Significance of the Encounter with the Dog in Flaubert's *Education sentimentale*." *French Forum* 4 (1979): 232–238.

Vallery-Radot, René. *The Life of Pasteur*. Translated by Mrs. R. L. Devonshire. London, 1919.

Veblen, Thorstein. *The Theory of the Leisure Class*. New York: Modern Library, 1934.

Vigarello, Georges. *Le Propre et le sale: L'Hygiène du corps depuis le moyen âge*. Paris: Seuil, 1985.

Virtanen, Reino. *Claude Bernard and His Place in the History of Ideas*. Lincoln: University of Nebraska Press, 1960.

Wagner, Anne. "Art and Property: Carpeaux's Portraits of the Prince Imperial." *Art History* 5 (1982): 447–471.

Watt, Ian. *The Rise of the Novel: Studies in Defoe, Richardson, and Fielding*. Berkeley: University of California Press, 1957.

Weber, Eugen. *France: Fin de Siècle*. Cambridge, Mass.: Harvard University Press, 1986.

———. *Peasants Into Frenchmen: The Modernization of Rural France, 1870–1914*. Palo Alto: Stanford University Press, 1976.

Wechsler, Judith. *A Human Comedy: Physiognomy and Caricature in Nineteenth-Century Paris*. Chicago: University of Chicago Press, 1982.

White, Hayden. *Metahistory: The Historical Imagination in Nineteenth-Century Europe*. Baltimore: Johns Hopkins University Press, 1973.

Williams, Raymond. *Culture and Society, 1780–1950*. New York: Columbia University Press, 1983.

Williams, Roger. *Gaslight and Shadow: The World of Napoleon III, 1851–1870*. New York: Macmillan, 1957.

———. *The Horror of Life*. Chicago: University of Chicago Press, 1980.

Williams, Rosalind. *Dream Worlds: Mass Consumption in Late Nineteenth-Century France*. Berkeley: University of California Press, 1982.

Wismann, Heinz, ed. *Walter Benjamin et Paris*. Paris: Cerf, 1986.

Wolin, Richard. *Walter Benjamin: An Aesthetic of Redemption*. New York: Columbia University Press, 1982.

Wright, Gordon. *France in Modern Times*. 3d ed. New York: Norton, 1981.

Young, Robert. *Darwin's Metaphor: Nature's Place in Victorian Culture*. Cambridge: Cambridge University Press, 1985.

Zeldin, Theodore. *France: 1848–1945*. 5 vols. Oxford: Oxford University Press, 1979–1981.

———. *The French*. New York: Vintage, 1984.

Index

Compositor:	Braun-Brumfield, Inc.
Text:	10/14 Janson
Display:	Janson
Printer and Binder:	Braun-Brumfield, Inc.